German Anti-Nazi Espionage in the Second World War

This book tells the dramatic story of the recruitment and training of a group of German communist exiles by the London office of the Office of Strategic Services for key spy missions into Nazi Germany during the final months of World War II. The book chronicles their stand against the rise of Hitler in the 1930s that caused them to flee Germany for Czechoslovakia and then England, where they resettled and awaited an opportunity to get back into the war against the Nazis.

That chance would arrive in late 1944 when the OSS recruited them for important missions that became part of the historic German Penetration Campaign. Some of the German exiles carried out successful missions that provided key military intelligence to the Allied armies advancing into Germany while others suffered untimely deaths immediately upon the dispatch of their missions that still raise troubling issues. In addition, a few betrayed the trust that the OSS had placed in them by collaborating with a Soviet spy network in England and secretly disclosing top secret OSS sources and methods used to carry out the German Penetration Campaign missions. These dual loyalties, however, did not prevent the United States military from awarding these men military decorations, which have been confirmed as the first such medals awarded to German nationals for their service to the Allied armies in World War II.

Jonathan S. Gould is a former New York City schoolteacher and curriculum writer. He is now an attorney admitted to practice law in the federal and state courts of New York specializing in commercial litigation.

Routledge Focus on the History of Conflict

The history of war and warfare often contains events and episodes that in themselves took place over a relatively short period of time but which have developed wider historical resonance. This series of books, part of the Routledge Focus series of short form volumes, usually somewhere between the average length of a journal article and a monograph, sheds a light on key topics within the history of conflict – taking a broadly international perspective and with all eras represented.

German Anti-Nazi Espionage in the Second World War
The OSS and the Men of the TOOL Missions
Jonathan S. Gould

German Anti-Nazi Espionage in the Second World War

The OSS and the Men of the TOOL Missions

Jonathan S. Gould

Routledge
Taylor & Francis Group

LONDON AND NEW YORK

First published 2019
by Routledge

2 Park Square, Milton Park, Abingdon, Oxfordshire OX14 4RN
52 Vanderbilt Avenue, New York, NY 10017

Routledge is an imprint of the Taylor & Francis Group, an informa business

First issued in paperback 2020

British Library Cataloguing-in-Publication Data
A catalogue record for this book is available from the British Library

Library of Congress Cataloging-in-Publication Data
Names: Gould, Jonathan S., author.
Title: German anti-Nazi espionage in the Second World War : the
    OSS and the men of the TOOL missions / Jonathan S. Gould.
Other titles: OSS and the men of the TOOL missions
Description: 1st edition. | Abingdon, Oxon ; New York, NY :
    Routledge, [2019] | Series: Routledge focus on the history of
    conflict | Includes bibliographical references and index.
Identifiers: LCCN 2018022500 | ISBN 9781138610736 (hardback :
    alk. paper) | ISBN 9780429465628 (e-book)
Subjects: LCSH: United States. Office of Strategic Services—
    Biography. | Gould, Joseph, 1915–1993. | World War, 1939–
    1945—Secret service—United States—Biography. | World
    War, 1939–1945—Secret service—Germany—Biography. | Ruh,
    Anton, 1912–1964. | Lindner, Paul, 1911—1969. | Gruber, Kurt.
    | Espionage—Germany—History—20th century. | World War,
    1939–1945—Military intelligence—United States—Biography.
Classification: LCC D810.S7 G648 2019 | DDC
    940.54/8673092331—dc23
LC record available at https://lccn.loc.gov/2018022500

ISBN: 978-1-138-61073-6 (hbk)
ISBN: 978-0-367-60683-1 (pbk)

Typeset in Times New Roman
by Apex CoVantage, LLC

Contents

List of figures   vi
Preface   ix
Historical background   xii

1   The HAMMER mission and the GRU   1

2   Mission into Landshut: The triumph of the
    PICKAXE mission   50

3   Gone Too Soon: The courageous life and tragic
    death of Kurt Gruber   62

4   Still Missing: The story of Werner Fischer and
    the ill-fated BUZZSAW mission   81

5   Conflict of Loyalties: The MALLET mission and
    Adolph Buchholz   92

    Epilogue   100

    Bibliography   103
    Appendices   111
    Index   188

Figures

Chapter 1

1.1	Logo of the Office of Strategic Services	32
1.2	General William J. Donovan, OSS Director, 1942	32
1.3	Major General William J. Donovan (top row/center), 1944	33
1.4	HAMMER mission agent Anton Ruh, January 1945	33
1.5	HAMMER mission agent Paul Lindner, London, January 1945	33
1.6	Marjorie and Paul Lindner on their wedding day, London, 1942	34
1.7	Paul Lindner, Sr., father of Paul Lindner, Berlin, Germany, November 1938	34
1.8	Freeda Lindner, mother of Paul Lindner, Berlin, Germany, November 1938	34
1.9	Paul Lindner, Sr. and daughter Inge, Berlin, 1938	34
1.10	HAMMER mission agent Paul Lindner, Paris, July 1945	35
1.11	Joan/Eleanor (J/E) transmitter-receiver used behind enemy lines by TOOL mission agents	36
1.12	Al Gross, inventor, J/E radio receiver/transmitter	37
1.13a	US Army Lt. Joseph Gould with London bookstore owner Morris Abbey, September 1944	37
1.13b	US Army Lt. Joseph Gould in London	37
1.14	Army Lt. Joseph Gould outside London flat, October 1944	37
1.15	Army Lt. Joseph Gould with his father, Samuel Goldberger, August 1942	38
1.16	Joseph Gould, president of the Screen Publicists Guild (center), at a meeting with members of the guild's executive council, 1940	38
1.17	Joseph Gould (seated far right) signing the first contract with Hollywood studios on behalf of the Screen Publicists Guild of New York, May 1942	39

1.18 Joseph Gould (seated second from left) at the Motion Picture Emergency Defense Council conference sponsored by the Screen Publicists Guild in late December 1941 at the Hotel Piccadilly in New York City. Garson Kanin, acclaimed theater and film director, was the keynote speaker, seated far right — 39

1.19 Army Lt. Joseph Gould outside OSS London mission training school, October 1944 — 40

1.20 OSS Labor Division Chief Arthur Goldberg (far right) with staff of the OSS Labor Desk in London — 40

1.21 Army Lt. Joseph at parachute training field with OSS London mission training staff, Ringway Air Field, Ruislip, England, November 1944 — 41

1.22 Staff of OSS Labor Division, London, England, with Joseph Gould standing second from right and Arthur Goldberg seated far left, November 1944 — 41

1.23 Jurgen Kuczynski, London, 1943 — 42

1.24 Ursula Kuczynski (aka Ruth Werner), 1938 — 42

1.25 Ursula Kuczynski, 1955 — 42

1.26 HAMMER mission agent Anton Ruh in East Berlin, Germany, 1960, while serving as head of the Customs Service for the German Democratic Republic — 43

1.27 Erich Henschke (aka Karl Kastro), Paris, January 1945 — 43

1.28 Silver Star award presented to families of HAMMER mission agents on May 5, 2006, at a ceremony held at the US Embassy in Berlin — 43

1.29 Colonel Donald Zedler, military attaché to the US Embassy in Berlin, and William Timken, US ambassador to Germany, presenting the Silver Star medals to Marjorie Lindner and Denis Ruh at the medal presentation ceremony held at the US Embassy in Berlin in May 2006 — 44

Chapter 2

2.1 PICKAXE mission agent Emil Konhäuser — 59

2.2 PICKAXE mission agent Walter Strüwe — 60

2.3 John G. Winant, Sr., US ambassador to Great Britain, 1941–46 — 60

2.4 John G. Winant, Jr. (fourth from right) with US Army Air Force unit before being shot down over Germany, Harrington Airfield, England, 1945 — 60

Chapter 3

3.1   CHISEL mission agent Kurt Gruber, 1944 — 74
3.2   Jessica Campbell Leith, wife of Kurt Gruber — 75
3.3   Young Kurt Gruber (bottom right) with his family in Ahlen, Germany, 1925 — 75
3.4   Karl Gruber, brother of Kurt Gruber, in coffin following shooting death during street brawl with Nazi storm troopers, Ahlen, Germany 1931 — 76
3.5   Residents of Ahlen, Germany, marching in protest of the murder of Karl Gruber by Nazi storm troopers, 1931 — 76
3.6   US Army Air Force Colonel Hudson Upham, 1944 — 77
3.7   A-26 aircraft used to fly OSS agents into Germany in the CHISEL mission — 77
3.8   Major John Walch was the navigator for the HAMMER mission into Berlin on March 2, 1945. He was killed while navigating the ill-fated A-26 aircraft that attempted to drop CHISEL mission agent Kurt Gruber into Ahlen, Germany on March 19, 1945. — 77
3.9   Hermann Kruse, 76, owner of family farm in Schwege, Germany, that CHISEL mission aircraft crashed onto in March 1945 — 78
3.10 Hermann Kruse with aviation investigators examining CHISEL mission aircraft debris discovered on Kruse farm in 2015 — 78

Chapter 4

4.1   BUZZSAW mission agent Werner Fischer, 1939 — 88
4.2   Heinz Schmidt, friend and mentor of Werner Fischer, London, 1944 — 89

Chapter 5

5.1   Adolph Buchholz, age 13 in 1928, Berlin, Germany — 97
5.2   Adolph Buchholz, East Germany, 1953 — 98
5.3   Hermann Matern, member of the Politburo of the Socialist Unity Party of East Germany which conducted interrogations of TOOL mission agents in 1953 — 98

Preface

The publication of this manuscript marks the end of a long journey that actually began in the spring of 1993 during a difficult time in my life. This was because my father Joseph Gould had just received a diagnosis of lung cancer that would take his life three months later. He was 78 years old and living in Washington, DC at the time. I was visiting him from my home in New York City. On a cool spring day, we were having lunch in my sister's house. We were talking about his wartime service in the Office of Strategic Services during World War II. Although I had knowledge of his work in the OSS, I was not aware of its historical significance nor of the men he recruited for these important spy missions from the German exile community in London in the fall of 1944.

One other moment during that conversation rekindled my interest in revisiting my father's work with the OSS. That was his disappointment in not receiving the recognition that he felt he deserved for his wartime service with the OSS. Part of this sense of disappointment may have stemmed from the fact that he never received the Bronze Star that senior military officers of the OSS in June 1945 had recommended that he be awarded by the US military. I first became aware of this fact in 2008 when the CIA declassified this medal recommendation together with the order of the War Department in 1946 that the award be made. While he did mention in a memoir of his wartime service he wrote in 1988 that he was aware that a decision had been made to award him the Bronze Star, he never actually received it during his lifetime. But in the fall of 2009, with the assistance of Congressman Charles Rangel of New York, I was able to successfully petition the US Army Military Awards Branch for the posthumous award of this medal. Three months later, I was presented with the Bronze Star by Congressman Rangel at a ceremony held in his Harlem office.

When this conversation with my father took place in April 1993, I had no idea that he had never been presented with the Bronze Star. I have no recollection of him mentioning this while growing up in Great Neck, Long

Island. But I was deeply moved by the feelings he shared with me that day. After he passed away in July 1993, I privately vowed to reexamine what I knew about his OSS service and to take whatever action was necessary to have the story of his unique wartime service become more widely known.

I was able to achieve this objective with the publication of an article that I wrote in 2002 and which was published in the historical journal of the Central Intelligence Agency – *Studies in Intelligence*. The article is titled "Strange Bedfellows: The OSS and the London Free Germans." It was based on my review of OSS records I found in his files and new files released to the US National Archives in 2000. The primary focus of that article was the HAMMER mission into Berlin, which is discussed in great detail in this book. I had uncovered these newly released files during my visit to the National Archives in 2001. I would not have found them without the aid of the late John Taylor, who served as the senior military archivist at the National Archives for sixty-three years. Mr. Taylor was instrumental in making me aware of the existence of these newly released mission files that I had never seen before.

My discovery of these files enabled me to learn more about the German nationals my father recruited and trained for these dangerous missions. In addition, I learned that the agents of the HAMMER mission into Berlin – Paul Lindner and Anton Ruh – had been recommended for the award of the Silver Star. And since I already had made contact with the families of the men, I learned that neither Lindner nor Ruh had been presented with this award for their service on the mission. Their return to East Germany in 1947, combined with the intensifying Cold War, were probably the reasons why this had not occurred. Nevertheless, with the assistance of a widely respected military lawyer – Grant Lattin – I was able to prepare a medal application for the posthumous award of the Silver Star that the US Army Decorations Board granted in September 2004.

As discussed in more detail in this book, political complications developed that delayed the presentation of the medals to the Berlin families. But with the help of the military attaché to the US Embassy in Berlin – US Army Colonel Donald Zedler – that day finally arrived. On May 5, 2006, I traveled to Berlin to attend the medal ceremony that took place at the US embassy. The medals were presented to the late Marjorie Lindner on behalf of her late husband Paul Lindner and to the late Denis Ruh, the son of Anton Ruh.

On my return to New York from Berlin, I decided that I would direct my energies to writing the full story of Joseph Gould and the men he recruited for the missions into Nazi Germany now known as the TOOL missions. This book is the realization of that goal. A number of my friends and colleagues provided support and encouragement that I would like to acknowledge.

First, I would like to thank Professor Volker Berghahn of Columbia University in New York City. He recently retired from that university after a long and distinguished career as an historian of German and modern European history. Professor Berghahn's support and guidance toward the development of the manuscript has been invaluable. In addition, I want to thank Professor Anne Nelson of the Columbia University School of International and Public Affairs. Throughout this period when I was drafting the manuscript, she provided valuable assistance and encouragement.

I also want to thank Barbara Gould Plesser of Martha's Vineyard, Massachusetts. She is my sister who supported and encouraged my work during this period. I also want to acknowledge the ongoing support and encouragement I have received from Ross Lewis of Jacksonville, Florida, and Vic Losick of New York City. Ross Lewis has been a close friend for many years and is a well-respected international photographer. He provided valuable advice and ongoing support that helped sustain my commitment to this project. Ross also introduced me to Vic Losick, an award-winning freelance cameraman based in New York. Vic's background in documentary film production and media informed his advice that I repeatedly sought. He continued to encourage me to work toward the completion of the manuscript. And finally, I want thank one of my lifelong friends – Bob Kremer – for his interest and support in developing the manuscript that has finally come to fruition.

I will always be grateful for the support I received from the families of the men my father recruited for the TOOL missions. They are all German nationals who grew up in East Germany. They include Sylvia Anders, daughter of MALLET mission agent Adolph Buchholz; John Strüwe and Charles Konhäuser, the sons of PICKAXE mission agents Walter Strüwe and Emil Konhäuser; and Katrin Ruh, whose father Anton Ruh, together with Paul Lindner, carried out the HAMMER mission into Berlin in March 1945. And I will always remember the late Marjorie Lindner, wife of HAMMER mission agent Paul Lindner, for her unwavering support and kindness that began in 2001 and continued until her death in 2007.

Historical background

In 1976, the United States government declassified top secret files of the Office of Strategic Services (OSS). This was the nation's first military intelligence service. These documents, for the first time, chronicled one of the OSS's most significant achievements: the successful penetration of Nazi Germany by over 200 American spies, following the Allied landing at Normandy in June 1944. From September 1944 through April 1945, the London office of the OSS dispatched over 100 missions into Germany. With agent recruits drawn from the ranks of Spanish Civil War veterans, political refugees and underground labor groups throughout occupied Europe, teams of OSS agents successfully pierced the Third Reich during this period. They gathered critically important military intelligence, which supported the advance of the Allied armies that culminated in the surrender of Nazi Germany on May 8, 1945.

The formation of the OSS

The Office of Strategic Services was organized in 1942 to replace its predecessor – the Coordinator of Information (COI). Formed in 1941, the COI found itself quickly embroiled in bureaucratic conflicts with the Office of Naval Intelligence, the Federal Bureau of Investigation and the Army's intelligence branch as to which agency could conduct covert and special operations.[1] The flaws exposed by this feud became apparent in December 1941. Although the COI had come into existence six months before the surprise attack at Pearl Harbor, the Office of Naval Intelligence had never allowed the COI to examine the intercepted Japanese radio traffic that foreshadowed that the attack was imminent.[2] This intelligence failure revealed the critical need for a centralized foreign intelligence agency.

In an effort to coordinate the gathering of intelligence and resolve the squabbling between the various American intelligence agencies, President Franklin Roosevelt created the Office of War Information (OWI) and the

OSS in 1942. OWI's mission was to handle matters of propaganda. The OSS, meanwhile, began the planning and preparation of "such special services as may be directed by the United States Joint Chiefs of Staff."[3] While this directive was vague, it allowed the OSS to set up its new staff in a way that American intelligence had never done before. The US Army and Navy would maintain their individual intelligence branches, but the OSS was to be the dominant agency in foreign intelligence gathering. By putting the OSS under the direction of the Joint Chiefs, FDR also made it possible for the military to have a direct relationship with the OSS so that military leaders would be able to use any intelligence that the OSS gathered in the field.[4] In June 1942, Colonel William J. Donovan was appointed by President Franklin Roosevelt to head the OSS.

One of the OSS's first organizational decisions was to form the Secret Intelligence unit (SI). And that led to the creation by SI of the Labor Branch, which was first established in July 1942. Its primary mission was to gather intelligence by working with underground labor organizations in order to learn about German industrial and production capabilities.[5] The Labor Branch consisted of individuals who "knew labor problems and who understood and respected the points of view of labor and its leaders . . . who had or could inspire their confidence."[6]

The OSS did not initially comprehend the value of labor groups in intelligence work. Before the creation of the OSS and its Labor Branch, an Austrian émigré and former communist named Paul Hagen approached the COI office in New York. Hagen had already distinguished himself in the United States by publishing *Will Germany Crack*, a 1942 book which argued that Nazi Germany's military and home front weaknesses persisted despite the fact that the German Army was conquering Europe. In April 1942, Hagen approached the COI's chief in New York, Allen Dulles.

In a memo to Dulles, Hagen pointed out the possible benefits of American cooperation with German underground movements. He outlined ways the US could contact these groups, primarily through a specialized agency that would work to build up contacts with underground groups in Germany, a potential cadre of anti-Nazi activists.[7] He also stressed and kept careful records about organized unrest in Germany. In a subsequent memo, Hagen maintained that there were more than six million foreign and conscripted workers inside Germany and a number of German labor émigrés in the United States, Britain and other neutral countries that could help build ties with German underground labor groups.[8] Hagen had laid the groundwork for the creation of the Labor Branch.

In 1942, Arthur Goldberg, chief counsel to the Congress of Industrial Organizations and future Supreme Court justice, was named chief of the Labor Branch. He also had contact with Hagen in New York. After few

xiv *Historical background*

meetings with Hagen, Goldberg recognized the untapped potential of labor intelligence and in a memo to General Donovan wrote:

> The working people of Europe have unparalleled access to strategic information. We must remember that they man the ships and the trains which transport the men and materiel of war. They pour the steel, dig the coal, process the food and make the munitions which are the sinews of war. . . . We can take advantage of the hatred of Hitler by members of the European labor movement. They fought the rise of fascism from its inception. They are its implacable enemy.[9]

By September 1944, the Allies recognized that Germany was not on the verge of collapse as they had imagined. This realization led Donovan and the military brass to conclude that without intelligence from inside Germany itself, the war might continue on indefinitely.[10] Now they were left with the question of how such a seemingly impossible task could be done; British intelligence had been saying for years that it couldn't, that the risks were too great, and that German security was too good.

There was only one branch in the entire OSS organization that had consistently prepared for the possibility of piercing the Third Reich: SI's Labor Branch.[11] William Casey, the OSS London officer and future director of the CIA, was the first high-level OSS staff member to call openly for the infiltration of Germany based on the Labor Branch's insight they had gained over the past two years. As Casey recalled after the war, "the Labor Desk people were the only people who had any preparation for working into Germany."[12]

Origins of the German Penetration Campaign

As the war against Nazi Germany intensified, the OSS mission in London emerged as the most critical intelligence outpost of the US military. Located at 72 Grosvenor Street in the Mayfair section of London, the OSS London office expanded quickly and became the focal point of Anglo-American intelligence relations in the war against Germany. One historian noted that "the London mission was the heart of OSS relations with British intelligence, and as such it personified the essence of that connection in the Allied war effort."[13]

As noted above, in June 1944, SI appointed William J. Casey as director of its London office. Casey, who later served as the director of the Central Intelligence Agency from 1980 to 1986 under President Ronald Reagan, was given full responsibility for organizing the penetration of Nazi Germany by OSS agents. This task of finding agents to parachute blind into the Third Reich "without reception committees, safe houses or friends . . .

who shared a common hatred of the Nazis"[14] was a challenge to Casey's leadership.

Casey's appointment as head of OSS London's SI operations came at a time when the military brass at the Supreme Headquarters of the Allied Expeditionary Force (SHAEF) in London had, with regard to military intelligence, little hope of accomplishing anything of consequence in Germany. In fact, as late as August 1944, high-level intelligence officers within SHAEF admitted that "it had *no* specific intelligence objectives within Germany and . . . had not done any planning for tactical intelligence inside Germany." As a result, SHAEF made it known to the OSS that

> any information regarding location, strength and movement of troops and supplies, together with the state of morale (inside Germany) was of interest.[15]

In response to SHAEF's request for military intelligence, the Labor Branch formulated the FAUST Plan for the penetration of Germany. The plan, named after the Goethe character featured in German literature known for his quest for knowledge and information, called for the training and infiltration of thirty secret agents that would be dropped inside Nazi Germany to establish a network of spies to collect and transmit military intelligence to the OSS. To achieve this objective, the Labor Branch sought to establish relationships with anti-Nazi elements, especially underground labor groups within Germany, who had conveyed their willingness to shelter those agents dropped behind enemy lines in furtherance of the FAUST Plan's aims.[16] On August 20, 1944, SHAEF approved the plan and directed the OSS to begin implementing it.

OSS recruitment of the German exiles

SI was now faced with the formidable task of finding agents to cover Germany. The current pool of potential recruits was scarce. But how and where would the OSS find German nationals in their mid-to-late '30s, conversant in the particular dialect of each German city targeted? And even if such persons existed, would they be willing to be trained and parachuted as enemy spies into their own war-torn country? SI's Labor Division, led by New York labor lawyer Arthur Goldberg, helped meet this challenge.

The Labor Division's efforts to cultivate relationships with underground anti-Nazi labor groups naturally led it to discover one potential source of agent recruits right in its own backyard: the Free German Movement. This group arose after the formation of the Moscow-based National Committee for a Free Germany by high-ranking German prisoners of war and communist exiles following the German Army's surrender at Stalingrad in January 1943. Its primary goal was to foment anti-Nazi resistance and become the nucleus of the post-war German government. With growing communities of anti-Nazi German émigrés drawn from the ranks of socialists, communists and social democrats in Britain, Sweden and France, the Free German movements in these countries sprang to life very quickly. Composed of nearly 1,000 members, the Free German groups served as popular front organizations under the more or less open leadership of German communists that supported the Allied war effort by providing information about conditions inside Nazi Germany, and by calling for Germans to rise up and overthrow Hitler.[17]

By September 1944, the search for suitable agents to lead the German penetration missions intensified. After learning that a growing community of anti-Nazi political exiles was living in the Hampstead section of London, the Labor Division assigned the task of initiating contact with their leadership to Joseph Gould, a 29-year-old army lieutenant from New York City. Gould's prior experience in organizing white-collar trade unionists made him well suited for the job.

After graduating from Columbia University's School of Journalism in 1936, Joseph Gould accepted a job as a motion picture publicist for United Artists, the film studio then owned by Hollywood screen legends Charlie Chaplin and Mary Pickford. He later organized the Screen Publicists Guild, which elected him as its first president in 1938.

His leadership of that white-collar trade union proved to be quite effective. During contract renegotiations in 1940, Gould led a picket line of Guild members outside the New York premiere of Disney's *Fantasia*; a better deal for the East Coast screen publicists, which doubled the weekly pay of its members, was signed shortly thereafter. This initial success in negotiating hard-won contracts with the film studios attracted the interest of film publicists and advertising department office workers employed in New York City by the eight major film companies. As a result, in July 1941, they voted overwhelmingly in an election held by the National Labor Relations Board for the Guild to represent them in future negotiations with the film studios.[18]

Within a year, this decision to select the Screen Publicists Guild as their collective bargaining agent yielded additional financial benefits by reason of the Guild's successful negotiation of a two-year contract with six major film studios. After eight tough months of negotiations, this agreement included substantial wage increases and retroactive pay for advertising office workers and publicists employed by Columbia Pictures, RKO, MGM, Universal Pictures, 20th Century Fox and Paramount Pictures.[19]

And following the Japanese attack on Pearl Harbor that brought the United States into the war, the Screen Publicists Guild in late December 1941 under

Gould's leadership took action to support the nation's war effort by organizing the Motion Picture Emergency Defense Conference that took place at the Hotel Piccadilly located off Times Square. The conference brought together members of the New York City film and theater industries and featured acclaimed theater and film director Garson Kanin as its keynote speaker.[20] Shortly thereafter, the Guild played a key role in the formation of the Film War Service Council.

Joseph Gould, who won reelection twice since he co-founded the Guild in 1938, served three consecutive terms as president of the Screen Publicists Guild. He also served as the Guild's representative on the War Activities Committee of the Motion Pictures Industry, which was formed by the industry to provide further industry-wide support for the war effort. It distributed many government-produced propaganda films and organized war bond drives.[21] But in June 1942, as the nation continued to mobilize in support of the war against the Axis powers, Gould's tenure as president ended as he was ordered by the US military to report for basic training at Camp Croft in South Carolina. And after completing special intelligence training at the OSS training camp in Prince William Forest Park in Virginia, he received orders to report to the OSS London office in June 1944.

Beginning in August 1944, Gould roamed through London neighborhoods in search of information about the Free German Movement in the UK. Employing a typical New Yorker's instincts, he decided to explore local bookstores. That hunch quickly yielded results when he encountered Morris Abbey, the friendly owner of a bookstore on New Bond Street.[22] Abbey took an immediate liking to Gould. He offered him an introduction to one of his regular customers – Dr. Jürgen Kuczynski, the renowned labor economist and leader of the Free German Movement in Great Britain.[23]

Prior to the outbreak of World War II, Kuczynski had earned a doctorate at the University of Heidelberg and then studied in the United States at the Brookings Institution. He returned to Germany from the United States in the late 1920s to edit the German Communist Party newspaper. With the rise of Hitler, Kuczynski went to Moscow in 1936 to meet with exiled German Communist Party leaders. He agreed with their suggestion that he rejoin his family in England where his father, Rene Kuczynski, was a well-known professor at the London School of Economics and the founder of the Free German Movement of Great Britain. In 1943, Jurgen Kuczynski succeeded his father to become the new leader of the Free German Movement.

So with a phone number supplied by Morris Abbey, Lt. Gould contacted Jurgen Kuczynski and arranged to meet with him at his flat in the Hampstead section of London. Gould wasted no time in asking for his help in recruiting German exiles to volunteer for dangerous missions inside Germany as OSS secret agents. Kuczynski responded favorably to Gould's request and shortly thereafter introduced him to a fellow German exile named Erich Henschke who set up a meeting at a London tavern where Gould was introduced to a group of four exiled German trade unionists. All of these men had gone underground in Germany after Hitler's rise to power and later fled to Czechoslovakia in the mid '30s where they continued their work with anti-Nazi underground resistance groups.

But with the heightened level of political repression that resulted from the German occupation of Czechoslovakia in March 1939, anti-Nazi resistance fighters in that country suddenly faced great peril. The British government had already formed the British Committee for Refugees from Czechoslovakia. This committee had been established in October 1938 to provide assistance for refugees created by the German annexation of the Sudetenland following the ill-fated Munich Agreement. This organization worked tirelessly to help refugees escape to Poland where they were given visas that allowed them to legally enter the United Kingdom. Later, the Czech Refugee Trust Fund was formed to provide these refugees with safe passage to England and their efforts successfully enabled over 8,000 people to escape Nazi persecution. Upon arrival, many of the refugees received assistance from the British Youth Peace Assembly.[24]

Among the beneficiaries of the Czech Refugee Trust Fund's work was the group of exiled German trade unionists that were introduced to Joseph Gould in late August 1944 by a German political refugee named Karl Kastro who, unknown to Gould at that time, was designated by the leadership of the German Communist Party in exile in England to provide assistance in recruiting these men for the missions into Germany. A German machine turner named Paul Lindner attended that meeting along with Toni Ruh, Lindner's lifelong friend from Berlin. Also in attendance was a coal miner from the Ruhr Valley named Kurt Gruber, and Adolph Buchholz, a metal worker from Spandau-Berlin. At that meeting, Gould presented them with an opportunity to join the war effort as spies for the OSS. He explained the pressing need of the Allies to obtain military intelligence as they entered Germany.

Following that luncheon, Lt. Gould continued to meet with these men in various homes in the London suburb of Hampstead and developed a sense of what they knew about current conditions inside Nazi Germany, what contacts they had, and who might shelter them after parachuting back into their homeland following years of exile. From an initial list of eleven potential agents given to Gould, seven were chosen for the TOOL missions, which were named HAMMER, CHISEL, PICKAXE, MALLET and BUZZSAW. In addition to Lindner and Ruh, Gould selected Buchholz and Gruber as well as Werner Fischer, Walter Strüwe and Emil Konhäuser. Karl Kastro was later hired as a consultant by the OSS to serve as a liaison with the families of the men during their mission training. All of the German exiles selected for the TOOL missions had gone underground after the Nazis destroyed the trade unions in Germany. All of them had grown up in the German towns and cities that later became the target of their missions. Even more critical was their age, which ranged from 30 to 41.[25] This was key because once dropped back into Germany, they would not likely arouse the suspicion of their countrymen whose younger conscript-age sons were most likely dead or wounded from six years of Hitler's war.

Internment of the German exiles

Following the fall of France in June 1940 that intensified the public's fear of a German invasion of England, the British government undertook a mass round-up of most Germans and Austrians now living in Britain, pro- and anti-Nazi alike. It was at this time that Winston Churchill issued his famous order: "Collar the Lot!"

The increase in the number of exiles interned led to a serious space problem within the UK, and following offers from the Canadian and Australian governments, more than 7,500 internees were shipped overseas in late June and early July 1949. Among those interned in those countries were some of the German exiles recruited by Army Lt. Joseph Gould for the German Penetration Campaign missions, including Paul Lindner and Werner Fischer (Canada) and Anton Ruh (Australia). Some of the other men recruited by Lt. Gould were interned off the coast of Ireland in camps set up by the British government on the Isle of Man; that group included Kurt Gruber, Adolph Buchholz and Walter Strüwe.

Tragically, in the early hours of Tuesday, July 2, 1940, 75 miles west of the Irish Atlantic coast, one of the converted steamships used to transport the internees to camps in Canada – the *Arandora Star* – was torpedoed and sunk by a German submarine. On board were 712 Italians, 438 Germans (including Nazi sympathizers and Jewish refugees), and 374 British seamen and soldiers. Over half lost their lives. It was this event that swayed public opinion towards the enemy aliens. By March 1941, 12,500 internees had been released, rising to over 17,500 in August, and by 1942 fewer than 5,000 remained interned, mainly on the Isle of Man. By that time, all of the anti-Nazi German exiles recruited by Lt. Gould had been released from internment by the British government.

Notes

1 Joseph Persico, *Roosevelt's Secret War: FDR and World War II Espionage* (New York: Random House, 2001), pp. 112–113.

2 William Casey, *The Secret War Against Hitler* (Washington, DC: Regnery Gateway, 1988), p. 7.

3 R. Harris Smith, *OSS: The Secret History of America's First Central Intelligence Agency* (Berkeley: University of California Press, 1971), p. 2.

4 Casey (note 2), p. 11.

5 George O. Pratt to David K. Bruce, OSS Memorandum, Plans for Proposed Operations on the Continent – Labor Desk, March 23, 1944 (Box 48, RG 226, NARA).

6 War Report of the OSS (Office of Strategic Services), U.S. War Department, Washington D.C., (Walker Publishing Company, 1976), p. 184.

7 Memorandum from Paul Hagen to Allen Dulles, How to Prepare Collaboration with the Anti-Nazi Underground Movement, April 10, 1942 (Box 12, Entry 106, RG 226, NARA).

8 Christof Mauch, *The Shadow War Against Hitler*, trans. Jeremiah Riemer (New York: Columbia University Press, 2003), pp. 170–171.

9 Joseph Persico, *Piercing the Reich: The Penetration of Nazi Germany by American Secret Agents During WWII* (New York: Viking Press, 1979), p. 19; (a copy of the Arthur Goldberg memo to OSS director William Donovan is attached to Appendix A).

10 Office of Strategic Services, Division of Intelligence Procurement Air Operations Final Report, Appendix, June 1, 1945 (Box 49, Entry 110, RG 226, NARA).

11 Persico (see note 9), p. 113, 319.

12 William Casey, interview by Joseph Persico, August 1976, Folder Casey (Box 1, Joseph Persico Papers), Hoover Institute, Stanford, CA, pp. 9–10.

13 *Kings and Desperate Men: The United States Office of Strategic Services in London and the Anglo-American Relationship by Brian Nelson Macpherson* (unpublished doctoral thesis, University of Toronto, 1995).

14 Persico (see note 9).

15 Macpherson (see note 13) footnote 8 on p. 165.

16 Memorandum from Colonel James Forgan, O.S.S Detachment, ETOUSA to Supreme Commander, SHAEF, August 16, 1944, Washington, DC, National Archives Records Administration (hereafter NARA), Record Group 226, Records of the Office of Strategic Services, Declassification No. NND843115.

17 Heike Bungert, The OSS and Its Cooperation with the Free Germany Committees, 1944–45, *Intelligence and National Security*, Volume 12, July 1997, p. 131.

18 Publicist Guild Wins, *New York Times*, July 18, 1941.

19 Screen Publicists Win Pay Increases, *New York Times*, May 6, 1942.

20 *Brooklyn Daily Eagle*, December 17, 1941; Kanin would later write and direct the Broadway version of *The Diary of Anne Frank* and *Born Yesterday*.

21 *SPG News*, Screen Publicists Guild of New York, February 1942.

22 Joseph Gould, *An OSS Officer's Own WWII Story: Of His Seven German Agents and Their Five Labor Desk Missions into Warring Germany*, unpublished manuscript (Washington, DC, 1989).

23 Bungert (note 17), p. 132.

24 Flora Lewis, *Red Pawn: The Story of Noel Field* (Garden City, NY: Doubleday, 1965), pp. 116–117.

25 Joseph Gould memoir (note 22).

1   The HAMMER mission and the GRU

This chapter will focus primarily on the two men who led the successful HAMMER mission into Berlin. While the agents of this mission – Paul Lindner and Anton Ruh – have since been posthumously awarded the Silver Star by the United States military for their performance of the mission, new documents from the East German archives show that they may also have secretly collaborated with agents of the GRU – the Soviet military intelligence service during World War II. This secret relationship enabled the GRU to gain access to top secret mission files and the sources and methods utilized by the OSS at the time. These documents add a troubling footnote to the historical record of the successful campaign conducted by the OSS to penetrate the Third Reich during the final months of the war.

Mission training

In November 1944, Lindner and Ruh began rigorous training under the direction of Lt. Joseph Gould, who had been designated the conducting officer for these missions. Lindner and Ruh were able to live at home with their families in Hampstead. They commuted daily to the OSS mission training school in Ruislip where they attended briefings dealing with a wide range of subjects designed to prepare them for their missions. Mondays were exclusively devoted to *order of battle*; Wednesdays for dealing with the SS and military patrols; Fridays for studying maps and reconnaissance photos showing the exact location within Germany where they would be dropped.[1] They also underwent parachute training at Ringway, which was located near the city of Manchester. This was the wartime base for the Royal Air Force parachute training school. It was charged with the initial training of all allied paratroopers trained in Europe. Agents of the British special agent unit called Special Operations Executive (SOE) were also trained to jump there.[2]

Lindner and Ruh also worked on the development of their cover stories and reviewed documents containing information on underground resistance contacts and safe addresses in Berlin. As the mission dispatch date grew closer, the OSS Schools and Training Division subjected Lindner and Ruh to "cover quizzes" to see if they had internalized their mission identities. And since these two men had been living in England for nearly seven years, it was necessary to have them outfitted at clothing depots stocked with the garments of European refugees who had fled Nazi persecution and which had been manufactured in Germany.

Probably the most difficult part of the TOOL mission training was the work done inside prisoner-of-war ("POW") camps maintained outside London by the US Army, where captured German Army officers and troops were being held. There were a number of reasons why this aspect of their training proved to be so important. First, because of their extended exile as German political refugees in England, Lindner and Ruh had lost touch with their homeland. The POW cage infiltration work gave them an opportunity to get a feel for wartime conditions in the German towns and cities they came from. This work also proved to be a great training ground for these men because it enabled them to live their own cover story.

Beginning in early 1945, Lindner, along with other German exiles recruited for these missions, were placed inside these POW cages, where they mingled for days before quietly slipping out with the aid of the OSS. Afterwards, they submitted detailed reports on the valuable information obtained from quiet conversation with German POWs. The following excerpts from these reports provide a snapshot into the hearts and minds of the soldiers of Hitler's army.[3]

On the prospects of losing the war

The German POWs encountered in the camp by Lindner continued to publicly express their faith in the Fuhrer, and in the secret weapons they believed were being developed by the Nazis that would enable Germany to turn the tide of the war around. Others rested their hopes on what they felt was the inevitable conflict that would soon arise between the US and the Soviet Union. But in private conversations with Lindner, most admitted that the war was lost but withheld stating such views for fear of physical harm from other POWs. Regardless of their private views, all still believed that the German soldier was superior but simply could not overcome the vast material superiority of the Allied armies.

On the morale of the German Army

A continuing theme throughout all of the reports submitted by the TOOL mission agents was the failure of leadership exhibited by their commanding officers on the front line. The German POWs repeatedly called them cowards who would run to shelter inside tanks at the first shot fired and leave them to fight alone without direction. The stories of high-ranking officer incompetence were never-ending. Some even claimed that their superiors would surrender positions in the field to induce capture rather than have to return home to war-ravaged Germany. One field commander even refused a private plane sent on the personal orders of Hitler and instead surrendered his unit to an Allied army officer rather than report back to the Fuhrer. And many low-ranking German soldiers complained that captured officers, like themselves, were not above currying favor from camp guards by offering valuable jewelry or watches in exchange for cigarettes, which triggered a flourishing black market inside the camp.

On the persecution of the Jews

When the subject of the Nazi persecution of European Jews came up, almost all of the captured POWs knew that the Allies would hold Germany responsible for the Holocaust. Most chilling was the predominant view in the camp that the Nazis should have waited until military victory was won before exterminating the Jews. This, according to one POW, would have enabled Germany to avoid "bringing the Jews of the USA and England into the frontline against us."[4]

According to Paul Lindner's report, all of the POWs knew of the "slave hells" where Jews and foreigners were worked to death. According to Paul Lindner, when he tried to elicit conversation about the death camps, "the POWs would smile back with a knowing glance and a twinkle of the eye that said: *you know yourself and I needn't tell you*." The feelings expressed on this subject by the German POWs demonstrated what "twelve years of Nazi education had taught the younger generation: *education for murder*."[5]

On the United States military

The German POWs envied American soldiers for their "good food and good pay" and for their abundant "war material." But they didn't hold a favorable opinion of US soldiers "who long for their home and for a speedy end of the war," which they felt was a "sign of weakness." Yet many of these German soldiers were pleased that they were "prisoners of the US" and were looking "impatiently to their being transported to America."

On the Soviet Union

The German POWs confessed to being "awfully frightened by the Russians" and that nobody in the camp believed that "Germany could conquer Russia." Instead, many of the POWs said that "it would have been better for Germany to attack Britain and they feel sure that they would have been victorious." They felt that if the Germans conquered Britain, then the US would not have been able to attack Germany in the West and would have had no other choice but "to send arms to Germany instead of Russia." Their fear of Russia was based on their belief that the Soviet Army would exact revenge on Germany because of the atrocities that the German soldiers inflicted on the Russian people.

On the resistance of European countries occupied by Nazi Germany

Many of the German POWs viewed the citizens of France and Belgium as "very ungrateful" because they were "treated nicely" by the German Army. And those who resisted the Nazis in these occupied countries were seem as "terrorists and bandits."

On life in the prisoner of war camps

The POWs also admitted that food in the camp was abundant and better than what their fellow soldiers or their families at home inside Germany were being fed. Moreover, they had no complaints about their housing or the supply of blankets and covers. But outside of talking, playing cards and cleaning their huts, the German POWs had nothing much to do but "kill time" and barter for cigarettes. And "being called a Nazi was regarded as an insult."[6]

Mission communication technology

In early 1943, the OSS formed the Communications Group to develop communications equipment that would aid the transmission of military intelligence from behind enemy lines. One of its radio operators heard about the work of a New Jersey inventor who had designed the first battery-powered handheld mobile "walkie-talkie." This man was Al Gross and in 1939 he was invited to demonstrate his invention to OSS chief William Donovan in Washington, DC. The meeting was so successful that Donovan recruited him into the OSS and made him a captain.[7]

Captain Gross collaborated with Lt. Commander Stephen Simpson and Dewitt R. Goddard, two radio technicians from RCA Laboratories in New York. Their work led to the development of the battery-powered Joan-Eleanor ("J/E") transmitter-receiver that resembled a modern-day cell phone: it measured 6 inches, weighed only 3 pounds, and was equipped with a collapsible antenna.[8] Each of the German exiles selected for the TOOL missions was trained to operate the J/E transmitter, which utilized very high radio frequencies. This enabled them to orally transmit military intelligence on the ground to planes hovering over Europe without detection from German Army short-wave radio operators.

The capture of British special operation agents dropped into Germany in late 1942 underscored the need for this new radio transmission technology that could elude electronic detection by the Nazis. Declassified documents found in the British archives in 2000 enabled historians to determine that these deaths were engineered by the notorious war criminal SS Major Horst Kopkow, a senior Gestapo officer responsible for counterespionage. Using short-wave radios equipped with direction finders, Kopkow's team was able to detect messages that these agents were attempting to send back to London using their radios. This fatal flaw in the radio transmitters sealed the fate of these British agents as the Gestapo's radio engineers were able to track the location of their signals. Nearly 116 agents were captured and hanged in Nazi concentration camps.[9] The newly developed J/E transmitter, with its ability to transmit voice messages using undetectable high frequencies, allayed Allied fears of such capture by the German Army.

The agents' radio transmitters had a range of about 20 miles. While behind enemy lines, the agents radioed their intelligence in plain language, which was received by the plane's radioman hunched in a small cabin installed in the rear fuselage that hovered over Germany at 30,000 feet. Equipped with a wire recorder, the Allied planes used for this purpose could receive a message from the agents in twenty minutes that would take three days to decode using conventional radio transmitters.[10]

They were also trained to decipher coded messages that would be transmitted to them through the British Broadcasting Corporation (BBC) radio in German when behind enemy lines. They were instructed to listen to these BBC broadcasts in order to learn the time and location of supply drops and J/E transmissions. To confuse German radio operators, the OSS asked the BBC to play alternate bars of Sindling's classical music composition *Rustles of Spring* as a signal to the agents that mission-related information would shortly be sent to them.[11]

The German attack in the Ardennes Forest: An intelligence failure

By late December 1944, most of the German exiles selected for the TOOL missions marked the Christmas season with a gala holiday dinner at Paul Lindner's home. This event was attended by Lt. Gould, who joined their wives and children to sing Christmas songs in German. Here, at a time when millions of Europe's Jews were being murdered, an oasis of admiration and mutual respect began to flourish between a Jewish US Army officer and his seven German recruits who shared a common goal: the destruction of Nazi Germany. But one last desperate thrust by Hitler's army dampened that holiday spirit and underscored the need to jump-start the OSS campaign to penetrate Germany.

The German counteroffensive through the Ardennes Forest in Belgium in late December of 1944 intensified the pressure from the Allied military command on the OSS to launch the German penetration missions. Known as the Battle of the Bulge, this last-ditch attack by the German Army was considered "the first and only serious reversal suffered by the Allied armies in its sweep from Normandy to the Rhine."[12] With the cover of heavy fog that hid the German military buildup, the attack came as a complete surprise, halted the Allied offensive, and cost American and British armies over 70,000 casualties.[13]

The Ardennes Forest attack by the German Army resulted "in the acute awareness that Allied forces were going into Germany blind and in a genuine appreciation of the intelligence that had been extracted from the [French underground] both before and after the [D-Day] invasion. And it caused an immediate demand for tactical intelligence."[14] With only three active OSS agents inside the Reich, the pressure on William Casey to get more agents into Germany began to mount.[15] Just as Lindner and Ruh had completed their training for their mission into Berlin, an unexpected challenge to their use arose within the OSS.

Political conflict within OSS London

The proposed use of the German exiles for the TOOL missions generated controversy within OSS London. Some had argued that the Free German Movement was no more than a Western subsidiary of the Moscow-based National Committee for a Free Germany. As they continued to proliferate in other Western European countries, the State Department, the FBI and conservative elements within the OSS suspected an "international Moscow line, a coordinated plan issued from Moscow to Bolshevize Germany after the end of the war."[16] One OSS officer within SI "found the prospect of arming Reds and positioning them where they could grasp power in Germany to be naïve."[17]

Special Intelligence chief Bill Casey challenged their use because of the strong objections expressed by British military intelligence. But Labor Division chief Arthur Goldberg opposed Casey on this issue. The matter was brought to OSS director William J. Donovan for resolution. Although Donovan was a Wall Street Republican lawyer with impeccable establishment credentials, he found Goldberg's arguments more persuasive. In particular, Goldberg asserted that the Joint Chiefs of Staff charter that created the OSS had expressly referenced the potential enlistment of irregular forces in fighting the war.[18] Donovan's ultimate decision to overrule Casey reflected his pragmatism in seeking assistance from anyone that could help the Allies defeat Nazi Germany. He was reported to have said "he'd put Stalin on the OSS payroll if it would help defeat Hitler."[19] On March 1, 1945, Donovan issued an order directing the immediate dispatch of the HAMMER mission into Berlin.

Destination: Berlin

Of the five TOOL missions, the HAMMER mission was the first sent into Germany and has achieved the most historical significance, mainly because "it would drive deeper into the Reich than any other mission before . . . to Berlin."[20] The German exiles chosen for this mission were – until their forced exile – lifelong natives of Berlin: Paul Lindner and Anton "Toni" Ruh. Both men were also close friends and had worked together in the anti-Nazi underground, until they successfully fled to England from Prague in early 1939. Both were ordinary working men who found themselves needed to perform a secret mission that could make a difference in ending the war.

Paul Lindner

On the evening that Joseph Gould accompanied Lindner and Ruh to Watton Airfield for their flight into Germany, Paul Lindner had just reached his 34th birthday. Born in Berlin, Lindner became active in the German labor movement at a very early age. By his 18th birthday, Lindner had become well known for his work as an organizer of the German Metal Workers Union. In 1930, Lindner spoke out publicly against the Nazi Party's proposal for labor conscription of German youth. His efforts helped sway public opinion against this plan – and helped earn him a place on the Nazi Party's enemies list. In 1932, Nazi storm troopers laid an ambush near his parents' home, where he was suddenly attacked and beaten. A year later, after Hitler's appointment as the German chancellor, Lindner was arrested again and taken by Nazi thugs to a private barracks where he was tortured and beaten for nearly twelve days; he suffered broken teeth and permanent kidney damage.[21]

After recovering from his injuries in a Berlin hospital, Lindner organized a hiking club that served as a cover for his underground work with the League of Labor Youth. By 1935, Lindner had trained over 400 young Germans in the basics of underground resistance work.[22] And he continued distributing anti-Nazi leaflets, painting anti-Nazi slogans on public street corners and providing aid to families whose breadwinners had disappeared into the first concentration camps. Inevitably, Lindner came under the Gestapo's radar and had to leave Berlin and his family in 1935 for Czechoslovakia. There he posed as a ski instructor to mask the illegal political work he continued to perform for the underground trade union resistance. For the next three years, Lindner helped Jews fleeing Nazi persecution to escape across the Czech border, and he collected information on secret German military installations for the Czech Army and evacuated children from the Sudetenland, which had just been ceded to the Nazis as a result of the Munich Agreement.[23]

After securing a visa through the Czech Refugee Trust Fund, Lindner traveled to Great Britain in 1939 and arrived in the small English town of Chatham, Kent. There he received aid from the local Youth Refugee and Relief Counsel, an organization formed by anti-fascist sympathizers to help German refugees adjust to life in England. Later, he met Marjorie Andrews, a native of the nearby village of Strood, and a volunteer from the Labor Party League of Youth. While she tutored him to learn English, they fell in love and later married following Lindner's return from deportation in Ottawa, Canada, where he had been interned in May 1940 with other German political refugees.

By late 1941, the British relocated Lindner to an internment camp off the coast of England on the Isle of Man. In August 1941, Lindner submitted an application to British immigration officials requesting release from the internment camp. In that application, Lindner asserted that he sought release and return to England "in order to help fight the Nazi regime." The British granted his application. Upon his release, Paul Lindner could have quietly sat out the war with other exiled German refugees. But he chose a different path and returned to England still fiercely committed to fighting the Nazi regime. Following their wedding in May 1942, Paul and Marjorie Lindner moved to the Hampstead section of London. Lindner soon obtained employment as a machine turner for a British firm and waited for his opportunity to rejoin the now global struggle to destroy Hitler.

Anton "Toni" Ruh

Toni Ruh's journey from underground resistance fighter to OSS secret agent also equipped him with skills needed for the HAMMER mission. Like Lindner, he was a Berlin native trained as a printer and lithographer. He started doing illegal political work with Lindner but was arrested and held for nearly six months until his release in early 1934. Ruh also sought refuge in Czechoslovakia after the Gestapo discovered a secret political leaflet shop he was operating in Berlin.

While residing in Prague, Ruh continued to smuggle leaflets into Germany. During this period, he actually returned to Berlin on six occasions – while being hunted by the Gestapo – to deliver forged passports to help Jews and other political dissidents flee Hitler's regime. After Germany occupied Czechoslovakia in 1939, Ruh was declared a political fugitive and hunted by the Nazis, but he evaded capture and successfully fled to England with the aid of the same Czech underground that assisted Lindner. After briefly settling in London, Ruh was also interned by the British government in June 1940, and he was then deported to Australia, where he lived until November 1941. Upon his return, he reunited with his wife, Elizabeth, resumed work as a welder for a British firm and began raising a family.[24]

The HAMMER mission begins

On March 2, 1945, Lt. Joseph Gould received an order to dispatch the HAMMER mission from Watton Airfield, where Lindner and Ruh would be flown out and parachuted into Berlin. One historian has described Gould as the "mother hen" of the HAMMER mission agents. While driving Lindner and Ruh to the airfield, Gould recalled being bothered "by the sensation that he was living through a movie scenario; Gould has described that night as being very emotional because he had committed the professional sin of growing too close to these men." As they boarded the plane, both men were carrying their J/E transmitters and forged "work orders" documenting their status as skilled defense workers exempt from military service. After taking deep swills of brandy from Gould's flask, they shook hands and were off. Four hours later, the mission aircraft, battered with the remnants of anti-aircraft fire, returned to Watton Airfield with the news that Lindner and Ruh had parachuted safely into a clear moonlit evening.[25] "The mission to Berlin was in."[26] The following account of the HAMMER mission, drawn from the declassified OSS files and interviews with surviving relatives, provides an extraordinary window into life among ordinary Berlin residents trying to survive the final days of chaos and destruction that marked the death rattle of the Nazi regime.[27]

After safely parachuting into a field about 30 miles outside the city, Lindner and Ruh buried their weapons and communications gear. They walked to a nearby station where they were able to catch a train to downtown Berlin. Because of blackouts, the trains were dark and overcrowded, enabling the HAMMER team to go unnoticed in those tense early moments of the mission. Although they came prepared to make contact with a member of the underground resistance, the darkness of night made it unsafe to confirm the address. So instead, Lindner and Ruh invoked the mission contingency plan and sought shelter from Lindner's parents, whom he had not seen since 1935. While Paul Lindner, Sr. and his wife, Freeda, had received letters from their son during his internment in Canada, they were completely unprepared for what became one of the special moments of the HAMMER mission – and the Lindner family.[28]

As they arrived to find his home miraculously untouched by Allied bombs, Lindner tapped on a front-door window. The noise awakened his parents. At first they did not believe that it was really their son who had finally returned after ten long years. But after concluding that only Paul could answer their very personal questions, a joyous reunion followed. Lindner later recalled his mother's emotional embrace, telling her son that "she knew that he would come home and fight the Nazis one day!"[29] In a city overflowing with households of sorrow and grief, this unexpected and very emotional reunion of mother and son after ten years in exile was especially poignant.

The HAMMER agents spent the first week of the mission with Lindner's family while quietly familiarizing themselves with the barely beating pulse of war-ravaged Berlin. Both men decided to remain illegal and not use their work papers because they felt it would impede their ability to execute the mission. And the mission objectives remained the same: collect strategically important information for transmission to the OSS via the J/E transmitter.

Their next destination also resulted in another family reunion – with Frau Treadup, Toni Ruh's sister. Her opposition to Hitler's regime had never wavered in his absence. Both Paul and Toni eagerly sought information about old friends that they felt would help with their mission. But she had to sadly inform them that all had been killed in action or had died in concentration camps. Two days later, on March 8, Lindner and Ruh returned to their landing point to retrieve their weapons, and the J/E communications equipment which was stored inside their gas masks. They also carried cigarettes and coffee used to barter for food, including a live sheep they would later slaughter and eat for dinner. Every evening, they would listen to German BBC broadcasts to learn dates of J/E contacts and supply drops at remote points outside of Berlin.

While walking through Berlin, the HAMMER agents were often accompanied by Paul's father, who possessed strong identification papers, thus enabling Lindner and Ruh to acquire much-needed credibility that kept them above suspicion. Some of the information transmitted to the OSS came from one of Paul's favorite teachers, whom he sought out and found at his home. But that night – March 18 – came more bombing that rendered it impossible for them to make contact with Allied planes they knew were coming to drop supplies and receive J/E transmissions. And because the Nazi regime imposed stiff border controls in a last-ditch effort to force Berliners to defend the city, no one could slip out of Berlin.[30]

On March 26, the HAMMER mission achieved its major breakthrough when it made a successful contact with an Allied plane hovering over Germany. They transmitted critically important military intelligence dealing with German troop movements, the location of operational munitions factories and, most important, the sinking morale of the German people.[31] In his memoirs, SI chief William Casey noted that a "big breakthrough had been achieved from the intelligence yielded by the HAMMER team, including important air-target data on a still-functioning power plant that kept key factories running . . . as well as detail on the importance of a Berlin transportation net and suggestions of key spots where (Allied) bombs could disrupt it."[32] Collecting that information over the prior two weeks, however, tested the limits of the survival skills of the HAMMER agents. Incessant Allied bombings dominated their every move. In order to avoid suspicion, Lindner and Ruh moved through a maze of public bomb shelters. They were often forced to break up fights between Berliners whose nerves were fraying from the unending Allied air assaults.

Mission at risk

During Lindner's exile from his family, his sister Inge had married a young soldier named Hans Gottwald. He had never met his brother-in-law Paul. Right after the March 26 transmission, Hans unexpectedly showed up at the Lindner home. He had been granted leave from his unit for destroying a Russian tank that earned him the Iron Cross. But he had no idea that his brother-in-law had returned to Germany as an enemy agent. This discovery inevitably led to an intense all-night dialogue between Paul, Toni and Hans that nearly threatened their survival –[33] and that of the HAMMER mission.[34]

But much to Paul's relief, Hans was "more good soldier than Nazi"[35] and responded to Paul's passionate arguments about the Nazi regime and Hitler's barbarism. Gottwald apparently recalled his own terrible experiences witnessing the carnage on the eastern front and began to question where he owed his loyalty. Was it to the Fuhrer – or to his family? This self-examination ultimately led to his decision to abandon his unit – and not report Paul and Toni to military authorities, which would have meant their immediate execution for treason. Paul decided to remain with his family, and his document-forging skills were then used to copy the stamp of Hans's Panzer unit. He then imprinted an extension on Gottwald's leave papers that passed muster when checked the next day during a visit to a German Army field office.[36]

In early April, the HAMMER agents had an encounter with a German patrol that nearly cost them their lives. On Easter Sunday, Lindner and Ruh had received a message through the BBC that food supplies were to be dropped at a contact point some 50 kilometers northwest of Berlin. But when they arrived at this location, Allied planes failed to respond to messages they sent through their J/E transmitter, so they wound up spending the night in an open field. At dawn, they woke up to find themselves surrounded by German Army troops. After gathering their gear, the HAMMER agents decided to quietly walk through the woods toward a nearby railroad station, but they were unexpectedly stopped by a lieutenant from the Herman Göring Division who asked to see their papers.

Lindner and Ruh must have encountered similarly tense moments during their pre-exile days in the Berlin underground and were obviously prepared for these situations. Both men had routinely carried dirty laundry in their duffel bags to make it appear as if they were just arriving from the outside to help with the defense of Berlin. So they used Toni Ruh's dirty underwear as a prop in a "Laurel and Hardy" routine they evidently had devised to escape these encounters with German patrols.

When this German soldier asked to see their papers, Paul immediately pulled out his Nazi Party membership card and work orders. While examining them, the soldier asked to see Toni's papers – and the contents of his bag that contained the J/E transmitter and other incriminating documents. Playing to the German soldier's "master race" indoctrination, Paul informed him that his friend was a dumb Czech who didn't understand German and that he would have to translate the soldier's instructions. This bought the HAMMER agents time to prepare their weapons, which they almost had to use. But the German lieutenant grew exasperated with Toni's snail-like search for his papers as he emptied one dirty sock after another and finally let them go. The HAMMER team had averted a close call, and they continued on their way to catch a train back to Berlin.[37]

Mission finale

By the second week of April, conditions in Berlin continued to hamper Lindner and Ruh's ability to respond to requests from the OSS via the BBC for more military intelligence. The combined effect of Allied bombing raids and incessant Russian artillery fire caused further chaos in the streets. On April 22, the HAMMER team received a coded BBC message from the OSS requesting that one of them cross over the battle lines and turn themselves in to a Soviet Army officer. The other was to stay behind until American troops arrived in Berlin. But the tightening Berlin defenses manned by German Army troops closed off all avenues of escape out of the city. So Lindner and Ruh decided to remain with Lindner's family until Russian troops reached the Neukölln district. They would not wait long.

Two days later, on April 24, the HAMMER mission would end – but only after some of the mission's most extraordinary events. That day marked a major breakthrough by the Soviet Army in the Battle of Berlin. Armies commanded by Red Army generals Zhukov and Konev met in the southern suburbs of Berlin and encircled German Army troops. Bitter street fighting broke out in the eastern and southern districts of the capital.[38]

The HAMMER team, along with brother-in-law Hans and Lindner's father, would soon become a part of that fighting when on April 22 they came upon a battle involving Russian troops trying to stop German soldiers from blowing up a bridge across the Teltow Canal near the town of Baumschulenbrücke. The German Army had deployed a special bridge demolition team. In addition, the commander of the platoon tasked with defending the canal – 1st Lieutenant von Reuss – reported that "a fire trench, a rocket projector and numerous machine gun positions were also put in place"[39] in an effort to prevent the Red Army from crossing the canal. And the Germans deployed nearly 15,000 troops in an ill-fated effort to prevent the Red Army from crossing the canal.

This is how one historian described the ensuing battle:

> Cracking the Teltow Canal line fell to General Pavel Rybalko and his Third Guards Tank Army. He spent all of 23 April bringing up 3,000 artillery pieces, mortars, and Katyusha rocket launchers, concentrating them on a narrow front. At 6:20 AM on 24 April, they all opened up, and then assault teams crossed the canal in collapsible boats to dig out strongpoints with flame throwers and explosive charges. The Germans didn't die easily, wiping out some of the teams or forcing them to fall back, but the defenders could only delay the inevitable. By early afternoon, Soviet armor was rolling across the canal on top of pontoon bridges, even while fighting continued to crush German resistance up and down the waterway.[40]

With weapons obtained just the day before, Lindner, his father and Anton Ruh would open fire. Then, more Russian soldiers arrived to join the battle – and started firing on Lindner and Ruh. However, they quickly stopped after realizing that they were anti-Nazi partisans. The German soldiers were quickly disarmed and taken prisoner by the Soviet Army. In addition, the HAMMER team successfully deactivated explosives set by the German Army and prevented one of the bridges from being blown up that would have hindered the advance of Soviet tanks. The Russian troops thanked them for their help.[41]

Shortly thereafter, Lindner and Ruh decided to end the HAMMER mission and report themselves as American soldiers to a Russian commander named Captain Martov. But in the climate of fear and suspicion that marked the final chaotic days of the war, the Soviet Army refused their offer and placed the HAMMER agents under arrest. Upon searching their belongings, the Russians subjected the agents to harsh interrogation after discovering OSS codebooks that they felt should have been voluntarily handed over. Moreover, the HAMMER team's request that the Russians guarantee their safety from harm by other Russian troops angered Martov. This was because they claimed to have witnessed Soviet Army soldiers brutalizing German civilians, especially women. According to the debriefing transcripts, Captain Martov reacted harshly to this accusation of misconduct and threatened to imprison Lindner and Ruh as enemies of the state.[42]

Unable to convince the Russians that they were OSS agents, Lindner and Ruh remained in Soviet custody for the next two months. They were moved repeatedly throughout Germany before finally being released to US Army personnel near Leipzig on June 16, 1945. From there, the HAMMER agents were flown to Paris, where they submitted to military debriefings about what happened to them during the nearly two months they conducted the mission inside Berlin.[43]

"Sonya" and the GRU

Almost immediately after the war ended in May 1945, Joseph Gould accepted a transfer to serve in occupied Berlin with the Office of Military Government. He received a promotion and assumed a new rank as a captain in the US Army. Captain Gould was then awarded the Certificate of Merit by the US military. He remained in Germany until his honorable discharge from the US Army in 1946, when he returned to his family in New York City and resumed his career in the film industry. With the Cold War between the US and Soviet Union heating up, Gould lost touch with the surviving agents of the TOOL missions who had returned to Germany. Following his discovery of an interview with Jurgen Kuczynski in the *Wall Street Journal* in 1975, Gould initiated correspondence with the German economist, who was now living in East Berlin while serving as an economic adviser to East German president Erich Honecker.[44]

The end of the Cold War in 1989 made it easier for Joseph Gould to consider visiting Germany for the first time since his US Army discharge. In August 1990, Gould traveled to Berlin and enjoyed a reunion with Jurgen Kuczynski. He also sought information on the fate of the surviving TOOL mission agents with whom he had lost touch after the war.[45] But sadly, Gould learned for the first time that all of his men were now deceased.

During that trip, Jurgen Kuczynski introduced Gould to his elderly sister – Ursula Kuczynski – during a quiet lunch at Kuczynski's home one afternoon. That meeting shook Gould's special memories of that important period in his life when he played a key role in the OSS German penetration campaign, which by this time had gained recognition as an important milestone in the history of US wartime intelligence. This is because Gould discovered that Ursula Kuczynski. Ursula Kuczynski was the notorious GRU agent who was operating a Soviet spy ring in England at the time when Gould first approached Jurgen for help in finding German exiles for the TOOL missions. In 1977, she had written *Sonya's Report* under the pen name Ruth Werner.[46]

Born in 1907, Ursula Kuczynski joined the German Communist Party in 1926. She was then recruited into the Soviet Army intelligence service – the GRU – in 1930 by Richard Sorge, its master spy in Shanghai. Given the code name "Sonya," she went to Moscow for radio communications training, where she learned how to transmit information to the GRU in Moscow. By late 1941, after completing assignments in China, Poland and Switzerland, she married an English citizen named Len Beurton and moved to Great Britain. She then rejoined her father and brother Jurgen, who had already emigrated there in the mid-1930s. After settling into a farm outside of Oxfordshire, Kuczynski set up her radio transmitter in the house attic and resumed her work as "Sonya" for the GRU.[47]

While living in England during the war, Werner transmitted atomic secrets to the Soviet Union in early 1942 that were given to her during secret meetings on the platform of a railroad station outside of London in 1941 by British physicist Klaus Fuchs, another German communist refugee – and a member of the UK's delegation to the Manhattan Project in Los Alamos, New Mexico. A year later, a Soviet mole within the British Foreign Ministry somehow got a copy of a top secret document called the Quebec Memorandum, which had memorialized agreements made between President Roosevelt and Prime Minister Winston Churchill in the summer of 1943. It was quietly delivered to Werner's Oxfordshire home. That document, considered one of the most top secret of the war, confirmed the development of the atomic bomb and each nation's vow to maintain the secrecy of the Manhattan Project without disclosure to their Soviet ally. Just three days before she gave birth to her third child in September 1943, Werner coded the memorandum and transmitted it to Moscow using her short-wave radio. This has been deemed by historians as a major breach of security within the British Foreign Ministry and it enabled Stalin to learn about the development of the atomic bomb by the US and Britain. She was later awarded the Order of the Red Banner by Stalin for her work in England for the GRU.[48] In 1949, Werner eluded the pursuit of British intelligence and hurriedly left England after gaining admittance to East Germany.[49]

At that first meeting at Kuczynski's home with Ruth Werner, Gould found himself deeply troubled to learn of her purported role in the recruitment of the German exiles for the German Penetration Campaign during the late summer of '44.[50] One year later, in 1991, Ruth Werner revised her memoirs in preparation of the English version of *Sonya's Report* and added a new chapter that referenced this meeting with Joseph Gould at her brother's home in Berlin in late August of 1990.[51]

According to Ruth Werner, she first became aware of the OSS interest in recruiting the German exiles from her brother Jurgen Kuczynski, following his initial meeting with Joseph Gould that had been arranged by bookstore owner Morris Abbey. Werner immediately notified the GRU and advised them of this development.[52] The Soviets immediately conveyed their interest in the use of the German exiles by the OSS for the TOOL missions. Werner then directed Jurgen to introduce Gould to a key member of the German Communist Party then living in London named Erich Henschke – *alias Karl Kastro*.[53] This was the same Karl Kastro who had assisted Gould with the agent recruitment process during that same period in the late summer of 1944 and who had been hired by the OSS as liaison to the families of the men recruited for the missions.

Erich Henschke was born in 1907 in Danzig to an Orthodox Jewish family and attended primary and secondary school in Berlin. In 1928, he joined the German Communist Party. In 1934, Henschke fled Germany and immigrated to the Soviet Union, where he attended the International Lenin School from 1934 to 1936. He briefly returned to Germany but had to flee to Czechoslovakia in order to avoid the pursuit of the Gestapo. From there he made his way to Spain, and according to recently declassified UK archive files, he served as a "broadcaster and propagandist for the Republican Army during the Spanish Civil War". There he operated a "loud speaker at the front," apparently urging on troops fighting Spanish government loyalists. Beginning in 1939, Henschke served as Director of the German-language Department in the radio station of the Republic of Spain in Madrid and adopted an alias – Karl Kastro.[54]

Later he went to France, where he was interned briefly and then was somehow able to gain safe passage to London in May 1939 with the aid of the Joint Committee for Spanish Relief. There he became a member of the leadership committee of the German Communist Party in exile while serving as an office clerk for the International Brigade Association.[55]

In order to release Henschke from his work for the German Communist Party exiled in England, Werner first advised her brother Jurgen that the GRU had demanded that he recommend to Joseph Gould that the OSS hire Henschke to serve as the liaison to the families of the men recruited for the missions. She then instructed Henschke to consult with the exiled German Communist Party leadership in England about the OSS interest in recruiting German exiles for the TOOL missions. According to Werner, the party leadership ordered Henschke and two other German communist exiles to compile a roster of potential candidates for the missions.[56] Henschke was the perfect candidate for this job because he had intimate ties to members of the German refugee community that had escaped Nazi persecution and fled to England with the aid of the Czech Refugee Trust Fund. And he knew what German towns and cities that the men chosen for the missions had left when they were driven underground after the rise of Hitler.

Shortly thereafter, Werner received photos and biographies of the seven German exiles selected for the missions from Henschke and claims to have passed them to the GRU in Moscow (most likely through the Soviet Embassy in London) for approval before this information was given to Lt. Gould by Erich Henschke during the agent recruitment period.[57]

Recently declassified OSS files released by the CIA in July 2000 appear to confirm some of the claims made by Ruth Werner in *Sonya's Report* with regard to Erich Henschke. The documents also indicate that Henschke was employed as a consultant to the OSS from October 1944 through July 1945. He performed a variety of tasks for the OSS. For instance, after the men were dropped into Germany, the OSS would contact Henschke after depositing hazardous duty compensation into Chase bank accounts set up in each agent's name. They requested that he inform the families of these transactions.[58] The late Marjorie Lindner, wife of Paul Lindner, recalls receiving word of the successful dispatch of the HAMMER mission from Erich Henschke.[59]

In addition, declassified OSS files reference Henschke in connection with the trip he took to France in early January 1945 with Army Lt. Joseph Gould. The purpose of the trip was to meet with leaders of the Paris-based Free Germany Committee, who provided the OSS with Berlin safe house information intended for use by the HAMMER and MALLET mission agents.[60]

Through his position as community liaison consultant to the OSS, Erich Henschke had clearly positioned himself to gain access to mission documents and top secret information during the mission training period. Since Werner claims to have passed everything – the J/E codes, agent cover stories, etc. – to the GRU in Moscow, she could have only received this information from Erich Henschke.

HAMMER mission agent Anton Ruh later testified in April 1953 at a secret interrogation of the Western exiles who worked with the OSS that during the mission training period "we had to make reports to Comrade Henschke about all methods used in the school, also about the education in parachuting, about the task assignments, about our work in the prisoner of war camps and also about the details from this apparatus (the J/E transmitter) which we also did on an ongoing basis. I was of the opinion that there must have been a connection between Henschke and others and that reports were passed on from there."[61] During the same Control Commission interrogation in April 1953, Kurt Hager, then the head of the German Communist Party in exile in the UK, testified that "Kastro passed information through Oxford . . . to a female comrade . . . everything he learned from the comrades [training for the TOOL missions]."[62] Werner later noted in an interview with the STASI secret police in East Germany in 1958 that at that time "she worked closely with Erich Henschke."[63]

He was the only member of the London Free German community involved with the OSS who knew of her work.[64] None of the men who led the TOOL missions knew of her existence – or Karl Kastro's real identity as an agent for the GRU. While the parties to this historical drama may have had divided loyalties, they shared a common goal: defeat Hitler and end Nazi tyranny.

In 2001, during the course of his research at the US National Archives, Jonathan Gould, the son of the late Joseph Gould, who had trained the German exiles for their missions, uncovered newly declassified HAMMER mission documents. They showed that the War Department had favorably acted upon a recommendation submitted by the OSS immediately after the war for the award of a military decoration to Lindner and Ruh for their conduct of the HAMMER mission.[65] But there was nothing in the archives to indicate that the medals had ever been presented to Lindner and Ruh. Both had returned to the Soviet zone in East Berlin in 1947 and essentially disappeared behind the Iron Curtain. Follow-up correspondence from Jonathan Gould in 2002 with the families of Lindner and Ruh confirmed that neither man had ever been presented with any medals by the US military.[66]

As a result, the families authorized Jonathan Gould to submit a medal application which contained numerous documents from the HAMMER mission file that Gould obtained from the US military archives. The medal application documented the specific accomplishments of Lindner and Ruh as they carried out the HAMMER mission and the military intelligence obtained by them for the Allied armies advancing into Nazi Germany.[67]

Since US law requires all medal applications seeking the posthumous award of a military decoration to be sponsored by a member of the United States Congress, Jonathan Gould approached the New York office of Senator Hillary Clinton in June 2003 with a request[68] that they evaluate the medal application for possible referral to the Army Decorations Board. After they completed their review of the medal application, Senator Clinton's office agreed to act as its congressional sponsor and contacted the Military Awards Branch to arrange for its referral.

By order of the Secretary of the Army, dated September 16, 2004, the Army Decorations Board approved the medal application and issued an order posthumously awarding the Silver Star to Paul Lindner and Anton Ruh. By correspondence, dated September 24, 2004, the Military Awards Branch informed Senator Clinton's office of this decision and mailed the orders, award certificates and engraved Silver Star medal sets to her office for future presentation to the designated family recipients of the deceased awardees.

Meanwhile, during the nearly one-year period between the submission of the medal application and the issuance of this order, Jonathan Gould had cultivated the interest of the German news magazine *Der Spiegel* in the story behind the medal application. Their interest stemmed from the potential historical significance of the story should the Army Decorations Board grant the medal application. This was because no German national had ever received such an award for military service to the Allies during World War II. Hence, if Lindner and Ruh received the Silver Star, they would be the first.[69]

As a result, Jonathan Gould began corresponding with Mr. Klaus Wiegrefe, a journalist with *Der Spiegel*, which is based in Hamburg, Germany. He later sent Mr. Wiegrefe a copy of the medal application during the summer of 2004. The subsequent announcement of the posthumous award of the Silver Star to Lindner and Ruh by the Army Decorations Board intensified Mr. Wiegrefe's interest in this story. Sometime in October 2004, he informed Jonathan Gould that he had been authorized by his editorial board to prepare an article on this subject.

On October 30, 2004, *Der Spiegel* published an article about the Silver Star awards and the HAMMER mission. The article was titled *False Friends*. Unknown to Jonathan Gould or his clients, Mr. Wiegrefe had learned that the German national archive in Berlin held declassified transcripts of testimony given by Lindner and Ruh in the spring of 1953 to the Central Party Control Commission of the East German Communist Party. These transcripts purportedly contained statements made by Paul Lindner, Anton Ruh and Erich Henschke, who was the German communist exile hired by Joseph Gould to serve as liaison between the OSS and the families of the German exiles recruited for the TOOL missions. According to the article written by Mr. Wiegrefe and published by *Der Spiegel*, these transcripts documented the article's assertion that both Lindner and Ruh were "Soviet spies" and "before becoming US agents, they were sworn into the Soviet secret service by the acting KPD liaison."[70]

On December 22, 2004, Jonathan Gould received an email from Ross Sparacino of the US Army Human Resources Command. In his email,

Mr. Sparacino advised him that "his office is in the process of securing concurrence from several federal agencies, including the State Department, for possible approval of the awards."[71] Jonathan Gould then asked him why he needed this information given that the award had already been made by order of the Army Decorations Board and that the medal certificates and medal sets had been sent to Senator Clinton's New York office. Mr. Sparacino responded that while "the Decorations Board did make a positive determination on Mr. Lindner and Mr. Ruh, as a matter of Department of Defense policy, concurrence must be obtained before these decorations can be officially presented since both individuals are not U.S. citizens."[72] Mr. Sparacino also noted that the concurrent review by these federal agencies had to occur "to prevent any possible embarrassment to the US Government if, for some reason, derogatory information comes to light concerning Mr. Lindner and Mr. Ruh."[73]

Upon receipt of this email, Jonathan Gould immediately contacted Senator Clinton's office regarding this development. Senator Clinton's office informed him that subsequent to their discovery of the *Der Spiegel* article, a decision was made by her office to return the medals to the Army Decorations Board for reasons that differed from those put forth by Mr. Sparacino. According to Senator Clinton's senior staff, they took this action because they were unable to determine the logistics of presenting the Silver Star medals to the families of the deceased awardees because of their status as foreign nationals.[74]

These conflicting explanations led Jonathan Gould to conclude that the *Der Spiegel* article was the reason behind the actions taken by Senator Clinton's office and the US Army Human Resources Command since the need for a concurrent review had never been mentioned before. This conclusion was reinforced when Jonathan Gould received a subsequent email from Mr. Sparacino three weeks later asking whether he knew anything "about a German newspaper article about Mr. Lindner and Mr. Ruh concerning an accusation that they were in fact Soviet spies."[75]

In early March 2005, Jonathan Gould obtained copies of the transcripts of the testimony given by Lindner and Ruh to the Central Party Control Commission referenced in the *Der Spiegel* article. The investigation of the German exiles in England and the hearings conducted by the East German Communist Party Control Commission in 1953 were not known by Jonathan Gould at the time the HAMMER mission medal application was presented to Senator Clinton's office. Neither Lindner nor Ruh had ever told their families of their appearance in front of the Control Commission. The publication of the *Der Spiegel* article alerted both Jonathan Gould and the Berlin families to the existence of these transcripts for the first time.[76]

The Control Commission transcripts that resulted from this investigation conducted in 1953 by the East German government had focused on all of the German communist exiles, including the men selected for the missions into Germany by the OSS. Next to the German Jews, the German communists who had joined the Communist Party (hereinafter "KPD") suffered the harshest treatment from the Nazi Party once Hitler assumed total power in 1933. Many KPD members who led anti-fascist resistance in Germany faced death or imprisonment. Ultimately, the complete destruction of any political opposition by Hitler forced them to flee Germany for Czechoslovakia and then to England.[77]

As previously noted, the men who later volunteered for the TOOL missions, including Lindner and Ruh, were among those who received aid from the British and were later evacuated from Prague to England just days before the German occupation of Czechoslovakia in March 1939. As a result, they became part of the community of German political exiles who resettled in the West, either in Sweden, France or Great Britain, for the duration of World War II. Many struggled to find work and nearly all were later forcibly interned in July 1940 by the British government and held in camps set up in Canada or Australia out of the mistaken fear that the exiles would aid the expected German invasion of England. Most interned exiles were permitted to return to their families in England by 1942.[78]

Once the war in Europe ended, the German political exiles in England sought repatriation to the Soviet zone of occupation in East Berlin. However, the Soviet occupation authorities refused to grant a collective entry visa so that all of the exiles could immediately return at once. Instead, the German communist exiles had to file individual applications for repatriation. This policy reflected the emerging suspicions of the German communist exiles harbored by the leaders of East Germany.[79]

The outbreak of the Cold War intensified those suspicions. In the early 1950s, the Soviet Union pressured the leadership of the East German government to launch an investigation of the Western exiles out of fear that some had been secretly recruited as agents of US or British intelligence. The Central Party Control Commission, which was led by Hermann Matern, a hard-nosed veteran member of the East German[80] Politburo, was charged with the responsibility of carrying out this investigation.

The Control Commission was the instrument of Stalinist terror directed against members of the East German Communist Party whose loyalty was called into question. And with regard to the men of the TOOL missions, despite the fact that the Soviets had apparently sanctioned their recruitment, Lindner, Ruh and Erich Henschke – as well as Jurgen Kuczynski and his sister Ursula – were summoned by the Control Commission to testify.

The testimony given to the Control Commission by Ursula Kuczynski and her brother Jurgen Kuczynski confirmed their work with the GRU in England during the war. According to her transcript, Ursula Kuczynski first began transmitting intelligence reports to the GRU in Moscow that had been given to her by her brother Jurgen, including top secret reports from the United States Strategic Bombing Survey which Jurgen Kuczynski was recruited to work on by the United States Army.[81]

With regard to the request from Army Lt. Joseph Gould for the names of German exiles who would volunteer for the TOOL missions, Ursula Kuczynski testified that she contacted the GRU – presumably through her short-wave radio transmitter – after receiving news of this development from Jurgen Kuczynski, who first received this request during his initial meetings with Joseph Gould in September 1944. She told the Control Commission that the GRU responded favorably to the idea because the information that could be obtained from this relationship would be "useful."[82]

In *Sonya's Report*, Ursula Kuczynski asserted that Erich Henschke had been designated as the liaison to the OSS by the German Communist Party in England and that she had been introduced to Henschke by Jurgen Kuczynski. She also claimed to have passed on all of the photos and resumes of the potential roster of nearly thirty German communist exiles to the GRU in Moscow for approval.[83]

Moreover, it does appear that certain senior members of the German communist exile leadership other than Henschke and Jurgen Kuczynski had knowledge of Ursula Kuczynski's work in England for the GRU. In particular, she told the *Times* of London in 1980 that a man named Hans Kahle was one of her agents,[84] and he is referenced by Paul Lindner during his testimony. According to Lindner, Kahle approached him about volunteering for the HAMMER mission in 1944, and then instructed him to see Erich Henschke about it.[85] Anton Ruh, during these same interrogations, stated that he too received orders from the leadership of the German Communist Party in exile to volunteer for the HAMMER mission.[86]

In *False Friends*, Klaus Wiegrefe claims that "shortly before becoming US agents, they [Lindner and Ruh] were sworn into the Soviet secret service by the acting KPD liaison [meaning Erich Henschke] who allegedly said to them: 'As of today, you must remember that you are working for our Soviet friends, and you must consider all questions as if you were under the command of the Red Army.'"[87] The impression given by this statement is that Lindner and Ruh appeared in front of Erich Henschke and took some sort of oath while being "sworn in" as agents for Soviet military intelligence. Paul Lindner did tell the Control Commission that Erich Henschke made this statement to him about being under the command of the Red

Army – *and that he was not to tell the others* (the other TOOL mission recruits) *about this.*[88]

There is nothing in Anton Ruh's transcript or in any other document to indicate that Ruh was also present when this statement was made by Henschke about the men being under the command of the Red Army. Nor does Henschke reference any other private conversations with Lindner or Ruh on any matter relating to the OSS missions. In fact, Henschke testified that he wasn't authorized to tell anyone about his ties to Red Army intelligence.[89] Nor is there anything in any of the Control Commission transcripts indicating that Anton Ruh was "sworn in" as an agent for the GRU or was ever told by Erich Henschke that he should understand that he was working under the command of the Red Army. In sum, the image of Lindner and Ruh being *jointly* sworn in at some ceremony presided over by Erich Henschke is not corroborated by any other document and does not appear to have happened.

As referenced above, Lindner and Ruh ended the HAMMER mission when they followed instructions conveyed to them by the OSS and surrendered themselves to Russian military officers on April 25, 1945. The Soviet Army did not greet them as fellow members of the Red Army and instead held them in custody for nearly two months, although they were not treated harshly.[90] The picture that Lindner and Ruh conveyed to the OSS during the post-mission debriefings is generally similar to what they told the Control Commission – with some significant omissions. For example, neither Lindner nor Ruh disclosed during their interrogation that they had considered trying to escape Russian custody, which is what they told the OSS. Nor did they tell the Control Commission that they protested the harsh treatment of German civilians, especially women, by the Soviet Army as they took control of war-torn Berlin. These protests, according to the OSS debriefings, did not sit well with the Russian Army officer to whom they were first brought and who threatened to arrest them.

Anton Ruh also testified that the statements they gave to the Soviet Army after they surrendered themselves were sent to Moscow for corroboration. But, according to Ruh, they were not deemed credible by Soviet authorities, who refused to believe they were agents of the GRU. If true, this testimony would further undermine the assertion by *Der Spiegel* that Lindner and Ruh had been "sworn in" as GRU agents. These documents from the OSS archives dealing with the HAMMER agents' post-mission custody by the Russian Army combined with their individual testimony simply does not support the contention that Lindner and Ruh were "Soviet spies" working under the command of the Red Army, as the *Der Spiegel* article attempts to portray them.

At the same time, Paul Lindner did admit during the Control Commission interrogation that in November 1944, he secretly met with Erich Henschke in his apartment at night after mission training sessions in London and provided information "to the greatest detail" on the methods of training and the highly advanced radio communication technology that the OSS had developed for these missions. Lindner also told the Commission that he gave the radio communications code given to him by the OSS to Henschke, which would have enabled him to monitor OSS communications to the agents when behind enemy lines through the BBC German broadcasts.[91]

Anton Ruh also stated that he reported to Erich Henschke and privately believed that "there must have been a connection between Henschke and others" and that the information was passed on to some unknown third party. Furthermore, Ruh also admitted during the Control Commission interrogations in March 1953 that when he returned to England after the war and resumed his job with a British defense technology firm that he secretly removed from one of the company's factories what he described "as a special instrument for shooting in fighter planes." Ruh told the Control Commission that he gave this device to Erich Henschke,[92] who then delivered it to Ursula Kuczynski at her home in Oxfordshire.[93] This does suggest that Ruh was working for the GRU upon his return to England in August 1945.

The only area where there is consistency between the testimony of Erich Henschke and Paul Lindner concerns the latter's disclosure of an alleged meeting that was to take place with a Soviet military operative at a certain location in Berlin during the HAMMER mission. According to Lindner, that meeting was arranged by Henschke "without informing the Americans."[94] Furthermore, Lindner advised the Control Commission that Henschke provided him with a certain "code phrase" or password that he was to use to identify himself when this Red Army officer arrived for this meeting. Lindner apparently took this assignment very seriously. This is evident because he told the Commission that if he had been able to make contact with this officer from the Red Army in Berlin, he would no longer follow any further commands from the OSS and instead would only obey instructions received from the Red Army for the remainder of the HAMMER mission.[95]

Lindner testified that he reported to the location in Berlin as instructed but that the meeting never actually took place because the Soviet military officer did not show up.[96] This fact is confirmed by the testimony of Ursula Kuczynski, who admitted during her appearance before the Control Commission in 1953 that the meeting was never actually arranged at all and was, as she put it, "fake."[97]

The Control Commissions transcripts do indicate that mission-related information was passed to Erich Henschke by both Lindner and Ruh. In sharing this top secret information with Henschke, both Lindner and Ruh breached the overseas employment contract that they signed with the OSS to maintain the secrecy of the HAMMER mission and never divulge any mission-related information.[98] But it is also possible that the dangers faced by Lindner and Ruh in that Control Commission hearing room caused them to color their testimony and possibly make untrue statements to make sure they cleansed themselves of any suspicion of being double agents because of their work with US intelligence.[99]

Finally, despite whatever mission-related information either Lindner or Ruh *may* have secretly reported to Erich Henschke, there is no evidence that these actions compromised the HAMMER mission. The OSS mission files confirm that Lindner and Ruh achieved the mission's primary objective: obtaining and transmitting vital military intelligence to the OSS.

Certainly, the OSS appreciated the work of the HAMMER team. Consider the letter submitted to both Lindner and Ruh by Colonel John A. Bross after they returned to England after completing the mission. Colonel Bross was the OSS officer in charge of training and deploying the JEDBURGH teams of OSS agents that supported Operation OVERLORD – the Allied landing in France on D-Day. This is what he wrote to Lindner and Ruh shortly after their discharge from the OSS in late August 1945:

> This organization has recommended you for a decoration which we hope will be awarded before long. In the meantime, we should like to express our appreciation for the heroic and extremely valuable work that you did for us. As the nature of your duties must still remain secret, it is, unfortunately, impossible to set down in detail the many courageous acts that you performed; but it can be said that during hostilities, you behaved coolly and efficiently and displayed remarkable ability in exploiting every means for fulfilling your difficult task. The successful completion of your mission was of very great value to the armed forces of the Allies and contributed greatly to the defeat of the enemy.[100]

Presentation of the Silver Star medals to the families of the HAMMER agents

By September 2005, the State Department and the Military Awards Branch had completed their review of the medal application and found no reason to reconsider the posthumous award of the Silver Star to Paul Lindner and Anton Ruh. Consequently, they confirmed the award and requested that the office of New York Senator Hillary Clinton resume its sponsorship of the medal application and arrange for the presentation of the medals to the families of Lindner and Ruh. But her office refused to do this and repeatedly declined to return calls from Ross Sparacino, who was still holding the medals and the award certificates in his office in Washington, DC after they were sent back to him in late December 2004 by Senator Clinton's office.[101] The Clinton staff person who initially met with Jonathan Gould in June 2003 and advocated the referral of the medal application to the US Army Decorations Board would not provide any explanation as to why Senator Hillary Clinton's office had abandoned its support of the medal application, including the handling of the medal presentation to the families.[102]

At that moment, it was unclear to Mr. Sparacino what the Military Awards Branch was going to do. Whether or not some sort of ceremony would be held and where it would be held remained unanswered questions. But that quickly changed when Jonathan Gould called Mr. Sparacino to see if he would authorize the presentation of the medals at the US Embassy in Berlin. He liked the idea and authorized Gould to present it to US Army Colonel Donald Zedler, who was currently serving as the defense attaché at the Berlin embassy.[103]

Jonathan Gould prepared a package of documents for Colonel Zedler to review, including a copy of the medal application, the Control Commission transcripts of Lindner and Ruh, and an affidavit which discussed the background to the medal application and the issues raised in the *Der Spiegel* article. Colonel Zedler agreed to go forward with the event and authorized it to be held at the US embassy on May 6, 2006.[104] Colonel Zedler had many relatives who were residing in Berlin when the HAMMER mission took place in March 1945 and had suffered under Hitler's regime. He was clearly aware of the chaos and ongoing destruction of the city that Lindner and Ruh encountered when they parachuted into Berlin in early March 1945.[105]

At the medal presentation ceremony held at the US embassy, both Colonel Zedler and his aide – Colonel Michael Kersey – were in attendance. In addition, William R. Timken, US ambassador to Berlin, who had just been appointed to the position by President George W. Bush, also attended and opened the proceedings with some brief remarks. Numerous friends and relatives of the families of the men were there, along with Mr. Karsten Voigt, then a member of the Federal Foreign Office, the German foreign ministry.

Before presenting the medals, Colonel Zedler spoke to the gathering and noted that both Lindner and Ruh had shown what he called "civil courage" in volunteering for and carrying out the HAMMER mission. Zedler later added, "We wanted to honor two courageous people who fought together with us for one thing: to bring the Nazis down."[106] In an interview with a prominent Berlin newspaper, Colonel Zedler also noted that the political views of the awardees were of secondary importance. Even though it took years after the end of World War II and the Cold War to make the award, Colonel Zedler added that "we do not forget concerted action during times of war and perhaps the award can strengthen our alliance."[107]

After Jonathan Gould spoke at length about the mission and his father's legacy, Colonel Kersey was called to the podium to read aloud the wording of the Silver Star award certificates, which praised Lindner and Ruh for "gallantry in action against the enemy." The certificate also referenced some of the key results produced by the awardees in the course of carrying out their mission:

> Lindner and Ruh were inserted into Berlin by parachute to gather intelligence on the enemy's situation and movements. The team confirmed the location and operational status of the Klingenberg power plant that was furnishing electrical power to munitions plants, the location and continuing operation of both the Berlin railroad transportation system and freight yards. Both men were also able to gather intelligence on hidden factories and storage dumps, the effectiveness of Allied bombings, the treatment of Allied prisoners of war and the strength of Nazi control over the civil populations. Additionally, the team organized a small group of underground resistance contacts who collected and transmitted intelligence including valuable information about defense points in the north section of Berlin. The gallantry displayed by Mr. Ruh and Mr. Lindner was in keeping with the highest traditions of the military service and reflects great credit on both men, the Office of Strategic Services and the Army of the United States.[108]

The medals were then presented by Colonel Zedler to Mrs. Marjorie Lindner, wife of Paul Lindner, and to the late Denis Ruh, son of Anton Ruh. Until that moment, no military decorations had ever been presented to German nationals for service to the Allies during World War II.

The award of the Bronze Star to Joseph Gould

Following the end of the war in Europe in May 1945, Army Lieutenant Joseph Gould remained in the service of the United States Army. Because of his background in trade unions and labor relations, he was assigned to the Labor Relations Division of the Office of the Military Government, which was the occupation authority that administered the US zone in Berlin. That unit's purpose was to aid in the reconstruction of German labor unions, which had been destroyed by Hitler after he came to power in 1933.[109]

After Lt. Gould left London and resettled in Berlin to join other US labor leaders also assigned to this unit, the OSS office in London was directed to prepare recommendations for the award of US military decorations to Lt. Gould and the men he recruited and trained for the TOOL missions. OSS director General William Donovan assigned one of his close aides – Colonel William J. Forgan – to assemble a staff to write these medal recommendations. The OSS had decided to recommend the award of the Bronze Star to Lt. Gould.

On June 20, 1945, Colonel Forgan submitted the recommendation for this award to the US Army Commanding General of the European Theater for approval. In a nearly three-page memorandum, Colonel Forgan reviewed Lt. Gould's work in setting up the agent training school in London and then highlighted his successful recruitment of the German exiles for the TOOL missions. And with regard to the HAMMER mission into Berlin, the recommendation noted:

> The first men were parachuted successfully in the Berlin area, hundreds of miles beyond the region in which it had previously been believed possible to effect a successful drop. Contact was established with the agent team by means of the J/E equipment and maintained successfully at a critical time in the assault on Germany. Vital information was obtained as to conditions in Berlin, the disposition of troops in the Berlin area and remaining targets for bombing by the Air Force. Lt. Gould's services were at all times of the highest caliber and largely due to his devotion to duty, his interest and his resourcefulness, important operations were prepared and dispatched and extremely valuable intelligence was obtained and transmitted to the G-2's of SHAEF and the Army Groups and Armies.[110]

New documents obtained from the US National Archives show that in February 1946, the War Department in Washington, DC, subsequently considered the recommendation and approved the award of the Bronze Star to Joseph Gould. But for reasons likely related to the sudden dissolution of the OSS in September 1945, together with Lt. Gould's redeployment to the US zone in Berlin, he never received news of this decision and the medal was never presented to him while he remained in the US Army until his honorable discharge in March 1946. Joseph Gould's family does not recall any reference to the award after he returned to his wife and family in New York City in April 1946. For reasons that remain unclear, his files do not show that he made any inquiries about the award and it was never presented to him before his death in July 1993.

This was likely due to the formation of the Central Intelligence Agency in 1947, which was authorized to seal all of the OSS wartime mission files;

they remained classified until 1976 when some were declassified.[111] However, the personnel files of everyone who served in the OSS during the war remained under seal and were not released by the CIA until August 2008.[112] Among those newly released documents was the aforementioned Bronze Star medal recommendation prepared by Colonel Forgan in June 1945; until then it had never made the light of day.

Upon receipt of this document, Jonathan Gould drew upon his experience in preparing the HAMMER mission medal application and contacted his congressman – Charles Rangel of Harlem – and asked that his office notify the US Army Military Awards Branch of the release of the medal recommendation. In addition, Congressman Rangel requested that the US Army review the document and reaffirm the award and authorize him to present the medal to Joseph Gould's family.[113]

On December 1, 2009, the US Army Human Resources Command notified Jonathan Gould that the Army Decorations Board was convened to consider the application and voted to reaffirm the posthumous award of the Bronze Star to Joseph Gould. The medal set with accompanying citation was sent to Congressman Rangel, who subsequently presented the award to Jonathan Gould at a public ceremony in his Harlem office in January 2010.[114]

Postscript

In 1947, HAMMER mission agents Paul Lindner and Anton Ruh and their families were finally permitted to return to the Soviet zone in a divided Berlin.[115] From 1950 to 1957, Anton Ruh served as the director of the Office of the Control of the Traffic Goods, the predecessor to the East German Customs Service from 1950 to 1957. After holding various positions with the East German Communist Party, he was appointed ambassador to Rumania in 1963. He died suddenly in 1964 while serving in that position. He was 52 years old.[116]

Paul Lindner eventually became a citizen of the GDR in 1948. He held a number of different jobs, including as a translator for Radio Berlin International and later as the cultural director for Siemens Electrokohle, and finally as a Party Secretary for KWO Cable Works. He died of a stroke at the age of 58 on November 18, 1969.[117]

Jurgen Kuczynski, the brother of Soviet spy Ursula Kuczynski, was later revealed to have also worked for the GRU in England and to have introduced atomic scientist Klaus Fuchs to his sister in 1940.[118] He survived the war and returned to the Soviet sector and later became an important economic adviser to East German president Erich Honecker. He published numerous books on labor history. He died at the age of 92 in 1997.[119]

Ursula Kuczynski, the sister of Jurgen and a key operative for the GRU in England during the war, managed to avoid the pursuit of British intelligence in 1949 after her role in receiving atomic secrets from Klaus Fuchs was revealed. She returned to East Berlin as a journalist and author. She was awarded both the Order of the Red Flag and the Order of the Red Banner by the Soviet Union for her work for the GRU. She died at the age of 93 in 2000.[120]

Erich Henschke, who operated under the alias Karl Kastro while in exile in Great Britain and had served as the liaison between the OSS and the men of the TOOL missions and their families, eventually repatriated back to the Soviet zone in East Germany in 1946. He later rose to prominence as editor in chief of *Berliner Zig*, a leading newspaper published in the GDR, a position he held until 1957. From 1958 to 1962, Henschke served in Red China as a correspondent for AND, an East German wire service. From 1962 to 1977, he held various staff positions for the GDR television network DDR-Fernsehens. Erich Henschke died in Berlin in 1988 at the age of 81.[121]

In July 1945, the United States Army reassigned Captain Joseph Gould for continued military service with the newly formed Office of Military Government (OMGUS) in the US sector located in Berlin. Sometime before he departed London to begin this new assignment, Joseph Gould met with Paul Lindner. This meeting occurred sometime after Lindner had returned to London after completing the HAMMER mission and had reunited with his wife Marjorie and their young son, Paul Jr.

Having witnessed the devastation of Berlin and the suffering of its citizens while carrying out the mission, Lindner feared for his elderly parents, Paul, Sr. and Freeda Lindner, who had survived the war and were still living in their home in the Berlin suburb of Neukölln. He apparently knew that Berliners faced near-famine conditions in the coming months and grew increasingly concerned about the welfare of his parents.

According to the sons of Paul Lindner, who shared this story in 2002, their father had asked Joseph Gould to make contact with his parents and to find a way to help them. Gould made a promise to Lindner that he would figure out some way to aid his elderly parents. He left for Berlin in early August 1945.

Sometime after he arrived in Berlin to begin his work with OMGUS, Gould first made contact with Lindner's parents to find out exactly where they lived. He then commandeered a US military jeep and persuaded an unidentified soldier to accompany him in the vehicle. They apparently slipped out of the city and were traveling toward the Lindner home in Neukölln when they came upon an abandoned farm or estate where numerous sheep were grazing unattended.

At that moment, Gould must have decided that delivering the sheep to Lindner's parents was the way he could help them survive the coming winter. They loaded the sheep on the jeep and drove to the Neukölln home of Paul Lindner, Sr. and Freeda Lindner. When they arrived, they were greeted warmly by Lindner's parents. After unloading the animals, they steered them toward a small barn attached to the Lindner home.

According to Paul Jr. and his brother Toni, the family cared for the sheep until it was time to slaughter them for much-needed food that helped them survive those terrible days. They never forgot the special kindness of Joseph Gould for what he did for them that day. Joseph Gould had kept his promise to Paul Lindner, who remained in England with his wife and family until he was finally able to return home in June 1947.

Captain Joseph Gould was honorably discharged from his service to the United States Army in February 1946, and he returned to his wife Betty in New York and resumed his career as a film publicist and producer. In 1955, Joseph Gould was appointed the advertising manager for the United Artists Corporation, which had just been sold by film legends Charlie Chaplin and Mary Pickford. He developed and supervised the print advertising campaigns for such renowned films as *Around the World in Eighty Days* and *Man with a Golden Arm* starring Frank Sinatra.

In 1960, Gould left United Artists and joined Paramount Pictures, where he won recognition for his work on the advertising and publicity campaign for the wildly successful film *Psycho*, which was directed by Alfred Hitchcock. He later formed his own advertising agency that developed the print advertising campaigns for the *Boston Strangler*, starring Tony Curtis, and *Patton*, the film about the controversial US World War II general George Patton. Joseph Gould left the film business in 1988 to become the Director of Public Affairs for the Center for Defense Information in Washington, DC. He died on July 11, 1993 at the age of 78.

OSS director William J. Donovan did not survive a political dispute with President Harry Truman, who ordered the dissolution of the OSS in September 1945. He later served as a special assistant to United States Supreme Court Justice Robert Jackson, the chief prosecutor at the Nuremberg War Crimes trial, before returning to his law practice on Wall Street in 1949. He died in a New York hospital in 1959 at the age of 76.[122]

William J. Casey, the New York lawyer who became director of the London office of Special Intelligence in 1944 and opposed the use of the German exiles for the TOOL missions due to his suspicion that they were agents of the Soviet Union, returned to his tax law practice in New York City. He became active in the Republican Party and served as the manager of Ronald Reagan's presidential campaign in 1980. He was appointed director of the Central Intelligence Agency in 1981 by President Reagan and served in that position until his death in 1987 at the age of 74.[123]

Figure 1.1 Logo of the Office of Strategic Services

Figure 1.2 General William J. Donovan, OSS Director, 1942

Figure 1.3 Major General William J. Donovan (top row/center), 1944

Figure 1.4 HAMMER mission agent
Anton Ruh, January 1945

Figure 1.5 HAMMER mission agent
Paul Lindner, London,
January 1945

Figure 1.6 Marjorie and Paul Lindner on their wedding day,
London, 1942

Figure 1.7 Paul Lindner, Sr., father of
Paul Lindner, Berlin, Ger-
many, November 1938

Figure 1.8 Freeda Lindner, mother of
Paul Lindner, Berlin, Ger-
many, November 1938

Figure 1.9 Paul Lindner, Sr. and daughter Inge, Berlin, 1938

Figure 1.10 HAMMER mission agent Paul Lindner, Paris, July 1945

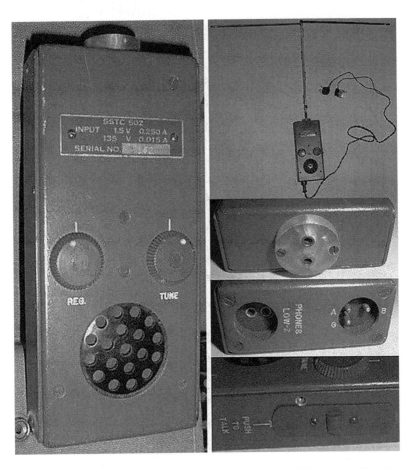

Figure 1.11 Joan/Eleanor (J/E) transmitter-receiver used behind enemy lines by TOOL mission agents

Figure 1.12 Al Gross, inventor, J/E radio receiver/transmitter

Figure 1.13a US Army Lt. Joseph Gould with London bookstore owner Morris Abbey, September 1944

Figure 1.13b US Army Lt. Joseph Gould in London

Figure 1.14 Army Lt. Joseph Gould outside London flat, October 1944

Figure 1.15 Army Lt. Joseph Gould with his father, Samuel Goldberger, August 1942

Figure 1.16 Joseph Gould, president of the Screen Publicists Guild (center), at a meeting with members of the guild's executive council, 1940

Figure 1.17 Joseph Gould (seated far right) signing the first contract with Hollywood studios on behalf of the Screen Publicists Guild of New York, May 1942

Figure 1.18 Joseph Gould (seated second from left) at the Motion Picture Emergency Defense Council conference sponsored by the Screen Publicists Guild in late December 1941 at the Hotel Piccadilly in New York City. Garson Kanin, acclaimed theater and film director, was the keynote speaker, seated far right

Figure 1.19 Army Lt. Joseph Gould outside OSS London mission training school, October 1944

Figure 1.20 OSS Labor Division Chief Arthur Goldberg (far right) with staff of the OSS Labor Desk in London

Figure 1.21 Army Lt. Joseph at parachute training field with OSS London mission training staff, Ringway Air Field, Ruislip, England, November 1944

Figure 1.22 Staff of OSS Labor Division, London, England, with Joseph Gould standing second from right and Arthur Goldberg seated far left, November 1944

Figure 1.23 Jurgen Kuczynski, London, 1943

Figure 1.24 Ursula Kuczynski (aka Ruth Werner), 1938

Figure 1.25 Ursula Kuczynski, 1955

Figure 1.26 HAMMER mission agent Anton Ruh in East Berlin, Germany, 1960, while serving as head of the Customs Service for the German Democratic Republic

Figure 1.27 Erich Henschke (aka Karl Kastro), Paris, January 1945

Figure 1.28 Silver Star award presented to families of HAMMER mission agents on May 5, 2006, at a ceremony held at the US Embassy in Berlin

Figure 1.29 Colonel Donald Zedler, military attaché to the US Embassy in Berlin, and William Timken, US ambassador to Germany, presenting the Silver Star medals to Marjorie Lindner and Denis Ruh at the medal presentation ceremony held at the US Embassy in Berlin in May 2006

Notes

1 HAMMER Mission File, NARA Record Group (hereafter RG) 226, Records of the Office of Strategic Services (hereafter) 148 (Box (hereafter B) 102, Folder (hereafter F)), pp. 1751–1753.
2 RAF Ringway, *Wikipedia.*
3 POW cage reports submitted by TOOL mission agents Paul Lindner (NARA, RG 226, E148, B101, F1740–42); Adolph Buchholz (NARA RG 226, E210, B47, F915); and Walter Strüwe (NARA, RG 226, E210, B298, F12123).
4 Lindner POW cage report (see note 3) (a copy of this report is attached to Appendix E).
5 POW cage report of Adolf Buchholz, who was also recruited by Army Lt. Gould and later dropped into Berlin in April 1945.
6 Ibid.
7 Obituary of Al Gross, *Los Angeles Times*, January 14, 2001.
8 Al Gross, *Encyclopedia.com*, 2004.
9 A Skeleton in the Closeted World of Espionage, *History Today*, September 2004, Volume 54, Issue 9.
10 *Flypast*, Key Publishing, Lincolnshire, United Kingdom, 1999.
11 HAMMER Mission File, OSS Record Group 226, NARA.
12 Charles V.P. von Luttichau, The German Counteroffensive in the Ardennes, United States Army in World War II, Ch. 20 (cited at http://trailblazersww2.org/ardennes.htm).
13 Battle of the Bulge, United States Holocaust Museum website.
14 *Kings and Desperate Men: The United States Office of Strategic Services in London and the Anglo-American Relationship* by Brian Nelson Macpherson (unpublished doctoral thesis, University of Toronto, 1995), p. 172 (citing "Final Report on SI Operations"). According to Joseph Gould, the need for this intelligence was specifically demanded by Generals George Patton and Alexander

Patch of the US Army and UK General Henry Wilson; Joseph Gould, *An OSS Officer's Own WWII Story: Of His Seven German Agents and Their Five Labor Desk Missions into Warring Germany*, unpublished manuscript (Washington, DC, 1989), pp. 7–8.

15 Ibid.
16 Heike Bungert, The OSS and Its Cooperation with the Free Germany Committees, 1944–45, *Intelligence and National Security*, Volume 12, July 1997, p. 132.
17 Joseph Persico, *Piercing the Reich: The Penetration of Nazi Germany by American Secret Agents During WWII* (New York: Viking Press, 1979), p. 166.
18 Joseph Gould, *An OSS Officer's Own WWII Story: Of His Seven German Agents and Their Five Labor Desk Missions into Warring Germany*, unpublished manuscript (Washington, DC, 1989), p. 7.
19 Persico (note 17), p. 167.
20 Ibid., p. 171.
21 Biographical profile of Paul Lindner prepared by Army Lt. Joseph Gould, HAMMER Mission File, October 1944, OSS Record Group 226, NARA; application for internment release from Paul Lindner to Under Secretary of State of UK Aliens Department, August 5, 1941 (NARA, RG 226, E115, B43, F563, E148, B101, F1740–F1742) (a copy of the internment release application is attached to Appendix B).
22 Paul Lindner internment release application (note 21).
23 Profile of Paul Lindner compiled by Army Lt. Joseph Gould, OSS Labor Division, December 1944 (NARA RG 226, E148, B101, F1740–F1742; E115, B43, F563).
24 Memorandum from Lt. Joseph Gould, HAMMER Mission File, December 5, 1944, OSS Record Group 226, NARA.
25 Persico (note 17), p. 174.
26 HAMMER Mission Dispatch Report, Army Lt. Joseph Gould, March 3, 1945, RG 226, NARA.
27 HAMMER Mission, Labor Division, OSS War Diary, Volume 6, pp. 421–456, OSS Record Group 226; transcript of HAMMER team interrogation of Paul Lindner and Anton Ruh, conducted by Comdr. Graveson and Lt. Sutton, June 27, 1945, OSS Record Group 226, NARA.
28 Ibid.
29 Ibid.
30 Ibid.
31 Transcript of J/E radio transmission, March 28, 1945, HAMMER Mission File, OSS Record Group 226, NARA.
32 William J. Casey, *The Secret War Against Hitler* (Washington, DC: Regnery Gateway 1988), pp. 196–199.
33 Marjorie Lindner, wife of HAMMER mission agent Paul Lindner, telephone interview from Berlin, March 10, 2001.
34 Casey (note 32).
35 Persico (note 17), p. 212.
36 Casey (note 32).
37 Ibid.
38 Ian Kershaw, *Hitler: Nemesis 1936–45* (New York: W.W. Norton and Company, 2000), p. 809.

39 Transcript of J/E radio transmission, March 28, 1945, HAMMER Mission File, OSS Record Group 226, NARA.
40 Sean Mcateer, *500 Days: The War in Eastern Europe*, Kindle edition (Red Lead Press, 2009).
41 Casey (note 32).
42 Transcript of interrogation of HAMMER mission agents, June 27, 1945, RG 226, NARA.
43 Ibid.
44 Correspondence between Joseph Gould to Jurgen Kuczynski, May 17, 1977, through August 1990, when Joseph Gould visited with Kuczynski at the latter's home in Berlin.
45 Correspondence from Joseph Gould to Marjorie Lindner and Ellen Buchholz, September 1990.
46 Ruth Werner, *Sonja's Rapport* (Berlin: Verlag Neus Leben, 1977).
47 Obituary, Ruth Werner, *Guardian*, July 11, 2000.
48 Chapman Pincher, *Treachery: Betrayals, Blunders and Cover-ups: Six Decades of Espionage Against America and Great Britain* (New York: Random House, 2009) (Chapter One: A Momentous Message).
49 *Sonya's Report* (note 46), pp. 250–252; 288–289.
50 Meeting with Joseph Gould in Washington, DC, September 1990.
51 *Sonya's Report* (note 46), p. 265.
52 Ibid., pp. 306–308.
53 Bungert (note 16), p. 132.
54 Erich Henschke, aka Karl Kastro, Metropolitan Police file, United Kingdom National Archives, KV2/3908/1321715.
55 Ibid.
56 *Sonya's Report* (see note 46).
57 Ibid.
58 Memorandum to file, Joseph Gould, May 18, 1945, OSS Records, Record Group (RG) 226, NARA.
59 Interview with Marjorie Lindner, widow of deceased HAMMER mission agent Paul Lindner, March 19, 2001.
60 Memorandum from Thomas Wilson to Lillian Traugott of the SI Labor Division, December 22, 1944 (HAMMER Mission File), RG 226, NARA.
61 Central Committee Control Commission interrogation transcript of Anton Ruh, March 30, 1953. BArch, SAPMO, DY 30/IV 2/4/123.
62 Central Committee Control Commission interrogation transcript of Kurt Hager, March 1953. BArch, SAPMO, DY 30/IV 2/4/123.
63 Report on interview with Ursula Kuczynski by East German secret police in 1958.
64 *Sonya's Report* (note 46), p. 263.
65 Memorandum submitted to Paul Lindner and Anton Ruh from Colonel John Bross, Office of Strategic Services, mission to Great Britain on September 30, 1945; see also letter from Major James H. Kaylor to Captain W. Blake-Budden, May 20, 1946, regarding medal recommendations submitted on behalf of Paul Lindner, Anton Ruh, Walter Strüwe and Emil Konhäuser for their service on OSS missions into Germany.
66 Telephone conversation with the Marjorie Lindner, widow of HAMMER mission agent Paul Lindner, July 2001; affidavit of Marjorie Lindner, August 11, 2002 (attached to the HAMMER mission medal application (see note 50)).

67 The HAMMER mission medal application was prepared by this author and presented to the office of Senator Hillary Clinton in June 2003 for referral to the US Army Military Decorations branch for consideration of a posthumous award of a military decoration to the deceased German nationals – Paul Lindner and Anton Ruh – for their service on the HAMMER mission into Berlin in March 1945.

68 Correspondence between Jonathan Gould and Senator Hillary Clinton of New York, July 11, 2003; correspondence between Senator Hillary Clinton of New York and Benjamin Lane, U 32S Total Army Personnel Command, July 11, 2003, regarding referral of HAMMER mission medal application for consideration of a posthumous award of a military decoration to deceased German nationals for their service to the OSS.

69 Letter from Lt. Colonel Deborah W. Ivory, Chief, Military Awards Branch, October 19, 2001 (disclosing results of their review of WWII records "maintained by this office and [which] found no awards to German nationals").

70 False Friends, *Der Spiegel* (see footnote 80) (a copy of the *Der Spiegel* is attached to Appendix F).

71 Email correspondence between Jonathan Gould and Ross Sparacino, US Army Human Resources Command, dated December 22, 2004, and January 26, 2005.

72 Ibid.

73 Ibid.

74 Telephone conversation between Jonathan Gould and Eric Bederman, member of the staff of the New York office of Senator Hillary Clinton, December 22, 2004.

75 Ross Sparacino email correspondence (see note 71).

76 Correspondence between members of the families of HAMMER mission agents Paul Lindner and Anton Ruh and Jonathan Gould, December 1, 2004, regarding claims made in the *Der Spiegel* article titled False Friends.

77 *The Last Revolutionaries: German Communists and Their Century*, Catherine Epstein (Cambridge, MA: Harvard University Press, 2003), Chapter 3, Persecuted: At Home and Abroad After 1933.

78 Collar the Lot! Britain's Policy of Internment During the Second World War, United Kingdom National Archives, July 2, 2015 | Roger Kershaw (http://blog.national archives.gov.uk/blog/collar-lot-britains-policy-internment-second-world-war).

79 Epstein (note 77), pp. 137–139.

80 Ibid. (background on the establishment of the Central Party Control Commission in the German Democratic Republic as vehicle for interrogating the Western exiles), pp. 137–139.

81 Ibid.

82 Ibid.

83 Control Commission transcript of interrogation of Ursula Kuczynski Beurton by Herman Matern, September 1953, SAPMO-BArch DY 30/IV 2/4/123.

84 German Passed WWII Secrets Through Sister's Spy Ring, *Times of London*, January 28, 1980.

85 Control Commission transcript of interrogation of Paul Lindner by Herman Matern, April 1, 1953, in Stiftung Archiv der Parteien und Massenorganizationen der DDR im Bundesarchiv Berlin (hereinafter referred to as SAPMO-BArch) DY 30/IV 2/4/123, Bl. 272–282.

86 Control Commission interrogation transcript of Anton Ruh (see note 112).

87 False Friends (note 70), October 30, 2004.

88 Ibid.
89 Control Commission transcript of interrogation of Erich Henschke by Herman Matern March 30, 1953, (SAPMO-BArch) DY 30/IV 2/4/123, BL 155–173.
90 Debriefing of HAMMER mission agents regarding events on the ground in Germany after they surrendered themselves to Red Army troops who held them from April 25, 1945, to June 16, 1945, when they were released back to the US military.
91 Ibid.
92 Central Committee Control Commission interrogation transcript of Anton Ruh, March 30, 1953. BArch, SAPMO, DY 30/IV 2/4/123, pp. 343–344.
93 In her book titled *Sonya's Report*, Ursula Kuczynski also claims that after the war she learned that during the HAMMER mission, Toni Ruh was also given shelter in Berlin by a longtime friend named Dora Selchow, who helped Ruh bury his J/E radio in her yard. Selchow later dug it up and purportedly gave it to a Soviet military officer right after the Red Army entered Berlin in April 1945. In his Control Commission interrogation, Ruh also confirmed this account regarding Dora Selchow and the J/E transmitter, which he admitted was given to this Red Army officer. *Sonya's Report* (note 46), p. 263 (see note 93) (Control Commission transcript of Anton Ruh).
94 See note 86 (Control Commission testimony of Paul Lindner).
95 Ibid.
96 Ibid.
97 See note 84 (Control Commission transcript of interrogation of Ursula Kuczynski Beurton).
98 United States Government Overseas Agent Employment Contracts, individually signed by Paul Lindner and Anton Ruh on February 23, 1945 (see paragraph 4(b) where agents agreed to keep "forever secret this employment and all information obtained by reason thereof").
99 Jurgen Kuczynski and the Search for a Western Spy Ring in the East German Communist Party in 1953, Professor Matthew Stibbe, Professor of Modern European History, Sheffield Hallam University, *Contemporary European History* (2011), p. 64, 73 (citing allegations by the Control Commission that some of the German communist exiles recruited by Army Lt. Joseph Gould for the TOOL missions later "had been turned into spies for the CIA"). In view of this climate of suspicion of the Western exiles who worked with the OSS, those who appeared in front of the Control Commission were likely aware of the need to demonstrate their loyalty to the regime.
100 See note 66, Letter from Colonel John Bross.
101 This information regarding the return of the medal and certificates was obtained by Jonathan Gould from a telephone call with Ross Sparacino, Military Awards Branch, in January 2005.
102 See note 75. This was the second attempt by the author to reach Eric Bederman at the New York office of Senator Hillary Clinton regarding the issue of the presentation of the Silver Star medals and certificates to the families of the deceased awardees Paul Lindner and Anton Ruh. Mr. Bederman declined to respond to these inquiries from Jonathan Gould as well as separate inquiries from Mr. Sparacino of the US Army Military Awards Branch. As a result, Mr. Sparacino favorably responded to the suggestion from Jonathan Gould that an approach be made to the office of the military attaché at the United States Embassy in Berlin.

103 Telephone calls and emails between Jonathan Gould and Robert Shelton, United States Navy and aide to Colonel Donald H. Zedler, military attaché to the United States Embassy in Berlin, Germany, September–December 2005.
104 Meeting with Robert Shelton and Colonel Donald H. Zedler, Defense Attaché, US Embassy in Berlin, May 4, 2006.
105 This information regarding Colonel Zedler's awareness of the conditions in Berlin at the time that the HAMMER mission was sent in on March 2, 1945, was shared with Jonathan Gould during this meeting in his office at the US Embassy in Berlin the day before the medal presentation ceremony was held.
106 Secret: Operation Hammer, Lars Broder Keil, *Berlin Morning Post*, May 21, 2006.
107 Ibid.
108 Excerpt from Silver Star medal certificate posthumously presented to the families of HAMMER mission agents Paul Lindner and Anton Ruh at a ceremony held at the United States Embassy in Berlin, May 5, 2006 (a copy of the medal certificates are attached to Appendix C).
109 Carolyn Woods Eisenberg, *Drawing the Line* (Cambridge: Cambridge University Press, 1996), p. 151 (fn. 91).
110 Recommendation for the award of the Bronze Star to Joseph Gould, J.R. Forgan, OSS Theater Commander, London, June 20, 1945 (a copy of the medal recommendation is attached to Appendix D).
111 According to Joseph Persico, the CIA declassified the OSS War Report in 1976; this document was the first document dealing with the OSS campaign to penetrate Nazi Germany to be declassified. See Joseph Persico, *Piercing the Reich: The Penetration of Nazi Germany by American Secret Agents During World War II* (New York: Viking Press, 1979), p. ix.
112 Press Release, Central Intelligence Agency, OSS Personnel Files Released, September 11, 2008.
113 Letter from Congressman Charles Rangel to Army Lieutenant Bennett, Military Awards Branch, June 11, 2007.
114 *OSS Society Journal*, Summer/Fall 2010, p. 14.
115 Regional Advisory Committee, United Kingdom Immigration Division, UK National Archives, HO 396/126, HO 396/132 and HO 396/151.
116 Bernd-Rainer Barth: Ruh, Anton. *Who Was Who in the GDR?* 5th edition. Volume 2, Ch. Links, Berlin 2010, ISBN 978-3-86153-561-4; Affidavit of Denis Ruh, dated August 11, 2002.
117 Affidavit of Marjorie Lindner, dated August 11, 2002 (see note 49).
118 Obituary of Jurgen Kuczynski by David Childs, *Independent*, August 12, 1997.
119 Ibid.
120 RED SONYA: The Spy Who Lived in Kidlington, *Oxford Mail*, August 6, 2010.
121 Erich Henschke biographical note (note 89).
122 OSS director William J. Donovan died on February 8, 1959, in New York City. Obituary of William J. Donovan, Arlington National Cemetery website.
123 Obituary of William J. Casey by Eric Pace, *New York Times*, May 7, 1987.

2 Mission into Landshut
The triumph of the PICKAXE mission

Of the remaining TOOL missions, only one actually achieved its objective of gathering and transmitting military intelligence to the US military for use by their armies advancing into Germany. That mission was the PICKAXE mission into Landshut. The PICKAXE mission file maintained at the US National Archives documents the extraordinary success of this mission as it was carried out by these men.

Profiles of the PICKAXE mission agents

Walter Strüwe

Walter Strüwe was born in Bielefeld, Germany, in 1904. In 1919, he completed his apprenticeship as a bricklayer with the building construction trades. In 1925, he moved to Frankfurt and joined the Building Workers Union. From 1927 to 1937, Strüwe worked on various public works construction projects as a stone layer and assumed leadership positions in the building trade unions. But after Hitler assumed power in 1933, Strüwe went underground and performed political work for the Frankfurt trade unions, which included the printing and distribution of leaflets protesting Nazi economic policies.

Strüwe eventually became a leading figure in the Rhineland Communist Party. According to documents from the German archive, Strüwe helped print and distribute anti-Nazi leaflets in Frankfurt. But in 1935, after a coworker tortured by the Gestapo had disclosed Strüwe's identity and his political activities, a warrant for Strüwe's arrest for "high treason" was issued. Strüwe fled into the underground and eventually to Czechoslovakia. Strüwe, however, continued to maintain contact with the Communist Party underground in Dresden and made frequent trips there from Prague to meet with other workers still trapped in Germany.[1]

In April 1939, as the German Army moved to occupy Czechoslovakia, Strüwe managed to elude the Gestapo's pursuit by fleeing across the Polish border on skis. He later obtained a British visa with the aid of the Czech Refugee Trust Fund. After being interned by the British government in a camp located off the coast of Great Britain called the Isle of Man, Strüwe was released in December 1940 after the British government acknowledged that he genuinely harbored strong "anti-Hitler opinions." Strüwe then married Leonie Bursztin and settled in Manchester, where he found work as a bricklayer with various UK construction firms.[2]

Emil Konhäuser

Emil Konhäuser was born in Hof, Germany, in 1906. He later attended technical school and trained as a plumber in the building and construction trades. During the early 1930s, Konhäuser became active in the Municipal Workers Trade Union. But unlike his fellow PICKAXE agent, Emil Konhäuser's political resistance to the Nazi regime cost him two years of his life, which he spent in the Dachau concentration camp from 1933 to 1935. After his release, Konhäuser worked on the construction crew that built the German superhighway called the Autobahn. By that time, Konhäuser's work with the underground resistance in Hof forced him to seek exile with his family in Czechoslovakia. From 1935 to 1938, Konhäuser worked with the Political Refugees Committee in Prague and the Central Jewish Committee in Poland, where he continued "helping victims of Nazi terror."[3] In the early spring of 1939 and just prior to the German occupation of Czechoslovakia, Konhäuser and his family quickly left Prague and secured passage to England with the aid of the Czech Refugee Trust Fund.[4]

Mission training

Beginning in the winter of 1945, Emil Konhäuser and Walter Strüwe underwent extensive training in preparation for the PICKAXE mission under the direction of Lt. Gould, who had been designated the OSS training officer for the TOOL missions. Both men traveled to the OSS mission training school in Ruislip, where they attended briefings dealing with a wide range of subjects designed to prepare them for their missions, including military identification of German military armor and supply trains, as well as weapons, close combat, and counterespionage techniques. Later, Strüwe and Konhäuser received parachute training in a top secret training site at Ringway, near the English city of Manchester.[5]

As with the other German exiles recruited for the TOOL missions, fictional identities were developed for Strüwe and Konhäuser. Strüwe would later parachute into Landshut with work identification papers under the name of Frantisek Skala, a plumber from Czechoslovakia who fled to Germany to escape the advancing Russian Army. Konhäuser's passbook identified him as Guillaume Godart, a building construction foreman from Belgium who years earlier had been forcibly deported by the Nazis to Nuremberg.[6]

POW camp reports

Sometime in March 1945, both Walter Strüwe and Emil Konhäuser agreed to be placed inside prisoner-of-war camps maintained outside London by the US Army, where captured German Army officers were being held. This work also enabled them to gain some insight into the mindset of German soldiers and conditions inside Germany, especially given their long exile in England. Both men later submitted detailed reports to the OSS about their experiences inside these camps.

Report of Emil Konhäuser

Emil Konhäuser was placed in a POW camp outside London in March 1945. He spent four days in barracks housing noncommissioned German officers captured by the Allies. He did not mingle or speak with regular soldiers of the German Army who were separated from the officer barracks and housed in a separate POW camp. Konhäuser reported on conversations he had with these men on a range of subjects.

On the prospects of a German victory

The POWs that Konhäuser encountered believed that Hitler would soon launch a new offensive and "wipe out all Anglo-American military forces" then advancing into Germany from the west, and that this victory would result from the secret weapons that the Fuhrer would soon unleash upon them. Moreover, these German officers actually believed that whatever gains made by the Allies on the continent (since the D-Day invasion) came about because Hitler had pulled his "crack troops" in order to save them for more decisive battles.

One 22-year-old lieutenant, who was captured by Allied forces during the Battle of the Bulge in late December 1944, claimed that a captured German Army major disclosed to Allied interrogators that the Germans were about to deploy a large paratrooper force; it was later repelled by Allied forces who were waiting for them. But for this "treason," the new anti-tank weapons used by the Wehrmacht would have wiped out the enemy.

Many of the POWs that Konhäuser spoke with believed that Germany would ultimately win the war and they would return home to pleasant lives with their families. In their view, Hitler would have given up long ago and not held out to the bitter end and sacrificed the German nation. Moreover, the POWs believed that once a military victory had been won, the American people would soon find out what it meant to go hungry when Hitler plundered the US homeland for food and raw materials for shipment back to the Third Reich.[7]

On their African American camp guards

All of the German officers Konhäuser encountered said that they preferred the "Negro" camp guards because they allegedly spoke disparagingly of their senior officers. According to the POWs, this was because of the racist views that their white officers apparently held that led to demeaning treatment of the African American guards at this camp.[8]

Report of Walter Strüwe

Walter Strüwe filed a more detailed report on his experiences inside the POW camp, mainly because he spent nearly eight days there. He told the other POWs that he had been captured on the Western Front and had been evacuated to a hospital in England where he received treatment for injuries he suffered in battle. He was then transferred to this camp, which held ordinary soldiers but no hard-core Nazi fanatics.

After some initial conversations with other POWs while walking the grounds, Strüwe reported that the POWs admitted that the US military had been treating them relatively well and they were likely better off than those still at the front or enduring bombing raids on the homeland. In fact, Strüwe recalled not one instance where the POWs talked of escaping the camp.

Their meals consisted of potatoes, cabbage, lots of bread and "tinned" meat and fish, usually washed down with coffee. Their huts, however, were given little heat on cold nights and they were often forced to burn bedsheets in a stove to keep themselves warm. And the black market flourished in this camp; one POW offered Strüwe a silver case and pen for a pack of cigarettes.

Like the POWs in Emil Konhäuser's camp, most of the POWs told Strüwe that they believed that "miracle weapons" would soon be unleashed on the Allies that would enable Germany to turn the tide of the war in their favor. They refused to believe news broadcasts from the BBC about military victories won by the Allies as they marched toward Germany; it was pure propaganda, according to the POWs, who believed that once the war ended, they would return to their homeland and enjoy "a good and quiet life."

On Nazi war crimes

Strüwe also reported that the POWs were aware of the terrible war crimes committed by the German Army and the SS and feared they would be held accountable for them. Many admitted witnessing such crimes while fighting on the Russian front and feared the violent revenge that the Red Army would exact on them if they were not kept out of Germany.

On the Holocaust

As for the persecution of the Jews by the Nazis, all felt that Hitler should have waited until military victory was won before launching the campaign to exterminate them. According to Strüwe, the POWs now believed that the "Jews would exact revenge" on the German people.

On fear of the fate of their families in Germany

The POWs repeatedly voiced their concerns about whether their families could survive the Allied bombings in Germany. Strüwe recalled conversations in which he suggested that ending the war immediately was the only way they could be saved. He tried to discourage their belief that the Nazis could achieve a military victory.

Strüwe even revealed his real feelings about Hitler and the Nazis. At first, such statements were met with silence, but Strüwe's appeal to the "personal worries" of the POWs eventually led some to grudgingly agree with him. None of them threatened to harm Strüwe for these views. Strüwe then left the camp unnoticed and filed his report.[9]

Destination: Landshut

On April 4, 1945, William Casey, chief of the London office of Special Intelligence, delivered the order to dispatch the PICKAXE mission into Landshut to Army Lt. Joseph Gould. The original targets of the mission – Frankfurt and Nuremberg – were scrapped because of rapid Allied advances into Germany that had not been anticipated when the mission objectives were initially determined in January. As a result, the OSS decided that the city of Landshut near Munich would become the mission's new intelligence target. Strüwe and Konhäuser were to be dropped into an area of Germany they had no familiarity with, nor any contacts in the underground resistance to shelter them if necessary.[10]

With little time to prepare, the OSS drew up a revised list of intelligence gathering objectives for the PICKAXE agents, primarily dealing with troop movements and defense installations as well as the state of highway and railroad military transports carrying German infantry divisions and artillery battalions operating in the area around Landshut. The OSS also sought information from the PICKAXE team on the treatment of Allied prisoners of war in nearby German POW camps. In particular, a special request was made by John Winant, the US ambassador to Great Britain and a close confidant of Prime Minister Winston Churchill, to see if the men could obtain any information about the condition of his son – John G. Winant, Jr.[11]

Shortly after Hitler declared war on the United States, the ambassador's son left Princeton University and enlisted in the United States Army Air Force. A first lieutenant, John G. Winant, Jr. served as a B-17 pilot in the Eighth Air Force based in England. On his thirteenth combat mission, a bombardment of the German city of Munster, his Flying Fortress was shot down. He was reported missing in action in October 1943, and his fate made headlines on both sides of the Atlantic.

Lieutenant Winant was captured and placed by the Germans in a camp which also held leading politicians and other notables from occupied countries. It was believed that Winant and his fellow POWs had become "the personal hostages of the Nazi S.S. leader Heinrich Himmler, who was said to have ordered them to be taken to the Black Forest and executed."[12]

Dispatch of the PICKAXE mission

The PICKAXE mission was dispatched from an airbase located in the eastern French city of Dijon on April 4, 1945. The agents agreed to specific drop points in separate locations outside of Landshut. The dispatch went very smoothly. It took nearly a day for Strüwe to find Konhäuser after they landed by parachute that first night on the ground behind enemy lines. Strüwe and Konhäuser then decided to retreat into the woods outside Landshut, where they set up tents made of rain gear and buried their J/E transmitters.

The next morning, Konhäuser and Strüwe walked to the center of Landshut, where they observed more refugees and foreign workers than German military officers or soldiers. Having also noticed too many tight controls throughout the city, the PICKAXE team decided that they would not use their cover stories and register with authorities to legalize their presence in the area. The reason for this decision to remain illegal was simple: most of the foreign workers were being moved to other locations outside of Landshut on short notice. If they registered, the agents would be subject to these same orders, which they felt might prevent them from carrying out their mission. At the same time, they had plenty of counterfeit food ration cards that were passing muster without suspicion. As a result, Strüwe and

Konhäuser decided to operate illegally and remain in the forest outside of Landshut for the duration of the mission.

The PICKAXE team successfully transmitted important military intelligence using the J/E transmitter. According to their mission reports, bad weather and artillery fire hindered communication with Allied planes hovering over Landshut. Of the seven contacts, only two resulted in direct two-way communication. In some instances, the PICKAXE team transmitted military intelligence that was recorded and later used to achieve a military objective. According to Special Intelligence chief William Casey:

> We put another team, codenamed *PICKAXE*, into Landshut near Munich. The agents funneled massive amounts of information about rail and road traffic, communications centers and troop movements-down to shoulder patch and other marking descriptions to waiting Mosquitoes during no fewer than nine Joan Eleanor reports. One typical message cited heavy troop movements through the Landshut rail junction. The information was relayed to Air Force HQ the next morning. That night both railroad station and yards were heavily bombed. A follow up report on the damage was radioed up to a Mosquito 24 hours later.[13]

The transcripts of the J/E transmissions provide further details on the Landshut railway depot bombing, which occurred on April 16, 1945. According to a radio transmission two days later, the agents reported that all railway traffic had stopped and there were no trains running through Landshut, mainly because the Landshut station was now a pile of rubble. The team also reported that they saw no armored trucks moving through the area. They also observed lots of truck traffic on the roads leading to Munich and passenger cars transporting German military officers.[14]

This is how agent Emil Konhäuser later described the conditions in the area around Landshut:

> Things in our area of deployment were already all haywire. No clear frontlines, parts of the German army flooding back and forth, bombed-out transportation routes, ongoing American air raids, streams of refugees, scattered German artillery positions. We didn't see much of resistance, only [people] running and racing for bare life. During the day, we both moved inside the city and its environs, at night we hid in the woods.[15]

The next successful J/E transmission occurred on April 25. The PICK-AXE team reported that the railway lines were still paralyzed; that an entire division of Waffen SS troops were being transported by truck to the town of Erding; and that a Special Forces unit known as Grenadiere was also observed moving through Landshut. The agents also reported the discovery of a military message center located in the center of Landshut and that nearly 5,000 *unarmed* troops were moving on foot toward Munich. In addition, Strüwe and Konhäuser learned that the German Army had mined the bridges spanning the Isar River with explosives. The OSS London office, after having received the transcripts of these transmissions, was quite pleased with the team's work. This was evident from the comment made the next day by the radio operator in the plane hovering over Landshut "that everyone in London is quite satisfied and that they like your work very much."[16]

While there were no more successful J/E transmissions before the mission ended on May 1, 1945, the PICKAXE team did provide extensive reports to Allied military intelligence officers who recovered them that day. Of primary importance was the information they obtained regarding the failure of the Germans to persuade local residents to defend Landshut. While the German Army set up tank blocks and mined railway and highway bridges with explosives, hardly anyone from Landshut came out to actively defend the city against the encroaching Allied armies. That result may have been due to the efforts of Strüwe and Konhäuser who, while mingling with local residents on food lines, assured them that they had nothing to fear from the Americans as long as they didn't actively fight to defend the city with the German Army.

The agents also reported that they overheard conversations between local residents admitting that even though they did not believe that the war could be won, they were still fearful of the Gestapo and even of the approaching American armies because of remarks made by Goebbels on the radio that the "Americans were committing atrocities and deliberately starving German civilians."[17]

The Allied military command also sought further intelligence on whether the rumors about the so-called National Redoubt were real. This was the English term used to describe the possibility that Adolf Hitler and the armed forces of Nazi Germany would make a last stand in the alpine areas of Austria, Bavaria and northern Italy in the closing months of World War II in Europe. In German this concept was called the Alpenfestung (Alpine Fortress). Although there was some German military planning for a stand in the Alpine region, it was never fully endorsed by Hitler and no serious attempt was made to put the plan into operation. This was reported in *Time* magazine in February 1945:

> But what of the top Nazis who cannot hide? With a compact army of young SS and Hitler Youth fanatics, they will retreat, behind a loyal rear-guard cover to the Alpine mountain range which reaches from southern Bavaria across western Austria to northern Italy. There immense stores of food and munitions are being laid down in prepared fortifications. If the retreat is a success, such an army might hold out for years.

Prior to the dispatch of the PICKAXE mission, senior Allied military officers did believe that Hitler was going to lead elite German troops into the Bavarian Alps using his mountaintop retreat as a base to organize a last stand. Their task: engage in a guerilla war with Allied armies in order to force a negotiated peace with the German government. Allied intelligence in Switzerland was warning that an underground railway had already been constructed and that a large supply of munitions and poison gas was being stockpiled.[18]

The presence of the PICKAXE team working in this section of the country proved useful with regard to the US military's fear of the rumored National Redoubt. Here is what the director of OSS Special Intelligence, William Casey, wrote in his wartime memoir:

> The PICKAXE team we had dropped into Bavaria in early April toured southern and eastern Bavaria. They sent a complete report via Joan Eleanor that did its best to demolish the myth [of the Redoubt]. PICK-AXE had found no evidence pointing to any German ability to mount serious resistance in the Bavarian mountains. The report was at once transcribed and the summary sent to SHAEF.
>   (Supreme Headquarters Allied Expeditionary Force)[19]

Based on transcripts of debriefings given by Strüwe and Konhäuser to Allied military officers in late June 1945 and transcripts of numerous con-versations between the agents and radio operators in planes hovering over southern Germany, there is no doubt that the PICKAXE mission achieved its main objective: transmitting military intelligence to the OSS later pre-sented to the senior military officers commanding troops in that area of Germany.

On May 5, 1945, Walter Strüwe and Emil Konhäuser were recovered by the American military and flown to Paris for mission debriefings. Shortly thereafter, the men returned to London and rejoined their families. Before their discharge from the US Army, the OSS submitted a recommendation to the US military in Washington, DC, that Strüwe and Konhäuser be awarded the Silver Star. Written by Colonel James R. Forgan, the recommendation cited "exceptionally meritorious and courageous action in volunteering for and successfully carrying out a secret and dangerous mission behind enemy lines which benefitted the Armies of the Allied Nations in the prosecution of the war."[20] On July 13, 1945, both men were discharged from the US Army and rejoined their families.[21]

As to the fate of Lt. John Winant, Jr., the son of the US ambassador to Great Britain, he eluded further efforts by the SS to hold him as a special hostage and was eventually found unharmed after making his way to a US Army outpost in Austria just one day before the Nazis surrendered to the Allies on May 8, 1945.[22]

Both Strüwe and Konhäuser remained in England until 1947 when their application for repatriation into Germany was finally granted by the Soviet Union. Walter Strüwe and his wife Leonie returned to Frankfurt, Germany, and later moved to Dresden. They lived out their lives in East Germany. Walter Strüwe died on April 24, 1976. Emil Konhäuser eventually returned to his hometown of Hof, Germany. He died of a heart attack in West Germany on July 14, 1971.[23]

Figure 2.1 PICKAXE mission agent Emil Konhäuser

Figure 2.2 PICKAXE mission agent
Walter Strüwe

Figure 2.3 John G. Winant, Sr., US
ambassador to Great Britain,
1941–46

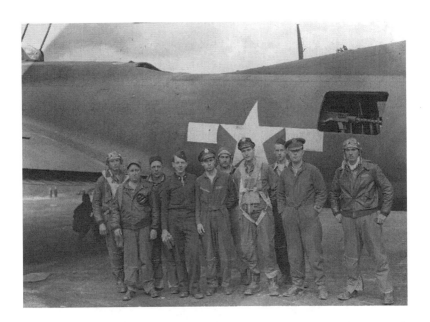

Figure 2.4 John G. Winant, Jr. (fourth from right) with US Army Air Force unit
before being shot down over Germany, Harrington Airfield, England,
1945

Notes

1 Biographical profile of Walter Strüwe drafted by Army Lt. Joseph Gould, OSS Labor Division, November 1944; Personal History statement, dated October 27, 1944, drafted and signed by Walter Strüwe, OSS Records, RG 226, US National Archives NARA
2 Ibid.
3 Ibid.
4 United Kingdom Immigration Office, Regional Advisory Committee Report: Emil Konhäuser, HO 396/48, United Kingdom National Archives.
5 OSS Mission training records, PICKAXE Mission, NND #974395, NARA, November 1944.
6 Cover Detail memorandum drafted by M.B. Wolf to BACH Unit, January 13, 1945, OSS Records, RG 226, US National Archives NARA.
7 POW Cage Report, Emil Konhäuser, OSS Records, RG 226, US National Archives NARA NND #974395.
8 Ibid.
9 POW Cage Report, Walter Strüwe, RG 226, OSS Records, US National Archives NARA NND #974395.
10 POW Cage Report, Walter Strüwe, OSS Records, US National Archives NARA NND #974395.
11 PICKAXE Mission report, prepared by Emil Konhäuser and Walter Strüwe, May 14, 1945, p. 9, RG 226, OSS Records, US National Archives NARA.
12 Obituary of John Winant, Jr. by Wolfgang Saxon, *New York Times*, November 2, 1983.
13 William J. Casey, *The Secret War against Hitler* (Washington, DC: Regnery Gateway, 1988), p. 200.
14 Transcripts of radio transmissions sent by Emil Konhäuser and Walter Strüwe while carrying out the PICKAXE mission, RG 226, OSS Records, US National Archives NARA NND #974395.
15 See note 11 (PICKAXE Mission Report).
16 Transcripts of radio transmissions between Emil Konhäuser and Walter Strüwe and US Air Force pilots hovering over Germany while carrying out the PICK-AXE mission, RG 226, OSS Records, US National Archives NARA NND #974395.
17 Ibid.
18 Ada Petrova, *The Death of Hitler: The Full Story with New Evidence from Secret Russian Archives* (New York: St. Martin's Press, 1995).
19 Casey (see note 13).
20 Medal recommendation for the award of the Silver Star, submitted by Colonel James R. Forgan, June 19, 1945 (a copy of the medal recommendations for both agents is attached to Appendix G).
21 Text of mission debriefing of PICKAXE mission agents conducted by E. Brooks, June 27, 1945, OSS Records, US National Archives NARA; PICK-AXE Agent Release of WALTER STRÜWE and EMIL KONHÄUSER, signed by Leonard Appel, OSS London, July 13, 1945, OSS Records, US National Archives NARA.
22 (Note 12).
23 Affidavits of John Strüwe and Charles Konhäuser, dated December 15, 2006, attached to PICKAXE Mission medal application submitted to the Military Awards Branch in January 2007 by Jonathan Gould, Esq.

3 Gone Too Soon

The courageous life and tragic death of Kurt Gruber

This chapter will focus exclusively on the CHISEL mission and the German exile recruited for this mission into the Ruhr Valley in northern Germany by Army Lieutenant Joseph Gould. His name is Kurt Gruber. While he died in the service of the war against Hitler, his sacrifice has gone relatively unnoticed – until now.

Birth of a coal miner

Kurt Gruber was born on May 13, 1912, in Hamm, which is located within the Westphalia district of Germany. His family later moved to the nearby coal mining town of Ahlen, where he was raised along with his older brother Karl. In 1928, he left school and became an apprentice in the Westphalia district coal mines under the tutelage of his father Eduard. He then joined the Ruhr District coal miners' union and was elected chairman of its Central Youth Council. By 1929, Gruber organized the youth federation to fight the rise of Nazism and led over 100 youth groups scattered throughout the entire Ruhr Valley coal mining region. He convened meetings of the Youth Council to deliver lectures on the growing danger of Hitler's Nazi Party and their plans to murder European Jewry.[1]

A letter written about Kurt Gruber in 2006 by a boyhood friend and fellow coal miner named Kurt Julius Goldstein and which reflected Gruber's courage in standing up to the Nazis in the early 1930s illustrates the strong impact he had on the youth of Ahlen, where both men grew up. Goldstein would later wind up as a slave laborer in the coal mines of Auschwitz-Birkenau, where he toiled from mid-1942 until the death camp was liberated in January 1945. The SS then marched him and other inmates to the Buchenwald concentration camp, where he was held until it was liberated by American troops in April 1945. He later became the leader of the International Auschwitz Committee until his death at 93 in September 2007.[2]

Goldstein, who had been a young Jewish man facing the growing anti-Semitism of the Nazi Party, later shared his memories of Gruber's leadership during those turbulent times:

> Kurt Gruber was the director of the anti-Nazi youth federation that I joined in August, 1928. From this time on, I participated under the leadership of Kurt Gruber in all activities of the youth federation that were directed against the rise of Nazism in our home region, western Westphalia. I remember a series of club-evening lectures by Kurt Gruber on the subject of "what we have to expect from Hitler's *Mein Kampf*."
>
> When I was at the Auschwitz camp between 1942 and 1945, I often came to think of Kurt Gruber, because in these lectures he turned our attention to the anti-Semitic plans that Hitler had developed in this book, for there were many of us young Jewish people in this anti-Nazi youth federation.
>
> He was also the author of pamphlets against the Nazis which our youth federation issued before all elections for the Landtag. Under Kurt Gruber's leadership we also went to the conventions of Nazi organizations where Kurt Gruber appeared as a speaker against the Nazis. We worked together in this fashion until late in 1930. At this point, Kurt Gruber was elected to the district leadership for the Ruhr area of our organization. We continued to be in close contact until January 1933 when the Nazis created their terror regime in Germany.[3]

Even more daring was Gruber's successful campaign to prevent Nazi storm troopers from marching through the working-class neighborhoods of Westphalia. In 1930, Gruber published pamphlets about the Nazis and distributed them to local politicians campaigning for the parliamentary elections in the Ruhr Valley. Gruber's campaign against the Nazis knew no bounds. But there was a price to pay, as the Nazis started to hunt down and attack all known anti-fascists. On March 24, 1931, Karl Gruber, the brother of Kurt Gruber, was murdered during a street brawl in Ahlen by the Nazi storm troopers who were vying for control of the Westphalia coal miners' union. The murder of Karl Gruber immediately triggered an outpouring of grief and protest from nearly 3,000 villagers of Ahlen who marched in support of their fallen comrade. Kurt Gruber later wrote that he was the real target of the Nazis that night.[4]

Life in the underground

Following Hitler's rise to power in 1933, the Nazis started hunting for Gruber. They tried taking his father hostage to achieve that end. But a friend managed to get a note from an imprisoned Eduard Gruber to his son. It read: "Never give yourself up, son, no matter what happens to me." For the next eighteen months, Gruber, operating under the alias "Paul," went underground and continued to fight the Nazis. Moving from house to house throughout the Ruhr district and later in Berlin, where he was sheltered by his uncle, Gruber's work focused primarily on developing underground basement facilities for printing German Communist Party leaflets.[5]

By 1936, Gruber suffered a nervous breakdown brought on by the issuance of an arrest warrant for "high treason" against the Reich. That warrant appears to have intensified the pressure on the Gestapo to capture Gruber.[6] According to Gruber's stepdaughter, he once told his wife how one night in 1935 he narrowly escaped being captured. The Nazis had posted wanted signs with Gruber's photo on them in railway stations throughout Berlin. One night, someone noticed him walking through one of these stations and alerted the Gestapo, who chased him down the street until Gruber reached an intersection where the local trams were running. As one of them approached, its conductor saw this scene unfold in front of him and slowed down so that Gruber could hop aboard. Its passengers then gathered around to shield him until the conductor accelerated and sped away, leaving the exhausted secret police behind. Gruber had apparently shared this story a number of times to show that many Germans hated the Nazis but felt powerless to do anything. This incident led Gruber to leave Nazi Germany for Czechoslovakia.[7]

From his new base in Prague with other German communist exiles, Gruber continued his work developing printing facilities. He used various cover stories, posing as a plumber, a commercial traveler selling bicycles or an unemployed man looking for work. And he continued to elude the Gestapo while providing underground assistance to political prisoners and their families in Germany, making numerous and very dangerous trips into Berlin.[8]

Escape to England

By the winter of 1939, Gruber was again forced to run from the Nazis as the German Army began its march into Czechoslovakia. On February 23, 1939, with the aid of the British Committee for the Rescue of the Czech Refugees (BCRC), Gruber was evacuated by plane from a remote Prague airfield to Holland and then England. He temporarily settled in Croydon, a suburb of South London. There, Gruber worked odd jobs as he tried to adjust to life in England. But in July 1940, the British government, fearing a German invasion of the homeland following Hitler's conquest of Europe, issued orders that all German exiles be interned indefinitely. Gruber was interned in a camp on an island controlled by the British government in the middle of the Irish Sea called the Isle of Man. He was later released in May 1941 and returned to London.[9]

Still struggling to find meaningful work, Gruber decided to return to the coal mines, which he viewed as the best way he could help fight the war against Hitler. As Gruber wrote in *I Am a German Coal Miner*: "I am going [back] down in the pits to produce the coal so necessary for the fight against fascism." This decision led Gruber to move to Scotland and he eventually settled in Glasgow.[10] In February 1943, he spoke at the opening of an anti-Nazi art exhibit in Edinburgh titled "We Accuse" and briefed reporters on the state of the anti-Nazi resistance inside Germany.[11] By March 1943, Gruber found work in the coal mines operated by the Glasgow-based Cadzow Coal Company.

A new life and family in Glasgow

Gruber's decision to return to mining was timely because it coincided with the growing crisis that would threaten England's wartime defense industries. The military conscription of England's coal miners caused a severe shortage of coal. The nation needed men to take their place in the mines. This led to the successful campaign spearheaded by defense minister Ernest Bevin to draft nearly 50,000 men who were ordered to report for work in the nation's coal mines. They were later dubbed the *Bevin's Boys*.[12] No doubt, Gruber's decision to offer his coal mining skills to the war effort was welcomed by the British authorities. In the fall of 1943, Kurt Gruber joined the Scottish Mineworkers Union and rose through the ranks to become one of its leaders. He rallied the mineworkers to forego actions against the coal mine owners for the sake of defeating German fascism.[13] He later accepted employment from the Jas. Nimmon Coal Company which operated the Bishopbriggs coal mines near Glasgow.

Sometime in early 1944, Gruber began to circulate in social circles within the Glasgow coal miners' community and met a woman who worked as a private secretary in the union office. Her name was Jessie Campbell Leith. Kurt Gruber fell in love with her. They were married in September 1944. Jessie Campbell Gruber would later become pregnant with the couple's first child. They were planning to return to Germany after the war, but in November 1944, fate intervened when Gruber answered the call of the OSS and the German Communist Party in exile. He accepted the invitation to meet in a small London tavern with a New York white-collar trade unionist and army officer from the OSS Special Intelligence Branch operating out of its London office. The army officer was Lt. Joseph Gould and he persuaded Gruber to volunteer for a dangerous espionage mission that sought military intelligence within the heart of the Ruhr Valley.[14]

Recruitment and training for the CHISEL mission

Beginning in January 1945, Kurt Gruber underwent extensive training in preparation for the CHISEL mission into the Ruhr Valley under the direction of Lt. Gould. Along with the other German exiles, he commuted daily from his London home that he shared with his new wife to the OSS mission training school in Ruislip. There, he attended briefings dealing with a wide range of subjects designed to prepare him for his mission, including military identification of German military armor and supply trains, weapons and close combat, and counterespionage techniques as well as special training dictated by the mission's objectives. And like the other German exiles recruited for these missions, Gruber underwent parachute training at the RAF training base at Ringway, located near the city of Manchester.

Later, the OSS developed a fictional identity for Kurt Gruber and produced impeccably forged papers identifying him as Pawel Novak.[15] Like the other German exiles recruited for the TOOL missions, Kurt Gruber was also trained to operate a newly invented radio transmitter which utilized very high frequencies that enabled its operator to orally transmit military intelligence on the ground to planes hovering over Europe without detection from German Army short-wave radio operators. He also learned to decipher coded messages that would be transmitted to him behind enemy lines through BBC radio broadcasts in German. Gruber was instructed to listen to these broadcasts in order to learn the time and location of supply drops and radio transmissions.

On February 23, 1945, Kurt Gruber signed an overseas agent employment contract with the OSS which provided hazardous duty compensation and death benefits. Gruber named his new wife, Jessie Campbell Leith, as his beneficiary. The dispatch of the CHISEL mission was quickly approaching. Kurt Gruber was ready to begin his mission. More than twelve years of underground resistance, internment and exile in Czechoslovakia, England and Scotland would end upon landing by parachute into Hamm, the designated drop point of the mission – and his birthplace.

Tragedy mars the dispatch of the CHISEL mission

The events surrounding the dispatch of the CHISEL mission on the evening of March 19, 1945, foreshadowed the tragic fate that Gruber and the flight crew would suffer. The prior mission dispatch dates had been canceled due to bad weather in England. A week went by before word was sent out in the late afternoon of March 19 that the mission was going to go that evening and that Lt. Gould was to bring mission agent Gruber to Harrington Airfield immediately.

After arriving at Harrington and hastily consuming a dinner of corn, coffee and oranges, Lt. Gould and Gruber moved quickly to an office where Gruber was instructed to change into his mission gear. He later met with the pilot and flight navigators to confirm the drop point. Shortly thereafter, United States Air Force Colonel Hudson Upham appeared. At that time, Colonel Upham was commander of the 492nd Bomber Group, otherwise known as the "Carpetbaggers." This was the bomber group that flew German penetration missions into Europe.

When Commander Upham was appointed the new commanding officer of the 492nd Bombardment Group in December 1944, his arrival coincided with the decision by the senior military brass in London to resume the OSS agent missions that had previously been thought to be unnecessary because of the mistaken belief that the war would end by Christmas. "The resumption of the relationship between the 492nd and the OSS began badly and went downhill."[16] Aside from Colonel Upham's lack of experience in supervising the deployment of the A-26 agent missions into Nazi Germany, many of the experienced air crews stationed at Harrington Air Base in England had already been transferred to other locations in Europe where they piloted aircraft used for night bombing raids inside the Reich.

In addition, the remaining crews "showed little enthusiasm or understanding of OSS missions."[17] Moreover, Colonel Upham, according to one historian, "resented having to assign his B-24s to OSS missions." As a result, for the next few months, Colonel Upham and Colonel Stephen Simpson "battled bitterly over who had operational control over agent flights, the Air Force or the OSS."[18] Against this backdrop of rising tensions between the 492nd Bombardment Group and the OSS, the conflict that night at Harrington Airfield involving the dispatch of the CHISEL mission unfolded, which led to the tragic events that followed.

So after placing Kurt Gruber inside the plane slated to be used to dispatch the CHISEL mission, Lt. Gould encountered Commander Stephen Simpson, who had flown the recently dispatched HAMMER mission into Berlin. The aircraft used for that mission had sustained serious damage from anti-aircraft fire and needed to be repaired.[19]

Commander Simpson advised Lt. Gould that because the plane required additional repairs, he was not certain whether it was safe to fly. In addition, Simpson confided that Commander Upham had been putting pressure on him all day after the latter had purportedly received a direct order from "an unnamed general" to dispatch the mission that night. And when Colonel Upham became angry at the crew's warnings about the plane's flightworthiness, he threatened to fly the mission himself. This elicited a harsh reaction from the navigators scheduled to pilot the CHISEL mission plane and nearly ignited a mutiny when they refused to board the aircraft. Aside from the fact that the crew slated to fly the CHISEL mission agent into Germany had told Simpson that they "had not sufficient rest," they also were apparently alarmed at the prospect of Colonel Upham piloting the aircraft because of his "brief flying time in flying the A-26 aircraft that was going to fly the mission."[20]

In a report marked TOP SECRET which was not declassified until many years after the war, Commander Simpson wrote about what happened that night on the Harrington Airfield tarmac just before the aircraft finally took off:

> On March 19th orders were given and cancelled several times to fly the CHISEL mission (the first A-26 operation). It was brought to everyone's attention that the A-26 needed a 100 hour check and the radio altimeter needed recalibrating. The Loran and Gee navigation systems needed checking and that Lieutenant Emmel had insufficient flying experience in the A-26 – he had only flown it twice at night. Major Tresemer had only been in an A-26 once before and had been completely bewildered by "ground pilotage" at such a speed. None of the crew – pilot, navigator or bombardier had ever flown together before, and were unfamiliar with the ship as a whole.
>
> It was finally decided to put the ship into the hanger for repair and inspection. At 4 o'clock Commander Simpson heard a rumor that Colonel Upham had again changed his mind and proceeded to headquarters to find out that this was true. Upon advising Colonel Upham that both engines were down, that the altimeter was not operating properly he was told to call the hanger and get the ship back into commission and have it ready by 7.30.
>
> The whole crew advised the Colonel that it would be impossible to get the flight plan and mission organized by that time, but the Colonel stated that this was an order from headquarters and it had to be done. The weather section added to the unease of the crew, stating that a bad front would be crossing the area and conditions on the continent were not good. The mission finally got off the ground after instructions from Lt Fogarty on operating the special apparatus in the ship they were not familiar with. Final statements were made by the pilot, navigator and bombardier to Colonel Upham that the trip was not feasible.[21]

But Commander Upham refused to consider these warnings and ordered the A-26 to lift off from Harrington and proceed to its destination. It never returned.

Mission aftermath

On March 26, 1945, the War Department in Washington filed a Missing Aircraft Report which officially confirmed that the plane and its crew were missing. Numerous contact messages were sent to Gruber's radio transmitter from planes hovering over the Ruhr Valley, but none were acknowledged.[22] In May 1945, the OSS sought assistance from the US Army unit then occupying the Ruhr Valley to search for the plane's wreckage, but nothing was found at that time. By August 1945, with still no wreckage found, Gruber and the flight crew that included four US servicemen were all declared dead.[23]

The OSS chose to notify Jessie Campbell Gruber by letter that the plane had not returned and that Gruber was presumed dead. The OSS honored its contract with Kurt Gruber and paid her the death benefit as Kurt Gruber had requested.[24] She continued to request more information about what happened to her husband. However, the OSS London office denied these requests from Jessie Campbell Gruber. It never disclosed to her the events that unfolded at Harrington Airfield that night when Colonel Hudson Upham ordered the mission to go despite the warnings of the crew that if the heavy rains predicted for Germany occurred, the aircraft, already battered from its trip to Berlin, was not safe to fly. The emotional trauma suffered by Gruber's wife from the loss of her beloved husband later took its toll when she suffered a miscarriage and never gave birth to Kurt Gruber's child.[25]

In August 2008, the Central Intelligence Agency declassified thousands of OSS personnel files. Among those files was the recommendation written in June 1945 by a senior OSS officer for the posthumous award of the Bronze Star to Kurt Gruber. The Bronze Star medal has been awarded to persons who, while serving in the Army of the United States during World War II, "distinguished themselves by heroic achievement or service."[26] The author of the medal recommendation – Colonel James Russell Forgan – wrote that Kurt Gruber, "by leaving his wife and volunteering for such a dangerous mission, knowing that he was going to be dropped blind into the Ruhr Valley and that capture by the German Army would have meant immediate execution for treason, had displayed outstanding gallantry worthy of the *Bronze Star*." Colonel Forgan concluded his recommendation by observing that Kurt Gruber had sacrificed his life in support of the war against Hitler and that "his bravery and desire to serve the Allied Armies was of the highest order."[27] He was just 32 years old.

For reasons likely due to a new statute passed in July 1945 by Congress authorizing the award of the Medal of Freedom to foreign nationals, the War Department did not act on the Gruber medal recommendation until

February 1946. At that time, the issue of whether the US military could actually approve recommendations for the award of military decorations to so-called enemy nationals was considered for the first time. A vigorous inter-office debate ensued among high-ranking military officers in Washington, DC. Ultimately, the War Department decided to authorize the Decorations Board to approve the awards of military decorations to German nationals like Kurt Gruber because they had "served the Allied cause." But in Gruber's case, the Decorations Board concluded that Kurt Gruber should be awarded the Medal of Freedom instead of the Bronze Star. While still honorable, the criteria for the issuance of the Medal of Freedom did not warrant a finding of gallantry and heroism but instead required evidence that the proposed awardee "performed a meritorious act or service which aided the United States in the prosecution of the war against Nazi Germany."[28]

Based on correspondence received from Cate Joyce, the daughter of Jessica Campbell Leif from a second marriage that took place a few years after Gruber's death, the United States military in England appears to have contacted Gruber's widow at her London home sometime in the spring of 1946 with the news of the War Department's decision to posthumously award the Medal of Freedom to her late husband. They continued to deny knowledge of what had happened to Gruber other than to repeat that he had gone missing and was presumed dead. And those US military officers charged with the responsibility of presenting the Medal of Freedom to Gruber's widow imposed harsh conditions on her. According to Cate Joyce, just before Jessie Campbell Leith Gruber's death in 2004, she told Joyce that representatives of the US Army arrived at her doorstep one day in 1946 and requested that she accompany them to an undisclosed military installation somewhere in England *while wearing a blindfold*. She was led into a room and presented with the Medal of Freedom. And then the military officer in charge of the medal presentation led her out in the same blindfold to a waiting military vehicle. Mrs. Gruber remained blindfolded until they reached her London home.[29]

By July 1946, the US military learned through various sources never publicly disclosed that the plane had crashed very close to the mission drop point near the small German town of Schwege and all of its occupants were killed. The cause of the plane crash was never conclusively determined by the United States military. The bodies were initially recovered by the local police and the German military and then buried in a military cemetery. Subsequently, the US military received information from German authorities as to the location of this cemetery and disinterred all of the bodies in order to confirm their identities. One of the bodies was dressed in civilian clothing and was later identified as Kurt Gruber.[30] Shortly thereafter, he was laid to rest with the remainder of the

CHISEL mission crew in the Ardennes American Cemetery in Neuville-en-Condroz, Belgium.[31]

According to documents found in the East German archive, Jessie Campbell Leith Gruber, during visits after the war from Erich Henschke, aka Karl Kastro, expressed bitterness at the treatment she received from the US military. She was never told about the results of the investigation referenced above and never knew that Kurt Gruber had been laid to rest in an American cemetery in Belgium that she could have visited during the course of her life. It was not until 2009 that the Scottish family of Kurt Gruber's widow, Jessica Campbell Leith, learned of his fate and his final resting place from documents and correspondence sent to them by Jonathan Gould. The OSS and the US military knew immediately what had happened that troubled night at Harrington Airfield. Did they fear disclosure of those events to Gruber's widow? Or were they simply maintaining the secrecy of the CHISEL mission to protect sources and methods of its wartime intelligence gathering? Those questions remain unanswered.

Mission investigation leads to a breakthrough

The post-war top secret classification of the CHISEL mission file by the United States military and later by the Central Intelligence Agency left many unanswered questions about what exactly happened when the aircraft flying Kurt Gruber to the Ruhr Valley to carry out the CHISEL mission crashed somewhere in the north German village of Schwege. Was the plane shot down by German anti-aircraft fire or by enemy fighter planes? Or did it crash in bad weather over Europe after it took off from the Harrington Airfield in England on the night of March 19, 1945? And where exactly was the crash site? While the CHISEL mission file maintained at the US National Archives in Washington, DC, contains some documents indicating that the military had learned sometime in 1946 that the plane had apparently crashed, it was never determined what caused it to go down. The file indicated that the aircraft planned to drop Kurt Gruber by parachute into an area near his hometown of Ahlen in order to carry out the CHISEL mission's objectives of transmitting intelligence about the movement of German troops in that area.[32] Moreover, the US military had confirmed that the bodies of the men had initially been removed from the site of the crash by German authorities and later buried at a military cemetery in Achmer.[33] But until recently, military historians had yet to find out what really happened that night.

Nearly seventy years after the crash of the CHISEL mission aircraft, new information has just been uncovered by a team of German aviation historians and an enterprising freelance reporter for a local newspaper based in the Wittager Land Region, which is located in the northern part of Germany. That region includes the small village of Schwege. The team of aviation historians, headed by Dr. Martin Frauenheim, had undertaken an investigation of the crash based on rumors and isolated leads that it had gathered in recent years.

On a cold morning in early February 2015, Gertrud Premke, the freelance reporter, followed up a lead suggesting that the crash may have occurred somewhere on a farm in the village of Schwege. On foot, Ms. Premke had decided to walk through the village and question residents on what they might have known about what happened that night in March 1945 when the plane came down. Ms. Premke had been given the name of Kruse as the owner of that farm. She then approached an elderly man operating a tractor and asked him what he knew. To Ms. Premke's surprise, the man – Hermann Kruse – was the son of Olinde Kruse, who had later told Hermann that she recalled hearing a "great noise" the night when the CHISEL mission aircraft crashed. Hermann Kruse recalled his mother telling him that because she was fatigued from a long day of farming her land, she went back to sleep. But the next morning – March 20 – Olinde Kruse began wondering what exactly she had heard and what had happened.[34]

She decided to investigate and took her son Hermann with her. Walking through their farmland, they soon came upon the gruesome sight of dead bodies and what turned out to be the wreckage of the CHISEL mission aircraft that had evidently gone down the night before. The chance meeting with Hermann Kruse, now 76 years old but still farming his family's land, was an unforeseen breakthrough that has led to the discovery of new evidence that sheds a much clearer light on the fate of the doomed CHISEL mission. Hermann Kruse told Ms. Premke that he still had vivid memories of that morning. He was a young boy, and he recalled the fear that enveloped him when he first observed the bodies of the crew strewn over his family's farm and the terrible wreckage of the Douglas A-26 aircraft that tragically failed to reach the CHISEL mission's destination. Instead it had apparently crashed into a wet moor on the Kruse farmland, causing the untimely deaths of four crew members and Kurt Gruber, then just 32 years old and awaiting the birth of his first child.[35]

Immediately thereafter, Hermann Kruse led the aviation historians and Ms. Premke to the small brook on the family farm where he recalled discovering the wreckage with his mother Olinde. He also remembered that his mother called the local police, who immediately came to the scene.[36] According to reports filed by the Schwege police and later by the German military, they were able to identify the mission crew from their military dog tags. They also found German currency and passport documents on or near the body of Karl Gruber identifying him as Pawel Nowak, his OSS alias, as well as the J/E radio transmitter that Gruber was planning to use to transmit military intelligence to planes hovering over the Ruhr Valley. All of the crew's personal effects – and the radio – were handed over to the German secret police.

In a report uncovered by the aviation historians, Ernest Grubendorf, then a German Air Force command officer, recalled arriving at the crash site after being notified by the local police in Schwege. He ordered Kruse farm laborers and a small group of Russian POWs to carry the bodies to a military vehicle that would transport them to the Achmer military cemetery where they were buried. Of further note from the Grubendorf report were certain observations he made at the scene of the accident. Specifically, there was *no* evidence that the plane had been shot down by anti-aircraft fire or German fighter planes. Grubendorf also determined that some of the bodies had been thrown over 150 meters as a result of the force of the impact when it crashed into this small brook on the Kruse farm. He also noted in his report that many parts of the aircraft were scattered all over the Kruse farmland.

Those aircraft parts were never removed by anyone and remained on the Kruse farm all these years – until now. They were recently found as the result of the forensic investigation conducted by the team of aviation historians who combed the Kruse farm to determine if any parts of the plane were still embedded in the land farmed by the Kruse family since the end of WWII. Using special metal detectors, Dr. Frauenheim's team found an array of parts scattered across the Kruse farm that apparently had not previously been searched. They included the aircraft nameplate with the inscription A-26 and the name of the US manufacturer (Beechcraft) as well as a rusted axle from the plane's cockpit.[37]

Between the damaged aircraft parts found at the site and the inspection of the aircraft by the officer from the German Air Force command which took place the morning after the plane fell out of the sky, there is no evidence to contradict the likely cause of this air crash: rainy and windy weather that battered the Ruhr Valley, no moonlight and the unsafe condition of the aircraft that had been damaged by anti-aircraft fire sustained while dropping the Berlin mission's agents into that war-torn city three weeks earlier.[38] The failure of Colonel Hudson Upham to heed the pleas of the aircraft's crew to postpone the dispatch of the CHISEL mission now appears to have sealed their tragic fate.

Colonel Hudson Upham's untimely death

After the war ended in April 1945, Colonel Upham was appointed commanding officer of the 306th Bomber Group, which remained in Europe for a specific project that sought to "map all of Europe using aerial photos."

He later was named chief of staff for the Traffic Division of the European Air Transport Service. However, on November 1, 1946, Colonel Hudson Upham, along with seven other US servicemen conducting a training mission during a flight headed for London, was tragically killed when the B-17 bomber that Colonel Upham was apparently co-piloting crashed into Mt. Blanc, then the tallest mountain in Western Europe on the border between France and Italy. According to a blog post on the US Army Air Force website, "the aircraft exploded and most of its pieces disappeared from the mountain."

With regard to the possible causes of the crash, according to a letter written by Brigadier General Lucas Beau of the above-referenced transport service to the commanding general of the US Air Force in Europe, General Beau "could not understand why they [the B-17] should have departed in such adverse weather conditions," which Colonel Upham apparently authorized. Three weeks after the crash and following the initial investigation into the circumstances surrounding this tragic occurrence, General Beau filed a report in which he apparently concluded that the flight plan agreed upon prior to the plane's departure may not have been adhered to.[39]

It took years before any trace of the doomed aircraft was found. In 2011, the family of Colonel Upham traveled to the site of the crash to search for his remains. A documentary produced in 2016 titled *B-17 Montblanc/Missing Aircraft* explored the circumstances behind the tragic flight of the B-17 that day.[40]

Figure 3.1 CHISEL mission agent Kurt Gruber, 1944

Figure 3.2 Jessica Campbell Leith, wife of Kurt Gruber

Die Familie des erschossenen Karl Gruber im Jahre 1938
vor ihrem Haus. Links steht ein Kostgänger.

Figure 3.3 Young Kurt Gruber (bottom right) with his family in Ahlen, Germany,
1925

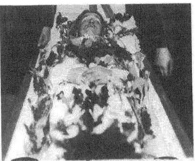

Zwei Bilder mit unterschiedlichem Bildausschnitt vom aufgebahrten Karl Gruber. Er liegt vor einem Lenin-bild und einer Fahne mit der Aufschrift: „Durch Klas-senkampf zur Freiheit". Vorne steht: „Karl Gruber – Von der braunen Mordpest im März 1931 erschossen." Die Totenwache halten vorne: der Bruder Kurt Gru-ber und Ernst Gerber, hinten: Willi de Graaf und Fritz Reimann.

Figure 3.4 Karl Gruber, brother of Kurt Gruber, in coffin following shooting death during street brawl with Nazi storm troopers, Ahlen, Germany 1931

Figure 3.5 Residents of Ahlen, Germany, marching in protest of the murder of Karl Gruber by Nazi storm troopers, 1931

Figure 3.6 US Army Air Force Colonel Hudson Upham, 1944

Figure 3.7 A-26 aircraft used to fly OSS agents into Germany in the CHISEL mission

Figure 3.8 Major John Walch was the navigator for the HAMMER mission into Berlin on March 2, 1945. He was killed while navigating the ill-fated A-26 aircraft that attempted to drop CHISEL mission agent Kurt Gruber into Ahlen, Germany on March 19, 1945

Figure 3.9 Hermann Kruse, 76, owner of family farm in Schwege, Germany, that CHISEL mission aircraft crashed onto in March 1945

Figure 3.10 Hermann Kruse with aviation investigators examining CHISEL mission aircraft debris discovered on Kruse farm in 2015

Notes

1 Agent recruitment profile of Kurt Gruber, from Army Lt. Joseph Gould to Thomas Wilson, December 8, 1944; responses to OSS agent recruitment questionnaire handwritten by Kurt Gruber, December 6, 1944; memo from Joseph Gould to George Pratt, Division of Intelligence Procurement, February 12, 1945, OSS Labor Division, OSS Records NARA.
2 Associated Press, Kurt Goldstein, Auschwitz survivor, October 1, 2007; Wikipedia, Kurt Julius Goldstein.
3 Letter from Kurt Julius Goldstein to Jonathan Gould, International Auschwitz Committee, September 27, 2006 (a copy of the letter from Kurt Julius Goldstein is attached to Appendix I).
4 Affidavit of Benedict Ruhmoller, mayor of Ahlen, North Rhine, Germany, January 10, 2007, paragraph 8 (review of Ahlen archives reveals article about battle for union control of Ahlen coal mines and death of Kurt Gruber's brother Karl Gruber during street altercation with Nazi storm troopers in March 1931).
5 Kurt Gruber, *I Am a German Miner: A German Miner in Britain Looks at Fascism* (Glasgow: National Union of Scottish Mineworkers, 1944); memorandum from Reich Attorney General to Hamm Attorney General regarding issuance of an arrest warrant for Kurt Gruber for high treason, May–October 1934.
6 See note 5 (memorandum from Reich Attorney General to Hamm Attorney General regarding arrest warrant targeting Kurt Gruber) and page 2 from *I Am a German Miner*, page 3.
7 Telephone interview with Cate Joyce, stepdaughter of Kurt Gruber, sharing recollection of her conversation with her mother and the first wife of Kurt Gruber, Jennifer Campbell Leith Gruber.
8 See note 1 (agent recruitment biographical profile); memo from George Pratt to Lt. Gould, March 19, 1945.
9 British Immigration Office, Kurt Gruber file, UK National Archive.
10 Ibid.
11 *Scotsman*, March 2, 1943.
12 Bevin Boys, Albert Gee, KURG Research Report No.7 (www.shropshiremines.org.uk/bmd/bevin).
13 See note 5 (excerpt from *I Am a German Miner*).
14 Joseph Gould, *An OSS Officer's Own WWII Story: Of His Seven German Agents and Their Five Labor Desk Missions into Warring Germany*, unpublished manuscript (Washington, DC, 1989).
15 Memo from Wilson to Joseph Gould, OSS London office, March 15, 1945; profile of mission cover identity named Pawel Novak; CHISEL mission training documents and overseas agent employment contract dated February 12, 1945; Schools and Training Branch Progress Sheet, January–February 1945, RG 226, OSS Records, NND, 974345, NARA.
16 Persico, Joseph, *Piercing the Reich: The Penetration of Nazi Germany by American Secret Agents During WWII* (New York: Viking Press, 1979), p. 159.
17 Ibid., pp. 180–181.
18 Ibid.
19 CHISEL Mission Dispatch Report submitted by Army Lt. Joseph Gould and Army Lt. Carl Devoe, March 20, 1945, RG 226, OSS Records, NARA.
20 Ibid.

21 Red Stocking Tragedy – Memorandum by Lt Comdr Stephen Simpson co-inventor of the "Joan-Eleanor" system concerning the loss of the A-26C on the first Red Stocking mission, *Flypast*, November 1999 (http://napoleon130. tripod.com/id312.html) (copies of Lt. Gould's dispatch report and Lt. Commander Simpson's memorandum are attached to Appendix H).

22 Missing Aircraft Report, issued by Office of European Theater Operations, May 3, 1945; 492 Bomb Operations. CHISEL Mission File, War Department Missing Aircraft Report, March 26, 1945, RG 226, OSS Records, NARA.

23 Ibid.

24 Memo to File from Army Lt. Joseph Gould, May 10, 1945; memo from Lillian Traugott, OSS Labor Division to Anthony Giuduci, August 27, 1945, CHISEL Mission File, Record of Payment of Compensation pursuant to Overseas Agent Employment Contract, August 23, 1945, RG 226, OSS Records, NARA.

25 Telephone conversation with Cate Joyce, London, England, June 2015.

26 The Bronze Star medal was established by Executive Order 9419, February 4, 1944.

27 Recommendation for the award of the Bronze Star to Kurt Gruber written by J.R. Forgan, OSS Theater Commander, June 20, 1945 (a copy of the medal recommendation is attached to Appendix J).

28 Memo from War Department General Staff regarding award of military decorations to enemy nationals, Feb. 28, 1946 to March 18, 1946.

29 Telephone interview with Cate Joyce (see note 7), June 2015.

30 The other US servicemen on board that night and who were also killed included 1st Lieutenant Oliver Emmel; Major John Walch; Major Edward C. Tressemer; and Frederick J. Brunner, a US Marine gunner who had already won the Silver Star in action in France in August 1944.

31 Cable from Paris to Washington, July 16, 1946.

32 Memo from Major Gordon Stewart to Army Lt. Joseph Gould, March 15, 1945, CHISEL Mission File, RG 226, OSS Records, NARA.

33 See note 147.

34 Gertrude Premke, *The Suicide Mission of Schwege: Reminiscence of an American Intelligence Aircraft that Crashed into Swampy Ground in March 1945*, published in local German newspaper *Wittlager Kreisblatt*, February 13, 2015.

35 Ibid.

36 Ibid.

37 Ibid. The name of the aviation historian is Dr. Martin Frauenheim and the forensic investigators are Matthew Zeisler and Johannes Haunert.

38 See note 139 regarding damaged condition of the A-26 that flew the CHISEL mission that night.

39 Memorial Day: Family seeks clues of B-17 crash in 1946, *Peninsula Daily News*, May 30, 2011 (www.b17montblanc.org/lincidente.html).

40 www.indiegogo.com/projects/b17-mont-blanc-missing-aircraft-in-the-glacier.

4   Still Missing

The story of Werner Fischer and the ill-fated BUZZSAW mission

This chapter will focus exclusively on the BUZZSAW mission and the German exile recruited for this mission by Army Lieutenant Joseph Gould. His name is Werner Fischer. For reasons which will be explained below, his fate still remains a mystery. But the historical record does show that he died in the service of the OSS and he should be remembered for his sacrifice and his stand against Nazi tyranny.

Profile of Werner Fischer

Werner Fischer was born in Dresden in 1913. After completing his education at the Volkschule in 1931, he became an artificial limb maker and was employed by German firms that sold prosthetics to doctors and hospitals treating injured WWI veterans. But in 1933, he was arrested by the Gestapo for his political work with the Young Communist League and placed in a concentration camp for being a "misled youth." His incarceration apparently had little effect. He was eventually released after being held for nearly four months but was kept under surveillance by the Nazis for nearly two years. He was only 20 years old at that time.[1]

In 1934, the Young Communist League sent Fischer to the Soviet Union, where he lived for nearly two years while attending classes at the Lenin School in Moscow, which trained him to assume leadership positions in support of the German Communist Party's campaign to recruit young cadres.[2]

Despite the risk, Fischer returned to Germany and continued his underground political work until forced to take refuge in Czechoslovakia in 1937, where he joined other anti-Nazi German political exiles. His flight out of Germany came just in time. This is because Fischer's name was repeatedly referenced by witnesses at the trials of other anti-Nazi activists conducted by the Nazis. Their testimony led to the issuance of an arrest warrant by the

Gestapo. The charge: committing acts of "high treason" against the Reich for his work with the Communist Youth Federation and his role in the production and distribution of anti-Nazi leaflets.[3]

For the next eighteen months, while operating out of Czechoslovakia, Fischer continued to ignore the perils he faced for his active support of the underground anti-Nazi resistance; he made repeated trips back into Berlin as a courier to deliver documents to other anti-Nazi activists still operating illegally in Germany. In 1938, following the signing of the Munich Agreement, Fischer fled to Paris but was arrested immediately on account of the pending visit to that city by German foreign minister Joachim von Ribbentrop. He was held for about five days but somehow managed to escape to Orléans, a city 80 miles south of Paris, where he secured a visa to England from its Parliamentary Refugee Committee.[4]

In England, he registered with the Czech Refugee Trust Fund, an organization of British volunteers who helped evacuate nearly 8,000 European political exiles just days before the German Army occupied Czechoslovakia in March 1939. In the UK, Fischer became prominent in the growing circle of young Germans fleeing Nazi Germany for England and was eventually elected the leader of the Free German Youth Organization.[5]

In July 1940, the British government, fearing a German invasion of the homeland following Hitler's conquest of Europe, issued orders that all German exiles be interned indefinitely. According to documents obtained from the British archives, Fischer boarded the SS *Ettrick* on July 3; it was crammed with German POWs and anti-Nazi political exiles. The former troopship carrying Fischer sailed for Ontario, Canada, where he remained in an internment camp until January 1942. He was released on the condition that he accept employment with the W. Michaelis Company, which offered him a job because of his skill as an artificial limb maker. Fischer then returned to London and started work with this firm.[6]

Just before accepting recruitment into the OSS to carry out the BUZZ-SAW mission in late November 1944, Werner Fischer appeared on behalf of the Free German Youth organization and spoke at the International Youth Conference that had been organized by the World Youth Council. His words speak of his commitment to ending Hitler's tyranny:

> The youth of the world is relying on us, for we know humankind's enemy from up close. We know how he grasped power in Germany, using calumny, fraud and terror. And thus the world expects special efforts from us young German anti-fascists, and in the end, this is about the future of the young generation in Germany itself, as represented in us. We will not have done our duty until the land of our birth is no

longer a robbers' den but, with our help, a normal member of the family of nations. Only then can there be peace.[7]

Mission training

Beginning in January 1945, Werner Fischer underwent extensive training in preparation for the BUZZSAW mission into Leipzig under the direction of Army Lt. Joseph Gould, who had recruited Fischer for this mission. Like the other German exiles training for the TOOL missions, Fischer commuted daily from his London home to the OSS mission training school in Ruislip, where he attended briefings dealing with a wide range of subjects designed to prepare him for the mission, including military identification of German military armor and supply trains and counterespionage techniques. Along with the other German exiles recruited for the TOOL missions, Fischer also underwent parachute training at the Ringway Airfield near Manchester.[8]

The OSS also considered it necessary to equip Fischer with identification papers and crafted a fictional identity. He was slated to parachute into Leipzig and carry papers identifying him as Ernst Georg Lauterbach of Breslau, Germany. Described as an ardent supporter of Hitler, the fictional Lauterbach joined the SS in 1933. After serving in various posts, Lauterbach's papers stated that he left the SS for the Gestapo and later became one of its special agents posted to Leipzig. According to these mission identity papers, Lauterbach was charged with hunting down French foreign workers conscripted by the Nazis and suspected of committing acts of sabotage.[9]

Sometime in February 1945, in order to complete his training for the BUZZSAW mission, Fischer was placed by the OSS inside a prisoner-of-war camp outside London where captured German Army officers and troops were being held. He was instructed to engage in conversation with the POWs not only to obtain intelligence but also to live his cover story. After four days, Fischer slipped out of the camp and submitted a detailed report which primarily focused on the mindset[10] of the German POWs and their continued faith in Hitler's ability to lead Germany to a military victory over the Allies.[11]

According to Fischer's report, all of the POWs felt that the Germans suffered a defeat at Stalingrad because of the betrayal of the Italian Army. And many German POWs in this camp did not believe that the war was over. They told Fischer that they believed Hitler had developed secret weapons that would soon be unleashed to alter the course of the war.

The German POWs cautioned others not to believe the news they were receiving about the progress of the war from Allied camp commanders. In their view, the Americans were still struggling to defeat the German Army and whatever losses German soldiers sustained on the western front was the result of cowardice of their own military officers who refused to fight. Many German POWs in this camp also predicted that the Soviet and American armies would soon turn on each other. And none believed that a German defeat was possible because "Germans are the best fighters and superior human beings."[12]

Destination: Leipzig

Finally, in early April 1945, the order to dispatch the BUZZSAW mission into Leipzig was given to Lt. Joseph Gould, who prepared the final mission checklist. Werner Fischer was ready to begin his mission and return home to his family in Dresden after nearly eight years in exile. He was well equipped for the mission with the usual supplies: lots of cigarettes, sugar and coffee to be used, if necessary, to barter for food and information. He also carried small arms and a dagger as well as plenty of reichmarks.[13]

The BUZZSAW mission had certain objectives. Most important was the radio transmission of intelligence bearing on the movement of troops by the German Army. Fischer was instructed to make his way into Leipzig and observe the railway traffic throughout the city. In addition, the OSS sought intelligence on the condition of factories in the Leipzig metropolitan area producing armored cars, aircraft and ball bearings as well as on the state of oil production at plants operated by the German industrial cartel – I.G. Farben. Lastly, the OSS asked Fischer to find a way, if possible, to report on conditions at various POW camps where large numbers of US and British troops were being held, including the notorious Colditz prison camp.[14]

Dispatch of the BUZZSAW mission

Unlike the earlier TOOL missions, which had been dispatched out of air-fields in England, the BUZZSAW mission was launched from an air base in the eastern French city of Dijon on April 7, 1945. The OSS had initially requested permission from the Soviet Army to dispatch the mission from behind their lines because of its geographic proximity to Leipzig. That request was rejected by the Soviets. As a result, the mission was flown out of Dijon.[15] Fischer had been advised that he would receive a contact through his transmitter from a US Air Force plane within forty-eight hours of his landing in Leipzig. Having been advised by senior military commanders in London of the rumored retreat by Hitler and elite Waffen SS troops into the Bavarian Alps, the OSS sought immediate intelligence on local conditions and "the directional flow of troops or any sign of preparation for a definite enemy stand in that area."[16]

According to the air transport report filed by the navigator of the plane carrying Werner Fischer to Leipzig, it took off from the Dijon airfield during the evening of April 7, 1945, at around 10:30 PM and arrived at the drop point at around 2:30 AM. The report indicates that Fischer parachuted somewhere near Leipzig from an altitude of approximately 600 feet.[17] Lt. Gould appears to be the last person ever to speak with Werner Fischer since he accompanied him to the Dijon airfield that night and had sent him off on his mission. But no one in the OSS or the United States military ever heard from Werner Fischer again.[18]

The search for Werner Fischer

For the next four weeks, the OSS, with the aid of the United States Air Force, searched for Werner Fischer. Extensive efforts were made to recover him from his mission. According to the mission file, from April 11 through May 30, 1945, numerous messages in mission code were forwarded to the BBC for transmission to Werner Fischer. On April 11, navigators of the US Air Force filed a report after returning from a flight overlooking the area where Fischer had been dropped on April 7. They reported that they had tried to make contact with him via the J/E transmitter but were unsuccessful. During that same period, the OSS wired numerous cables to the US Army unit that had captured Leipzig and to the BBC requesting that they attempt radio contact with Fischer.[19]

But Werner Fischer failed to respond to any of these messages. In early August 1945, the OSS contacted the Soviet mission in Paris regarding Fischer. By the end of August, Soviet military authorities sent word with "regret" that they had been unable to locate Werner Fischer, who remained missing. However, correspondence recently found in the East German archives suggests that the Soviet military authorities knew what happened to Werner Fischer but had lied to the OSS. For within a month of the mission dispatch on April 7, 1945, a Soviet military officer somehow was able to make telephone contact with Felix Albin, a/k/a Kurt Hager, the leader of the German Communist Party in exile in England. In the fall of 1944, documents from the East German archive show that Hager had previously received word from the GRU, the Soviet military intelligence service, via Ursula Kuczynski, of its strong interest in having the German exiles volunteer for the TOOL missions, including Werner Fischer. In addition, according to these documents, the GRU insisted that Erich Henschke be released from his party work in England in order to focus his time and energy exclusively on the recruitment of the German exiles for the OSS mission project, as they called it. Also in this letter to Ulbricht, Henschke claimed he personally selected the men who later became the TOOL mission agents and that the GRU had reviewed this list of exiles before authorizing Henschke to present it to Army Lt. Joseph Gould.[20]

Now, in mid-April 1945, according to a letter submitted to GDR president Walter Ulbricht by Erich Henschke in October 1949, an unnamed Soviet military officer had apparently reached Hager in London and inquired about the identity of a man named Werner Fischer and whether or not he had been living as a political exile in England.[21] Albin apparently responded to this inquiry by informing the caller that "Fischer was our man." The contents of the letter strongly suggest that the caller had information that Werner Fischer had been a member of the German communists in exile in London. Henschke further advised Ulbricht that he confirmed Hager's communication regarding Fischer and that the Soviets had also "initiated a search" for Fischer but that the result of this search was "unknown."[22]

In late September 1945, following the surrender of Nazi Germany in May, the OSS was disbanded. Upon his discharge from the US Army and his return to New York in March 1946, Lt. Joseph Gould contacted former OSS chief William Donovan and asked for his help in finding out what happened to Fischer. But Donovan was not able to help Gould in his search for Werner Fischer.[23]

Marianne Bessinger, Fischer's fiancée, continued to search for him. Werner had just made her acquaintance at a social gathering in the fall of 1944 among German exiles who had fled Nazi persecution and resettled in London. Bessinger, a Jewish woman from Dresden, had left Germany to avoid potential deportation to a concentration camp. She had developed into a highly skilled ballet dancer and attracted the attention of leading dance companies in England for whom she performed, including the Royal Ballet Company in London.

Her relationship with Werner Fischer later blossomed in the winter of 1945 when they fell in love.[24] They planned to get married and return to Germany after the war. But the German Communist Party in exile in the UK urged Fischer to accept recruitment into the OSS and he agreed to become one of the seven German exiles to serve as agents for these special missions into the Third Reich. So Fischer had to leave Bessinger and postpone any wedding plans. He promised to reunite with his future bride after he completed the mission into Leipzig, but he never returned.

New documents from the UK files show that Bessinger continued her search for Fischer after he disappeared following the dispatch of the BUZZ-SAW mission on April 7, 1945. She was able to return to Dresden after the war ended to visit with Werner Fischer's parents, who told her that they had not received any contact from their son and did not know what had happened to him. As late as August 1947, Marianne Bessinger made a visit to the US embassy in London. She met with Major James Kaylor, seeking any news of the US government's search for Werner Fischer, but was advised that nothing had materialized.[25] Bessinger later hired an English lawyer to take up her cause[26] but eventually gave up and moved to the United States sometime in 1950 and started a new life in Westchester County, a suburb of New York City. There, she worked to establish a ballet training school for young girls. And during the 1950s, she developed a passion for table tennis and became one of the top players on the women's circuit during the 1950s. Marianne Bessinger died at age 71 in 1993.[27]

What happened to Werner Fischer?

In 2006, this author intensified his efforts to find out what happened to Werner Fischer. Leads provided by various individuals in Berlin led to the discovery of an article bearing on the disappearance of Werner Fischer penned by a well-known German author named Hans Jacobus. This man also fled to England in the late 1930s to avoid Nazi persecution and returned to East Germany after the war. In 1995, Jacobus published an article concerning the fate of Werner Fischer in *Neus Deutschland*, a once-prominent newspaper published in East Germany before the end of the Cold War.[28]

In that article, Jacobus contends that after the war a former German communist exile in England named Heinz Schmidt returned to East Germany and uncovered the truth about the death of Werner Fischer. Schmidt had been a member of the leadership body that governed the German Communist Party in England during the war and had close ties to Werner Fischer. According to Jacobus, Heinz Schmidt revealed to him just days before his death in 1989 that Fischer had met his untimely death just moments after landing in Leipzig on April 7, 1945. Apparently, his parachute landing had been observed by a group of Red Army soldiers who had already advanced into southern Germany from the east. And after surrounding Fischer, who could only produce his papers identifying him as Gestapo special agent Ernst Lauterbach, the Red Army soldiers summarily executed him.[29] Below is a translation of an excerpt from that article published in *Neus Deutschland*, a newspaper published in the German Democratic Republic:

> Back in the early spring of 1945, he said, Fischer had landed behind Nazi lines – directly into a Russian patrol! As a German Young Communist, he enthusiastically greeted the Red Army men, but they were enraged: three others had already been arrested in US uniforms and had also claimed to be German communists, but then they had shot [the Red Army men's] sergeant. They didn't believe a word of what Werner

Fischer said, and there was no way out for him. For these soldiers, whose country the Nazis had attacked and whose families they had killed, could not trust him. And so Werner was shot by the liberators of his country, for whose liberation he too has given everything. . . . Heinz Schmidt had traced all these events, down to the report sheets of the unit in whose section all this had happened. In long and painstaking work, officers of the Soviet Army investigated this tragic end of a merry and brave anti-fascist, and then informed Schmidt (of Werner's fate).[30]

Previously unseen documents found in 2007 at the office of the Dresden Civil Registry lend credence to the claims made in the Jacobus article regarding Fischer's tragic death. According to Mr. Peter Neubert of the Dresden Civil Registry, the Dresden Municipal Court issued an order, dated March 20, 1952, granting his family permission to amend Werner Fischer's birth certificate declaring that Werner Fischer had died on *April 7, 1945*.[31]

According to the BUZZSAW mission file, this is the same day that Werner Fischer was parachuted into an area around Leipzig by the OSS to begin the mission. Subsequent correspondence in 2007 with a woman identified as the daughter of Werner Fischer's brother – Heinz Fischer – revealed conversations she had with her grandfather about visits made by a group of Soviet military officers to the family home in Dresden after the war ended.[32] This evidence leads to the conclusion that the information provided to the

Figure 4.1 BUZZSAW mission agent Werner Fischer, 1939

Figure 4.2 Heinz Schmidt, friend and mentor of Werner Fischer, London, 1944

family by the Soviet military during these meetings was later presented to the Dresden Municipal Court and found persuasive enough for that court to grant the petition filed by the Fischer family to amend the birth certificate. How else could this information regarding Werner Fischer's death have been obtained in 1952? The BUZZSAW mission file, which included the aforementioned flight reports that referenced this same date – April 7, 1945 – was still sealed by the CIA and there is no evidence that the Fischer family or the Soviet military somehow gained access to this classified file while the Cold War was raging.

Together, these documents provide circumstantial evidence that Werner Fischer was shot and killed by soldiers of the Red Army who mistook him for a Gestapo agent within hours of his landing somewhere near Leipzig. And since there is no evidence to indicate that Fischer's body was ever recovered and afforded a proper burial, it appears likely that Werner Fischer was left for dead or hastily buried by the Red Army soldiers who tragically took his life. The only possible way to uncover the truth of what happened to Werner Fischer is to review classified WWII/Red Army documents that remain under seal in the Kremlin. Otherwise, the fate of Werner Fischer remains a mystery. He is still missing after all these years.

Notes

1 Memo from Army Lt. Joseph Gould to George Pratt, Division of Intelligence Procurement, OSS London office, March 6, 1945, Agent Recruitment Profile of Werner Fischer, Army Lt. Joseph Gould, November 30, 1944, OSS Records, Record Group 226, NARA.

2 Herbert Hilse, The Communist Werner Fischer, *Sächsische Zeitung*, February 6, 1978.
3 See note 1.
4 Ibid.
5 National Archives, KV2/367/C608886.
6 British Immigration/Alien Registration Dept, internment file on Werner Fischer, October 1939–January 1942, HO 396/132, United Kingdom National Archives.
7 Werner Fischer, British Immigration/Alien Registration Dept; London Metropolitan Police files, United Kingdom National Archives, KV2/3671/C608886.
8 BUZZSAW mission training documents, January 23, 1945, BUZZSAW Mission File, OSS Records, RG226, NARA.
9 Cover story memorandum of Ernest Lauterbach, fictional cover story for BUZZSAW mission agent Werner Fischer, BUZZSAW Mission File, OSS Records, RG226, NARA.
10 POW Cage report submitted by BUZZSAW mission agent Werner Fischer, February 1945, OSS Records, RG226, NARA.
11 Ibid.
12 Ibid.
13 See note 8.
14 Intelligence Targets in the Leipzig Area, BUZZSAW Mission File, OSS London, March 7, 1945, OSS Records, RG 226, NARA.
15 Joseph Gould, *An OSS Officer's Own WWII Story: Of His Seven German Agents and Their Five Labor Desk Missions into Warring Germany*, unpublished manuscript (Washington, DC, 1989).
16 Memorandum from E.M. Burke to Army Lt. Joseph Gould, OSS London office, April 2, 1945, OSS Records, RG 226, NARA.
17 Air Transport Operation Report, BUZZSAW Mission File, April 7/8, 1945, OSS London, OSS Records, RG 226, NARA.
18 Memorandum, Army Lt. Joseph Gould to file, BUZZSAW mission chronology and comment, May 10, 1945, OSS London, OSS Records, RG 226, NARA.
19 Air Transport Operation Report, BUZZSAW Mission File, April 14/15; 16/17, 1945, cables and transcripts of radio transmissions in German seeking information regarding the whereabouts of Werner Fischer following dispatch of the mission, OSS London, OSS Records, RG 226, NARA.
20 Letter from Erich Henschke to GDR president Walter Ulbricht, October 13, 1949, East German STASI files, Berlin Archive.
21 Ibid.
22 Ibid.
23 See note 14, Joseph Gould memoir.
24 Hans Jacobus, *Unsere Zeit/Zeitung der DKP* (Our Time – The Newspaper of the DPK (German Communist Party)), December 24, 1999.
25 Memorandum to file, Major James S. Kaylor, United States Army, Administrative Officer, October 17, 1947.
26 Correspondence from D.N. Pritt, the English solicitor hired by Marianne Bessinger, to Ellen Buchholz and Marianne Bessinger regarding Werner Fischer. SAMPO Berlin, SgY/V239/5/20, BL 51–59.
27 Obituary of Marianne Bessinger, *Table Tennis Today*.
28 Hans Jacobus, Werner Fischer: The Tragedy of a Liberator of Our Country, *Neus Deutschland*, November 12, 1995.

29 Ibid.

30 Ibid.

31 Correspondence from Peter Neubert, registrar, Civil Registry Office, Dresden, Germany, to Jonathan Gould, September 27, 2006 (with amended birth certificate of Werner Fischer declaring him dead on April 7, 1945).

32 Affidavit of Senta Stender, dated December 6, 2006, attached to the BUZZSAW mission medal application.

5 Conflict of Loyalties

The MALLET mission and Adolph Buchholz

The HAMMER mission was one of two TOOL missions that targeted Berlin. The other mission – MALLET – was also manned by a Berlin native. That man was metal worker Adolph Buchholz. He was born in 1913 and grew up in the Spandau section of Berlin. Nicknamed "Appel" for his reddish, round face, from 1928 to 1932 Buchholz organized young metal workers while employed by Deutsche Industries in Berlin. After Hitler came to power, Buchholz had already joined the German Communist Party and openly opposed the regime. His political activity attracted the attention of Nazi storm troopers who arrested Buchholz in 1934 for "high treason" and declared his group to be illegal. The Nazis later sentenced Buchholz to two years of hard labor. That prison term was served at the notorious Luckau Penitentiary outside of Berlin where brutal beatings of prisoners were common. Buchholz was finally released in October 1936.[1]

His incarceration at Luckau did not deter him from resuming his anti-Nazi resistance activity. But the pressure from the Gestapo intensified, and Buchholz then fled to Czechoslovakia in November 1937 and resettled in Prague, where he assumed a leadership role in the formation of the Freie Deutsche Jugend ("FDJ"), or Free German Youth. This was an anti-fascist group that united other young German refugees who resisted Hitler but had to flee Germany. But now these young Germans found themselves alone and separated from their families while exiled in Czechoslovakia.[2]

By September 1938, the surrender of the Sudetenland to Hitler and the coming German occupation of Czechoslovakia made it too dangerous for Buchholz and his Free German Youth refugees to remain in Czechoslovakia any longer. So with the aid of the Czech Refugee Trust Fund, Buchholz immigrated to Great Britain in November 1938, along with many members of the FDJ. There he resumed leadership of the Free German Youth until 1942. Buchholz remained an active member of the German Communist Party in exile.[3]

The Free German Youth attracted many young people, mostly Jewish, whose parents arranged for their escape from Nazi Germany and other European countries under German occupation. This group transport of children came to be known as the *Kindertransport*. Between December 1938 and September 1939, approximately 10,000 unaccompanied refugee children arrived in England. Most would never see their parents again as the Holocaust swept through Europe. And many turned to the FDJ for help in adjusting to life in England. At one point, nearly 700 young adults of the *Kindertransport* joined the Free German Youth.[4]

After being interned on the Isle of Man in July 1940 by the British government following the fall of France, Buchholz was released after eight months and later obtained employment as an iron molder with Langley Alloys in London, where he remained until he was recruited into the OSS by Army Lt. Joseph Gould for the MALLET mission in November 1944.[5]

In a letter that Buchholz wrote in October 1946[6] and recently found in the Berlin archives, Buchholz asserted that his involvement with the OSS began when he was summoned sometime during the summer of 1944 to meet with three prominent members of the German Communist Party in exile in London. In attendance at that meeting was Erich Henschke (aka Karl Kastro), Hans Kahle and Kurt Hager, who had also approached Paul Lindner about accepting an invitation to join the OSS and train for the HAMMER mission. When asked if he would volunteer for this mission, Buchholz agreed as long as they could assure him that both the German Communist Party and the "Soviet comrades" approved. Shortly thereafter, Buchholz met with Lt. Joseph Gould at a local tavern and in Paul Lindner's apartment in the Hampstead section of London. He later admitted in this 1946 letter that when questioned by Lt. Gould, he told him that he was active in leading the Free German Youth in England but did not disclose his membership in the German Communist Party.

The dispatch of the MALLET mission

On April 10, 1945, the MALLET mission was dispatched from London to obtain intelligence on Berlin troop movements, the operational status of ball bearing factories, and the dreaded V-3 multi-chambered gun that was rumored to be in production at a secret location in Kremmen, a northern district of Berlin.[7]

Buchholz had prepared to be parachuted into the Wannsee district of Berlin armed with documents identifying him as Max Buchner, a Berlin-based Gestapo agent.[8] From there, Buchholz, like the HAMMER team, was instructed to seek aid either from family members still living in Berlin-Spandau or from underground resistance contacts.[9] The following is the account of the aborted mission that Buchholz gave the OSS after he was recovered in November 1945. However, new documents obtained from the German archive show that Buchholz did not level with the OSS and provided a false account of what actually happened.

Before he safely landed from his parachute jump, Buchholz said that he had decided to find his sister Gertrude Huth, a resident of the Spandau section of Berlin. But weather conditions, according to Buchholz, complicated the drop and Buchholz unexpectedly found himself in the Gransee section of Berlin, some 75 kilometers north of Berlin-Spandau. As a result, Buchholz said that he buried his communications gear and somehow made his way to his sister's home by foot. At the time, she had no idea where he was or even if he was still alive. More than six years had gone by since he left Berlin.[10]

The next day, Buchholz claims to have made contact with persons associated with the anti-Nazi underground. After those meetings, Buchholz and his sister bicycled back to Gransee and quietly retrieved the J/E transmitter and other supplies he had previously buried. By April 15, Buchholz moved into his sister's home and trained her to operate the J/E transmitter and on the code used to translate the BBC messages. But according to Buchholz, the ongoing advance of the Soviet Army and continued Allied bombing raids made it too difficult for him to contact the OSS. Shortly thereafter, Buchholz received a BBC message from a separate radio that instructed him to turn himself in to a Soviet Army officer and wait for US occupation troops to arrive. This, according to Buchholz, is why he was not able to transmit any military intelligence or achieve any of the mission's stated objectives.[11]

On May 1 – the day after Hitler committed suicide – Buchholz left his sister's home. But shortly thereafter, according to the account he gave to the OSS in November 1945, he got caught in a crossfire between German and Russian armies and retreated. He then decided, according to the debriefing transcript, to dig up the radio gear and codebooks that were buried near his sister's home so he could prove his real identity. After retrieving them, Buchholz then claimed to have disposed of the radio gear, including the J/E transmitter, and codebooks by throwing them over the side of a bridge into some sort of canal.[12]

As a result, Buchholz claimed that he was left only with his cover story documents that identified him as a Gestapo agent. So when a Russian soldier stopped him the next day, Buchholz asserted during the OSS debriefing that because he was unable to produce evidence showing his real identity, he was taken into custody for interrogation by the Soviet Army.[13] Following this questioning, Buchholz told the OSS debriefers that the Soviet Army moved him throughout a network of work camps occupied by captured German Army officers.

The Soviet military eventually contacted the OSS mission to Berlin to arrange for Buchholz's release.[14] According to Lt. Gould's memoir, Buchholz was the favorite of the OSS training staff – "jovial, full of fun and warmth." So after accepting reassignment with the Office of Military Government in Berlin following Germany's surrender in May 1945, Gould continued to wonder about Buchholz's fate, especially since no one had heard from him after the mission was dispatched on April 10, 1945. The following excerpt from Gould's memoir poignantly describes their emotional reunion, which allayed his concerns:

> In August 1945, six months after Buchholz had parachuted [into Berlin], while in a mess hall at lunchtime, I heard myself called to the lobby. One of two very young Russian lieutenants there handed me a slip of paper, asking if I would sign this as receipt of one *A. Buchholz*. I signed and they departed. The body they left standing, smiling broadly as the crowd milled about, was the wan, nearly ragged figure of Dolf. He had lost 70 pounds. It had taken those months for him to convince the coldly angry Russians that he was not Gestapo, that he was a German working for the Americans. I took him to the OSS Berlin house and fed him. Dolf had returned to us.[15]

However, between the aforementioned October 1946 letter apparently submitted to Soviet occupation authorities in Berlin and his Control Commission testimony in 1953, Buchholz offered a much different account as to what actually happened after he parachuted into Berlin to start the MALLET mission. This is what he told them.

Despite signing a special agent contract in late February 1945 with the OSS in which he swore to maintain the secrecy of the mission, Buchholz's testimony to the Control Commission suggests that he breached that provision of the contract. He failed to honor that contract when he admitted to holding regular meetings with Erich Henschke, aka Karl Kastro, after he completed the mission training. As previously noted, Henschke was appointed the TOOL missions liaison by the OSS upon the recommendation of Jurgen Kuczynski. This introduction was approved by the Soviet military intelligence service (GRU) in Moscow and initially conveyed to Kurt Hager, a/k/a Felix Albin, the head of the German Communist Party in exile, apparently through Ursula Kuczynski, who operated under the code name Sonya in her dealings with the GRU.

During those meetings with Henschke, Buchholz disclosed top secret mission information, including the technical aspects of the radio communications technology. He also received instructions from Henschke that when he landed in Berlin, he was to meet with a Soviet military officer on May 1 at a predetermined location in Berlin. Henschke also provided Buchholz with a special code or password that he was to use if the Russians mistook him for a Gestapo agent and imprisoned him.

This testimony, when analyzed together with the Control Commission testimony of HAMMER mission agent Paul Lindner and Erich Henschke, clearly shows that at least some of the German exiles – whether knowingly or not – were helping the GRU to gain access to the secrets of the TOOL missions and in doing so were breaching the secrecy provision of the agent employment contract they signed with the OSS.

This view is further bolstered by Buchholz's testimony given to the Control Commission about what happened after he landed by parachute to start the MALLET mission in Berlin. Before beginning his journey to rendezvous with his sister at her house in Spandau, Buchholz buried his codebooks and the gadgets. He kept the radio so he could receive the BBC messages in German from the OSS. He did not pause to deliver a message using the J/E transmitter as he agreed to do during his final meetings with Lt. Gould. Instead he remained with his sister until April 25, when Soviet troops knocked on the door of her home and asked to see Buchholz. They had obtained his sister's address – and the special password – from Erich Henschke in London.[16]

According to Buchholz's transcript, after the Red Army officer tracked down Buchholz at this sister's home, it was apparent that this officer was not aware of his exile in England, and Buchholz was arrested and eventually moved to a location in Landsberg, which is located in the Lower Saxony region of Germany. During that period when he remained in Soviet custody, he admitted to giving them the J/E transmitter – and all other papers except his identification booklet, which he had destroyed. He did not throw them into a river as he claimed during his OSS debriefing in November 1945. And he also testified that he showed them how the J/E worked and explained the technology behind it. Buchholz even wrote this out on paper and gave it to his Soviet captors.[17]

He then informed the Control Commission that the Soviets sometime later finally released Buchholz from their custody after another Red Army officer obtained Buchholz's sister's address – and the special password – from a contact in England and went to her home in Berlin. There he learned that Buchholz had been arrested. So when Buchholz later correctly stated the same special password also given to him in England by Erich Henschke to this same Red Army officer who questioned him, he was able to confirm his real identity and was released. He was then provided with an apartment in Berlin to live in and permitted to move about freely. But this was offered on the condition that he continued spying on the Americans after they released Buchholz back into the custody of the OSS in August 1945. This explains why Buchholz provided false information to the OSS during the mission debriefing. He also made up the story that the reason the Soviets arrested him was because the Soviets had grabbed his ID booklet and actually believed he was Max Buchner, special agent for the Gestapo.[18]

After the monthlong debriefing, the OSS finally released Buchholz in late November 1945. While he remained in Berlin, he continued working for the Russians until they released him in April 1946. Buchholz continued to work with the "friends" (meaning the GRU) and told them everything he could about the "English things."[19] This ongoing relationship with the Soviet military lasted until 1949, when he was released from any further commitment to continue spying on the Americans in post-war Berlin.

Figure 5.1 Adolph Buchholz, age 13 in 1928, Berlin, Germany

Figure 5.2 Adolph   Buchholz, East Germany, 1953

Figure 5.3 Hermann Matern, member of the Politburo of the Socialist Unity Party of East Germany which conducted interrogations of TOOL mission agents in 1953

Postscript

Adolph Buchholz lived out his life in the German Democratic Republic. After marrying the woman he met in England – Ellen Eva – he settled down and raised a family. He wisely decided to capitalize on his skill as a metal worker and carved out a successful career in the East German steel industry. Beginning in 1952, he rose to the position of senior manager of the Maxhutte metallurgical plant, which employed over 6,000 people. Later he assumed senior positions in the government ministry which oversaw the metallurgy industry in the German Democratic Republic. Adolph Buchholz died in 1978.[20]

Notes

1 Personal History statement, Adolf Buchholz, October 11, 1944; OSS Agent Recruitment profile prepared by Army Lt. Joseph Gould, October 18, 1944; memo from Thomas Wilson to William Casey, Chief, SI Branch OSS London, OSS Records Record Group 226, NARA.
2 *Freie Deutsche Jugend*, Berlin.

3 Free German Youth (www.fdj.de/history).

4 Ibid.

5 Ibid.

6 Special Report from Adolf Buchholz, October 14, 1946.

7 Memo from Army Lt. Joseph Gould, Mission Objectives, February 6, 1945, OSS London, OSS Records Group 226, NARA.

8 Memo from Lt. Gould to George Pratt, Chief of Division of Intelligence Procurement, February 13, 1945, OSS London, OSS Record Group 226, NARA; Detailed Cover Story – MAX BUCHNER, MALLET Mission File, OSS Record Group 226, NARA.

9 Ibid. (Gould memo to Pratt).

10 Operation MALLET Debriefing Interrogation, November 13, 1945, OSS London, OSS Record Group 226, NARA.

11 Ibid.

12 Ibid.

13 Ibid.

14 Cable from Moore and Horton to Van Arkel, OSS London, September 19, 1945, advising that Buchholz was located in the Soviet zone by the Soviet Military Mission in Paris, OSS Record Group 226, NARA.

15 Joseph Gould, *An O.S.S. Officer's Own WWII Story: Of His Seven German Agents and Their Five Labor Desk Missions into Warring Germany*, unpublished manuscript (Washington, DC, 1989).

16 Central Committee Control Commission interrogation transcript of Adolf Buchholz, April 1, 1953. BArch, SAPMO, DY 30/IV 2/4/123.

17 In his testimony before the Control Commission in April 1953, Erich Henschke, the GRU agent who was introduced to Army Lt. Joseph Gould during the recruitment of the German exiles and later served as the exile community liaison to the OSS, asserted that his Soviet handlers told him after the war that they "had the device" (meaning the J/E transmitter receiver) and to his knowledge it had already been deployed in Poland, suggesting that the Soviets had somehow developed their own version through some sort of reverse engineering of the J/E transmitter.

18 See note 16.

19 Ibid.

20 Affidavit of Sylvia Anders, daughter of the late Adolf Buchholz, August 2002; Adolf Buchholz biographical note, *Who's Who in the GDR*.

Epilogue

Most historians who have studied the German Penetration Campaign generally agree that the intelligence obtained by them was limited. No secret weapons were uncovered, no Alpine fortress was discovered, nor were the agents successful in locating the whereabouts of the Fuhrer. Nevertheless, the intelligence unearthed and sent to Allied military commanders was considered to be useful. Reports on troop locations, war munitions production, the morale of the German home front and other relatively minute details are now viewed as having added to the targets that the Allies later bombed and better prepared the Allied military forces for German counteroffensives. The general consensus is that the missions carried out by the agents of the German Penetration Campaign did shorten the war's duration and reduced casualties. Moreover, historians now concur that the OSS's ability to penetrate the German heartland at all was a major breakthrough in the history of wartime intelligence gathering.[1]

Of the approximately 100 German penetration missions that originated from the OSS London office, the completed TOOL missions manned by the German exiles clearly contributed to the Allied war effort. According to one historian:

> SI/London's German operations thus provided the military with precisely the kind of information it wanted at a time when the exploitation of ULTRA[2] material declined given the German Army's increased use of land-line communications as it retreated in the Reich. Since reduced radio usage ensured that German troop movements and locations were betrayed less often, the utility of the agency reports relative to ULTRA grew accordingly. The military's repeated demands for agents on shallow missions to report tactical intelligence and their support of missions to the Elbe and the supposed Redoubt area, both indicate their need for intelligence on the state of German installations, defenses and troop movements as they drove deeper into the Reich. A post-war

assessment by G-2 12 AG specifically noted that OSS agents helped provide the balance of information regarding routes of enemy withdrawal. The high quality intelligence of OSS agents gave American G-2s timely insights into enemy defenses and the dubious prospects for a last stand bastion in the Alps.[3]

In its final report to the Joint Chiefs of Staff, Colonel G. Edward Buxton, the assistant director of the OSS and later as its action director of Strategic Services, praised the many agents of the German Penetration Campaign, including the men of the TOOL missions. In a memorandum to the US Joint Chiefs of Staff, he reported that:

> During the eight months preceding the unconditional surrender more than 100 OSS intelligence missions penetrated into Germany to obtain information on the enemy's situation and movements, on hidden factories and storage dumps, on the effectiveness of Allied bombings, on the treatment of Allied prisoners-of-war, and on the strength of Nazi control over the civilian population. Information from these missions reached Allied military headquarters promptly and in a steady stream throughout the rapid advances in March and April and into the last weeks of crumbling Nazi resistance.[4]

In contrast to the decision by the US military to acknowledge the service of the German exiles and recommend that they be awarded military decorations, there is no trace of any public recognition of these men by the East German government or any reference to these missions in its official historiography. For example, Anton Ruh's official file published by the East German Communist Party makes no mention of his work for the OSS or his service in carrying out the HAMMER mission.

Instead, some of the surviving agents of the TOOL missions, upon their eventual return to the Soviet zone in East Germany, were immediately suspected of disloyalty by their government. This was based on the unjustified fear that because of their work with the OSS, they had been turned by the British to spy on the newly formed German Democratic Republic. As a result, in 1953 they were forced to appear before the Control Commission of the East German Communist Party and answer questions about their work with US intelligence. In fact, surviving descendants of the TOOL mission agents now contend that their fathers had to make sure that their loyalty was not questioned or face possible exile or incarceration. They argue that the answers they gave to their Control Commission interrogators were not entirely accurate because of their fear of retribution should they candidly discuss their views about their work with the OSS and the men who trained them for their missions. None of the men questioned by the Control Commission were exiled or ever punished by their government for their service to the OSS. Those TOOL mission agents who survived their missions lived out their lives in the German Democratic Republic.

Notes

1 Nelson Macpherson, *American Intelligence in Wartime London: The Story of the OSS* (London: Routledge, 2004), p. 160; Joseph Persico, *Piercing the Reich: The Penetration of Nazi Germany by American Secret Agents During WWII* (New York: Viking Press, 1979), p. 334.
2 "Ultra was the designation adopted by British military intelligence in June 1941 for wartime signals intelligence obtained by breaking high-level encrypted enemy radio and teleprinter communications at the Government Code and Cypher School at Bletchley Park. Ultra eventually became the standard designation among the western Allies for all such intelligence." Wikipedia.
3 Nelson Macpherson, *Kings and Desperate Men: The United States Office of Strategic Services in London and the Anglo-American Relationship* by Brian Nelson Macpherson (unpublished doctoral thesis, University of Toronto, 1995) (citing G-2's Study of Operations for the period August 1 to May 9, 1945), p. 52.
4 Edward Buxton G., Memorandum of Information for the Joint U.S. Chiefs of Staff: OSS Penetration of Germany (see copy of memorandum attached to Appendix K).

Bibliography

General works

Bungert, Heike. The OSS and Its Cooperation with the Free Germany Committees, 1944–45, *Intelligence and National Security*, Volume 12, July 1997

Casey, William. *The Secret War Against Hitler*. Washington, DC: Regnery Gateway, 1988

Eisenberg, Carolyn Woods. *Drawing the Line*. Cambridge: Cambridge University Press, 1996

Epstein, Catharine. *The Last Revolutionaries: German Communists and Their Century*. Cambridge, MA: Harvard University Press, 2003

Gould, Joseph. *An OSS Officer's Own WWII Story: Of His Seven German Agents and Their Five Labor Desk Missions into Warring Germany*, unpublished manuscript, Washington, DC, 1989

Kershaw, Ian. *Hitler: Nemesis 1936–45*. New York: W.W. Norton and Company, 2000

Lewis, Flora. *Red Pawn: The Story of Noel Field*. Garden City, NY: Doubleday, 1965

Macpherson, Brian Nelson. *Kings and Desperate Men: The United States Office of Strategic Services in London and the Anglo-American Relationship*, unpublished doctoral thesis, University of Toronto, 1995

Mauch, Christof. *The Shadow War against Hitler*, trans. Jeremiah Riemer. New York: Columbia University Press, 2003

Mcateer, Sean. *500 Days: The War in Eastern Europe*, Kindle edition, Red Lead Press, 2009

Persico, Joseph. *Piercing the Reich: The Penetration of Nazi Germany by American Secret Agents During WWII*. New York: Viking Press, 1979

Persico, Joseph. *Roosevelt's Secret War: FDR and World War II Espionage*. New York: Random House, 2001

Petrova, Ada. *The Death of Hitler: The Full Story with New Evidence from Secret Russian Archives*. New York: St. Martin's Press, 1995

Pincher, Chapman. *Treachery: Betrayals, Blunders and Cover-Ups: Six Decades of Espionage Against America and Great Britain*. New York: Random House, 2009

Smith, R. Harris. *OSS: The Secret History of America's First Central Intelligence Agency*. Berkeley: University of California Press, 1971

Werner, Ruth. *Sonja's Rapport*. Berlin: Verlag Neus Leben, 1977

Historical background

Primary source documents

George O. Pratt to David K. Bruce. OSS Memorandum, Plans for Proposed Operations on the Continent – Labor Desk, March 23, 1944 (Box 48, RG 226, NARA)

Memorandum from Paul Hagen to Allen Dulles. How to Prepare Collaboration with the Anti-Nazi Underground Movement, April 10, 1942 (Box 12, Entry 106, RG 226, NARA)

Memorandum from Colonel James Forgan. OSS Detachment, ETOUSA to Supreme Commander, SHAEF, August 16, 1944, Washington, DC, National Archives Records Administration (hereafter NARA), Record Group 226, Records of the Office of Strategic Services, Declassification No. NND843115

Office of Strategic Services. *Division of Intelligence Procurement Air Operations Final Report*, Appendix, June 1, 1945 (Box 49, Entry 110, RG 226, NARA)

U.S. War Department. *War Report*, Walker Publishing Company, 1976, 184

William Casey, interview by Joseph Persico, August 1976, Folder Casey (Box 1, Joseph Persico Papers, Hoover Institute, Stanford, CA), 9–10

Secondary sources

Brooklyn Daily Eagle, December 17, 1941

Publicist Guild Wins, *New York Times*, July 18, 1941

Screen Publicists Win Pay Increases, *New York Times*, May 6, 1942

SPG News, Screen Publicists Guild of New York, February 1942

Chapter 1: The HAMMER mission and the GRU

Primary sources

Affidavit of Denis Ruh, dated August 11, 2002

Application for internment release from Paul Lindner to Under Secretary of State of UK Aliens Department, August 5, 1941 (NARA, RG 226, E115, B43, F563, E148, B101, F1740–F1742)

Biographical profile of Paul Lindner prepared by Army Lt. Joseph Gould, HAMMER Mission File, October 1944, OSS Record Group 226, NARA

Central Committee Control Commission interrogation transcript of Kurt Hager, March 1953. BArch, SAPMO, DY 30/IV 2/4/123

Central Committee Control Commission interrogation transcript of Anton Ruh, March 30, 1953. BArch, SAPMO, DY 30/IV 2/4/123, 343–344

Control Commission transcript of interrogation of Ursula Beurton by Herman Matern, September 1953, SAPMO-BArch DY 30/IV 2/4/123

Control Commission transcript of interrogation of Erich Henschke by Herman Matern, 30 March 1953, SAPMO-BArch DY 30/IV 2/4/123, BL 155–173

Control Commission transcript of interrogation of Paul Lindner by Herman Matern, 1 April 1953, in *Stiftung Archiv der Parteien und Massenorganizationen der DDR im Bundesarchiv Berlin* (hereinafter referred to as SAPMO-BArch) DY 30/IV 2/4/123, Bl. 272–282

Correspondence between Jonathan Gould and Senator Hillary Clinton of New York, July 11, 2003

Correspondence between Senator Hillary Clinton of New York and Benjamin Lane, U 32S Total Army Personnel Command

Debriefing of HAMMER mission agents regarding events on the ground in Germany after they surrendered themselves to Red Army troops from April 25, 1945 to June 16, 1945

Erich Henschke, aka Karl Kastro, Metropolitan Police file, United Kingdom National Archives, KV2/3908/1321715

HAMMER Mission, Labor Division, OSS War Diary, Volume 6, 421–456, OSS Record Group 226

HAMMER Mission Dispatch Report, Army Lt. Joseph Gould, March 3, 1945, RG 226, NARA

HAMMER Mission File, Record Group (hereafter RG) 226, Records of the Office of Strategic Services, NARA

Letter from Congressman Charles Rangel to Army Lieutenant Bennett, Military Awards Branch, June 11, 2007

Letter from Lt. Colonel Deborah W. Ivory, Chief, Military Awards Branch, October 19, 2001 (disclosing results of their review of WWII records "maintained by this office and [which] found no awards to German nationals")

Letter from Major James H. Kaylor to Captain W. Blake-Budden, May 20, 1946, regarding medal recommendations submitted on behalf of Paul Lindner, Anton Ruh, Walter Strüwe and Emil Konhäuser for their service on OSS missions into Germany

Memorandum from Lt. Joseph Gould, HAMMER Mission File, December 5, 1944, OSS Record Group 226, NARA

Memorandum from Thomas Wilson to Lillian Traugott of the SI Labor Division, December 22, 1944 (HAMMER Mission File), RG 226, NARA

Memorandum to file, Joseph Gould, May 18, 1945, OSS Records, Record Group (RG) 226, NARA

Memorandum submitted to Paul Lindner and Anton Ruh from Colonel John Bross, Office of Strategic Services, Mission to Great Britain on September 30, 1945

POW cage reports submitted by TOOL mission agents Paul Lindner (NARA, RG 226, E148, B101, F1740–F1742); Adolph Buchholz (NARA RG 226, E210, B47, F915); and Walter Strüwe (NARA, RG 226, E210, B298, F12123)

Recommendation for the award of the Bronze Star to Joseph Gould, J.R. Forgan, OSS Theater Commander, London, June 20, 1945

Regional Advisory Committee, United Kingdom Immigration Division, UK National Archives, HO 396/126, HO 396/132 and HO 396/151

Report on interview with Ursula Kuczynski by East German secret police in 1958, STASI Archive, Berlin, Germany

Transcript of HAMMER team interrogation of Paul Lindner and Anton Ruh, conducted by Comdr. Graveson and Lt. Sutton, June 27, 1945, OSS Record Group 226, NARA

Transcript of Interrogation of HAMMER mission agents, June 27, 1945, RG 226, NARA

Transcript of J/E radio transmission, March 28, 1945, HAMMER Mission File, OSS Record Group 226, NARA

United States Government Overseas Agent Employment Contracts, individually signed by Paul Lindner and Anton Ruh on February 23, 1945

Secondary sources

Al Gross, *Encyclopedia.com*, 2004

Archives July 2, 2015 | Roger Kershaw (http://blog.nationalarchives.gov.uk/blog/collar-lot-britains-policy-internment-second-world-war)

Battle of the Bulge, United States Holocaust Museum website Anton Ruh biographical note, *Who's Who in the GDR*

Charles V.P. von Luttichau. The German Counteroffensive in the Ardennes, *United States Army in World War II*, Ch. 20 (cited at http://trailblazersww2.org/ardennes.htm)

German Passed WWII Secrets Through Sister's Spy Ring, *Times of London*, January 28, 1980

Jurgen Kuczynski and the Search for a Western Spy Ring in the East German Communist Party in 1953, Professor Matthew Stibbe, Professor of Modern European History, Sheffield Hallam University, *Contemporary European History*, 2011

Obituary of William J. Casey by Eric Pace, *New York Times*, May 7, 1987

Obituary of William J. Donovan, Arlington National Cemetery website

Obituary of Al Gross, *Los Angeles Times*, January 14, 2001

Obituary of Jurgen Kuczynski by David Childs, *Independent*, August 12, 1997

Obituary of Ruth Werner, *Guardian*, July 11, 2000

OSS Society Journal, Summer/Fall 2010, 14

Secret: Operation Hammer, Lars Broder Keil, *Berlin Morning Post*, May 21, 2006

Ibid. *Collar the Lot! Britain's Policy of Internment during the Second World War*, United Kingdom National Archives

Red Sonya: The Spy Who Lived in Kidlington, *Oxford Mail*, August 6, 2010

A Skeleton in the Closeted World of Espionage, *History Today*, September 2004, Volume 54, Issue 9

Chapter 2: Mission into Landshut: The triumph of the PICKAXE mission

Primary sources

Biographical profile of Walter Strüwe drafted by Army Lt. Joseph Gould, OSS Labor Division, November 1944

Cover Detail memorandum drafted by M.B. Wolf to BACH Unit, January 13, 1945, OSS Records, RG 226, US National Archives NARA

OSS Mission training records, PICKAXE mission, NND #974395, NARA, November 1944

Personal History Statement, dated October 27, 1944, drafted and signed by Walter Strüwe, OSS Records, RG 226, US National Archives NARA

PICKAXE mission report, prepared by Emil Konhäuser and Walter Strüwe, May 14, 1945, 9, RG 226, OSS Records, US National Archives NARA

POW Cage Report, Emil Konhäuser, OSS Records, RG 226, US National Archives NARA NND #974395

POW Cage Report, Walter Strüwe, RG 226, OSS Records, US National Archives NARA NND #974395

Text of mission debriefing of PICKAXE mission agents conducted by E. Brooks, June 27, 1945, OSS Records, US National Archives NARA; PICKAXE Agent Release of WALTER STRÜWE and EMIL KONHÄUSER, signed by Leonard Appel, OSS London, July 13, 1945, OSS Records, US National Archives NARA

Transcripts of radio transmissions sent by Emil Konhäuser and Walter Strüwe while carrying out the PICKAXE mission, RG 226, OSS Records, US National Archives NARA NND #974395

United Kingdom Immigration Office, Regional Advisory Committee report: Emil Konhäuser, HO 396/48, United Kingdom National Archives

Chapter 3: Gone Too Soon: The courageous life and tragic death of Kurt Gruber

Primary sources

Affidavit of Benedict Ruhmoller, mayor of Ahlen, North Rhine, Germany, January 10, 2007, paragraph 8 (review of Ahlen archives reveals article about battle for union control of Ahlen coal mines and death of Kurt Gruber's brother Karl Gruber during street altercation with Nazi storm troopers in March 1931)

Agent recruitment profile of Kurt Gruber, from Army Lt. Joseph Gould to Thomas Wilson, December 8, 1944

British Immigration Office, Kurt Gruber file, UK National Archive

CHISEL Mission Dispatch Report submitted by Army Lt. Joseph Gould and Army Lt. Carl Devoe, March 20, 1945, RG 226, OSS Records, NARA

CHISEL Mission Training Documents and Overseas Agent Employment Contract dated February 12, 1945

Kurt Gruber, *I am a German Miner: A German Miner in Britain Looks at Fascism.* Glasgow: National Union of Scottish Mineworkers, 1944

Letter from Kurt Julius Goldstein to Jonathan Gould, International Auschwitz Committee, September 27, 2006

Memo from Major Gordon Stewart to Army Lt. Joseph Gould, March 15, 1945, CHISEL Mission File, RG 226, OSS

Memo from Joseph Gould to George Pratt, Division of Intelligence Procurement, February 12, 1945, OSS Labor Division, OSS Records, NARA

Memo from War Department general staff regarding award of military decorations to enemy nationals, February 28, 1946–March 18, 1946

Memo from Wilson to Joseph Gould, OSS London Office, March 15, 1945, profile of mission cover identity named Pawel Novak

Memo to File from Army Lt. Joseph Gould, May 10, 1945, Memo from Lillian Traugott, OSS Labor Division to Anthony Giuduci, August 27, 1945, CHISEL Mission File, Record of Payment of Compensation pursuant to Overseas Agent Employment Contract, August 23, 1945, RG 226, OSS Records, NARA

Memorandum from Reich Attorney General to Hamm Attorney General Regarding Issuance of an Arrest Warrant for Kurt Gruber for High Treason, May–October 1934

Missing Aircraft Report, issued by Office of European Theater Operations, May 3, 1945, 492 Bomb Operations. CHISEL Mission File, War Department Missing Aircraft Report, March 26, 1945, RG 226, OSS Records, NARA

Recommendation for the award of the Bronze Star to Kurt Gruber written by J.R. Forgan, OSS Theater Commander, June 20, 1945

Responses to OSS agent recruitment questionnaire handwritten by Kurt Gruber, December 6, 1944

Schools and Training Branch Progress Sheet, January–February 1945, RG 226, OSS Records, NND, 974345, NARA

Secondary sources

Associated Press, *Kurt Goldstein, Auschwitz Survivor*, October 1, 2007

Bevin Boys, Albert Gee, KURG Research Report No. 7 (www.shropshiremines.org.uk/bmd/bevin)

Gertrude Premke. *The Suicide Mission of Schwege: Reminiscence of an American Intelligence Aircraft That Crashed into Swampy Ground in March 1945*, published in local German newspaper *Wittlager Kreisblatt*, February 13, 2015

Memorial Day: Family Seeks Clues of B-17 Crash in 1946, *Peninsula Daily News*, May 30, 2011 (www.b17montblanc.org/lincidente.html)

Red Stocking Tragedy – Memorandum by Lt Comdr Stephen Simpson co-inventor of the "Joan-Eleanor" system concerning the loss of the A-26C on the first Red Stocking mission, *Flypast*, November 1999 (http://napoleon130.tripod.com/id312.html)

Scotsman, March 2, 1943

Wikipedia, *Kurt Julius Goldstein*

www.indiegogo.com/projects/b17-mont-blanc-missing-aircraft-in-the-glacier#/

Chapter 4: Still Missing: The story of Werner Fischer and the ill-fated BUZZSAW mission

Primary sources

Affidavit of Senta Stender, dated December 6, 2006, attached to the BUZZSAW mission medal application

Agent Recruitment Profile of Werner Fischer, Army Lt. Joseph Gould, November 30, 1944, OSS Records, Record Group 226, NARA

Air Transport Operation Report, BUZZSAW Mission File, April 7/8, 1945, OSS London, OSS Records, RG 226, NARA

Air Transport Operation Report, BUZZSAW Mission File, April 14/15, 16/17, 1945, cables and transcripts of radio transmissions in German seeking information regarding the whereabouts of Werner Fischer following dispatch of the mission, OSS London, OSS Records, RG 226, NARA

British Immigration/Alien Registration Dept., Internment file on Werner Fischer, October 1939–January 1942, HO 396/132, United Kingdom National Archives

BUZZSAW mission training documents, January 23, 1945, BUZZSAW Mission File, OSS Records, RG226, NARA

Correspondence from Peter Neubert, Registrar, Civil Registry Office, Dresden, Germany, to Jonathan Gould, September 27, 2006 (with amended birth certificate of Werner Fischer declaring him dead on April 7, 1945)

Correspondence from D.N. Pritt, the English solicitor hired by Marianne Bessinger, to Ellen Buchholz and Marianne Bessinger regarding Werner Fischer. SAMPO Berlin, SgY/V239/5/20, BL 51–59

Cover story memorandum of Ernest Lauterbach, fictional cover story for BUZZSAW mission agent Werner Fischer, BUZZSAW Mission File, OSS Records, RG226, NARA

Hans Jacobus, *Unsere Zeit/Zeitung der DKP* (Our Time – The Newspaper of the DPK (German Communist Party)), December 24, 1999

Intelligence Targets in the Leipzig Area, BUZZSAW Mission File, OSS London, March 7, 1945, OSS Records, RG 226, NARA

Letter from Erich Henschke to GDR president Walter Ulbricht, October 13, 1949, East German STASI files, Berlin Archive

Memo from Army Lt. Joseph Gould to George Pratt, Division of Intelligence Procurement, OSS London office, March 6, 1945

Memorandum, Army Lt. Joseph Gould to file, BUZZSAW Mission Chrono and Comment, May 10, 1945, OSS London, OSS Records, RG 226, NARA

Memorandum from E.M. Burke to Army Lt. Joseph Gould, OSS London Office, April 2, 1945, OSS Records, RG 226, NARA

Memorandum to file, Major James S. Kaylor, United States Army, Administrative Officer, October 17, 1947

POW Cage report submitted by BUZZSAW mission agent Werner Fischer, February 1945, OSS Records, RG226, NARA

Werner Fischer, British Immigration/Alien Registration Dept; London Metropolitan Police files, United Kingdom National Archives, KV2/367/C608886

Secondary sources

Hans Jacobus. Werner Fischer: The Tragedy of a Liberator of Our Country, *Neus Deutschland*, November 12, 1995.

Herbert Hilse. The Communist Werner Fischer, *Sächsische Zeitung*, February 6, 1978

Chapter 5: Conflict of loyalties: The MALLET mission and Adolph Buchholz

Primary sources

Adolf Buchholz biographical note, *Who's Who in the GDR*

Affidavit of Sylvia Anders, daughter of the late Adolf Buchholz, August 2002

CABLE from Thomas Moore to Van Arkel, OSS LONDON, September 19, 1945 advising that Buchholz was located in the Soviet zone by the Soviet Military Mission in Paris, OSS Record Group 226, NARA

Central Committee Control Commission interrogation transcript of Adolf Buchholz, April 1, 1953. BArch, SAPMO, DY 30/IV 2/4/123

Memo from Army Lt. Joseph Gould, Mission Objectives, Feb. 6, 1945, OSS London, OSS Records Group 226, NARA

Memo from Lt. Gould to George Pratt, Chief of Division of Intelligence Procurement, February 13, 1945, OSS London, OSS Record Group 226, NARA; Detailed Cover Story – MAX BUCHNER, MALLET Mission file, OSS Record Group 226, NARA

Memo from Thomas Wilson to William Casey, Chief, SI Branch OSS London, OSS Records Record Group 226, NARA

Operation MALLET Debriefing Interrogation, November 13, 1945, OSS London, OSS Record Group 226, NARA

Personal History statement, Adolf Buchholz, October 11, 1944, OSS Agent Recruitment profile prepared by Army Lt. Joseph Gould, October 18, 1944

Special Report from Adolf Buchholz to Soviet Zone occupation authorities, October 14, 1946

Secondary sources

Free German Youth (www.fdj.de/history)

Epilogue

Buxton, G. Edward. Memorandum of Information for the Joint U.S. Chiefs of Staff: OSS Penetration of Germany (see copy of memorandum attached to Appendix K).

Macpherson, Nelson. *American Intelligence in Wartime London: The Story of the OSS*. Routledge 2004, 160; Persico, Joseph. *Piercing the Reich: The Penetration of Nazi Germany by American Secret Agents During WWII*. New York: Viking Press, 1979, 334

Macpherson, Nelson. *Kings and Desperate Men: The United States Office of Strategic Services in London and the Anglo-American Relationship* by Brian Nelson Macpherson, unpublished doctoral thesis, University of Toronto, 1995 (citing G-2's Study of Operations for the period August 1 to May 9, 1945), 52

Appendices

APPENDIX A: Memorandum from Arthur Goldberg to General William J. Donovan, 1943   113
              Re: Labor Section of the OSS

APPENDIX B: Letter from Paul Lindner to UK Undersecretary of State, August 5, 1941   129
              Re: Request for release from internment

APPENDIX C: *Silver Star* certificates awarded to Paul Lindner and Anton Ruh, May 2006   132
              Re: HAMMER Mission

APPENDIX D: Recommendation for Award of *Bronze Star* to Joseph Gould, June 1945   137

APPENDIX E: P.O.W. Cage report from Paul Lindner, November 1944   142

APPENDIX F: German and English translation of *Der Spiegel* article titled FALSE FRIENDS November 1, 2004   154

APPENDIX G: Recommendation for award of the *SILVER STAR* to PICKAXE mission Agents Waiter Struwe and Emil Konhauser, June 19, 1945   161

APPENDIX H: Memorandum from Lt. Commander Stephen Simpson   168
              Re: Dispatch of the CHISEL Mission aircraft, March 20, 1945
              CHISEL Mission Dispatch Report from OSS mission conducting officer Lt. Joseph Gould, March 20, 1945

APPENDIX I: Letter from Kurt Goldstein to Jonathan Gould, September 21, 2006   174
              Re: Kurt Gruber (German and English translation)

APPENDIX J: Recommendation for the award of the *Bronze Star* to Kurt Gruber, June 1945 — 177

APPENDIX K: Undated memorandum from OSS Assistant Director G. Edward Buxton To Joint U.S. Chiefs of Staff — 180
Re: OSS Penetration of Germany

APPENDIX L: HAMMER Mission dispatch report from OSS mission conducting officer Army Lt. Joseph Gould, March 12, 1945 — 184

APPENDIX A

Memorandum from Arthur Goldberg to
General William J. Donovan, 1943

Re: Labor Section of the OSS

OFFICE OF STRATEGIC SERVICES
WASHINGTON, D.C.

May 10, 1943

To: General William J. Donovan

From: Arthur J. Goldberg   α.γ.ђ

Subject: The Labor Section of the Office of
          Strategic Services

Attached you will find the memorandum you asked me to prepare the other day. I trust that it will suit your purpose.

Attachment

Declassified by <u>009785</u>   APPROVED FOR RELEASE
Date *[illegible] 1977*   Date *[illegible] 1973*

THE LABOR SECTION OF THE OFFICE OF STRATEGIC SERVICES

Acting upon the assumption that this is a people's war and that a people's war requires a people's intelligence service, the Office of Strategic Services very early in its work established a section to maintain close contact with the underground labor movements of the Axis and occupied countries. These underground labor movements are important allies in the common struggle against the Axis powers. In every Axis and occupied country they constitute the bulwark of the movements or resistance. Although their organizations have been formally dissolved they, nevertheless, wage an unremitting struggle underground. They constitute a continuous and valuable source of strategic, military, naval and political intelligence. They also carry on continuous warfare behind the enemy lines in the form of sabotage and by guerrilla methods.

In recognition of this the Office of Strategic Services established a Labor Section for the purpose of cooperating with the underground labor movements of enemy and occupied countries in obtaining intelligence and in encouraging sabotage and resistance. In its work the Labor Section operates in close cooperation with the Joint A.F. of L - C.I.O. Relief Committee, headed by Mathew Holl and Sidney Willmen, and with the relief committee established by the Railway Labor Executives Association, representing the twenty-one standard railway organizations of the United States and headed by J.A. Phillips. Through these labor channels we have obtained and continuously are receiving a flow of vital and important information about the activities of the enemy. The underlying principle behind the operation is that throughout the occupied countries and in the enemy countries as well, there are countless thousands of devoted anti-Fascists who are willing to and do risk their lives to cooperate in communicating information and in sabotage activities so as to hasten the overthrow of the Axis powers.

The work of the Labor Section encompasses many projects by which intelligence from labor channels is obtained collected, analyzed and reported to the Joint Chiefs of Staff and to the other military and naval services. Illustrative of these projects is one which emphasizes a wide-spread plan for the utilization of the underground network of the International Transport Workers' Federation, the International Federation of Trade Union and other democratic trade union organizations which have underground organizations operating in occupied and enemy countries.

The International Transport Workers' Federation, which for brevity is often called the ITF, is the largest international union in the world and has among its affiliated members transport workers in five of the word's continents. The unions affiliated with the ITF are democratic trade unions of railwaymen, seamen, longshoremen, tramway and truck drivers and other transport workers throughout the world. Every worker who has anything to do with the movement of passengers or goods is eligible for membership in the ITF. The ITF has a eighty affiliated unions and is represented practically in every country on the globe. Prior to the advent of the Hitler regime in Germany and the occupation by the Nazis of countries in Europe, transport workers of the following countries were affiliated with the ITF:

Algeria	Dutch East Indies	Indo-China	Poland
Argentina	Dutch Guiana	Ireland	Portugal
Australia	Ecuador	Italy	Rhodesia
Austria	Egypt	Japan	Rumania
Belgium	Estonia	Kenya	Spain
Bolivia	Finland	Latvia	South Africa
Brazil	France	Luxemburg	Sweden
Bulgaria	Germany	Madascar	Switzerland
Canada	Great Britain	Mexico	Trinidad
Chile	Greece	Morocco	Tunisia
China	Holland	New Zealand	United States
Cuba	Hungary	Nicaragua	Venezuela
Czechoslovakia	Iceland	Norway	Yugoslavia
Denmark	India	Palestine	

The greatest strength of the ITF was in Europe. In Belgium the ITF had organized the general transport workers, railway, maritime, air, telephone, telegraph and other services, tramways and motor bus personnel. In Denmark the ITF was represented by the general transport workers, locomotive and railwaymen, seamen end maritime personnel. In Estonia the general transport workers, railway workers and, related transport trades were all members of the ITF. In Finland the ITF represented and still represents the general transport workers, railwaymen and seamen. In France the ITF had affiliated with it railwaymen, transport workers, dockers, longshoremen, river men, fishermen, seamen, and other maritime personnel. In Great Britain there were and now are affiliated with the ITF the railwaymen, locomotive engineers, firemen, clerks general transport workers, dockers, distributive and allied workers, bargemen, seamen and all maritime personnel. The ITF represented all general transport workers and municipal transport workers in Hungary. In Iceland they represented the sailors and fishermen; in Ireland the railwayman and general transport workers; in Luxemburg the railwaymen; in the Netherlands the general transport workers of all trades, the railwaymen and the seamen; in Norway the general transport workers, railwaymen, seamen and other transport trades; in Poland the railwaymen, general transport trades and the seamen; in Rumania the dockers and the general transport workers; in Sweden the general transport trades, the locomotive and railway personnel, seamen and all maritime personnel; in Switzerland the railwaymen and all general transport trades; in Yugoslavia the general transport trades, dockers, maritime workers, river men, fishermen, seamen and all mercantile marine personnel; in Greece all seamen and maritime personnel; in Austria the railwaymen and general transport workers; in Czechoslovakia the railwaymen and general transport Workers; in Germany the railwaymen, inland waterway men, dockers, seamen and all related trades; in Spain the railwaymen and general transport workers, including truck drivers.

The ITF also represents transport workers and railwaymen and seamen in the Argentine, Canada, China, Ecuador, India, the Netherlands East Indies, New Zealand, Australia, Palestine, Rhodesia and Trinidad.

When Hitler came to power, the transport workers' unions in Germany and the various countries occupied by Germany were among the first to be officially dissolved. In spite of this official destruction, however, the organizations, though driven underground, kept in regular communication with ITF headquarters, and the ITF underground communication system between its affiliates and its members has been rather effectively maintained.

Until 1939 the headquarters of the ITF were in Amsterdam. In that year they were moved to London where they are at present.

The attitude of the ITF toward the present war is one of militant support. This attitude remained unchanged during the period of the German-Soviet pact. The ITF has at all times resisted communist penetration, and does not follow the communist line.

In France, Holland, Belgium, Luxemburg, Germany, Italy, Norway, Denmark, Sweden, Switzerland, Portugal and Spain, functionaries and agents of the ITF are carrying on underground activities. Unlike the usual agents employed for sabotage or subversion, the members of the ITF do not have to be paid for their work. They are devoted to the task of interfering in every way with the successful exploitation of their countries by the Nazis. Furthermore, because of the strength of the ITF in the railway and maritime fields among the skilled employees of these industries, the members of the ITF have natural cover for their activities.

We are in cooperation with the ITF and are utilizing their facilities for penetrating the occupied and enemy countries of Europe. For example, Swedish seamen as part of their job regularly travel to the occupied countries of Europe and even to Germany itself. Swedish railwaymen have direct contact with the Norwegian underground and Swiss railwaymen with the German underground. Many of these workers are ITF people and are devoted to the principles of the ITF. We, in collaboration with the ITF are obtaining intelligence from these sources which should be most helpful in shortening this war.

Among the transport workers perhaps the most important are railway workers. With natural cover, going as a part of their job from place to place, they can, if cooperative and organized, become the key to an information system. Most of them are skilled and cannot be replaced. Many of them are resourceful. They are, on the whole, unusually intelligent. Such evidence as we have has indicated their desire to injure the enemy and to help United Nations. Prior to 1933 in Germany and prior to the dates of occupation in the occupied countries, these workers had strong unions, all affiliated with the International Transport Workers' Federation. Occupying key positions in the enemy's transportation system, these railway workers can do more than gather and carry information. They can be of tremendous help as saboteurs.

For many years the Railway Labor Exective Association, representing the twenty-one standard railway organizations of the United States has been in close contact with various of the European railway organizations which are affiliated with the International Transport worker' Federation. These contacts have been maintained to the present time and the leaders of the American railway labor organizations have exhibited great interest in augmenting and supplementing these contacts during the war in such a way as to be of assistance to the prosecution of the war by our Government. At our suggestion the Railway Labor Executives' Association is cooperating closely with the ITF in collecting intelligence through underground channels and in encouraging sabotage and resistance by underground labor groups in the occupied and enemy countries.

The participation of American railway labor organizations will be of great value in accomplishing the purposes of this undertaking. Representatives of the railway labor organizations in the United States have already established many personal friendships with the leaders of European railway labor organizations and, by working in close cooperation with the ITF, these friendships and contacts may be expanded. In addition, Swedish and English railwaymen have expressed a desire to have the participation of American railway labor representatives in developing their plans for the defeat of our enemies by working with railway workers in enemy and occupied countries.

The prestige and popularity of America is tremendous among the labor groups in the enemy and occupied countries. Therefore, the participation of American workers will greatly enhance the value of the work now being done and that planned by the ITF. This will make the ITF venture one of transport labor of the United Nations rather than that of transport labor which is European and Insular. Effective resistance and cooperation with our military effort can be multiplied and greatly expanded if it is known that our American workers' organizations are sharing with the ITF in the program.

The Railway Labor Executives' Association, with one or two exceptions, represents all of the railway brotherhoods, both operating and non-operating. This organization has recently set up a committee for the handling of their international problems. This committee will be staffed with a permanent secretary with an office in Washington and will carry the cover of a relief organization which is created for the purpose of assisting the needy railway workers who have been victimized by the war. This committee will be financed by contributions from the various railway unions and the personnel and administrative expenses will be paid from this fund. The resources of this committee can be drawn upon to assist not only in the relief of individual railway employees but also for the maintenance of contacts with their brothers in the occupied countries in order to encourage their activities in opposing the enemy. These activities include both the gathering of information about the enemy and encouragement of resistance. Our office has cooperated closely with this committee and the committee is prepared to do anything it can to assist our Government in the war.

Beyond the International Transport Workers' Federation and the American Railway Labor Executives' Association, there are those democratic labor unions associated with the International Federation of Trade Unions (IFTU) which maintains headquarters in London and with which the British Trade Union Congress and the American Federation of Labor are associated Thè IFTU has contact with personnel in enemy occupied and controlled territories who were formerly members of powerful unions in the manufacturing, mining, and distributive industries. This office has close working relations with the IFTU; they have proven to be a valuable source of intelligence for us.

Before the war the following National Labor Federations were affiliated with the International Federation of Trade Unions:

Country	Name of National Labor Federation	Last Available Membership Figures (pre-war)	Number of Unions Belonging to IFTU
Belgium	Confederation Generala Du Travail*X	582,000	24

Country	Name of National Labor Federation	Last Available Membership Figures (pre-war)	Number of Unions Belonging to IFTU
Czechoslovakia	Spolecna Ustredna*X	750,000	74
Denmark	De Samvirkende Fagforbund	526,000	
Estonia	Eestimaa Toolisuhingute*	16,000	48
Finland	Suomen Ammattiyhdi stysten	72,000	19
France	Confederation Generale Du Travail*	3,500,000	12,000
Great Britain	Trades Union Congress	5,200,000	216
			34
Hungary	Hunkasegyesuletek Szovetsege*	115,000	34
Ireland	Irish Trade Union Congress	275,000	50
Luxemburg	Commussion Syndicale*X	15,000	11
Netherlands	Verboad van Vakveriningen*X	310,000	29
Norway	Faglige Landsorganises jon*X *	340,000	34
Poland	(Three national federations) *X	500,000	
Rumania	Confederatia Generala*	60,000	12
Spain	Union General de Trabajadores*	2,000,000	43
Sweden	Landsorganisationen	950,000	45
Switserland	Cewerksohaftsbund	230,000	17
Yugoslavia	Ujedinjeni Radnicki*	65,000	37
Algeria	(See France)		
Argentina	Confederacion General	265,000	50
Australia	Australasian Council	600,000	

Country	Name of National Labor Federation	Last Available Membership Figures (pre-war)	Number of Unions Belonging to IFTU
Brazil	Uniao Geral dos Trabalhadores	13,000	
Canada	Trades and Labor Congress	235,000	2,000
	Canadian Federation of Labor	65,000	260
	All-Canadian Congress of Labor	30,000	288
Ceylon	Ceylon Trade Union Congress	15,000	
China	Chinese Association of Labor	500,000	
Cuba	Confederacion de Trabajadores	400,000	
India	National Trades Union Federation	165,000	63
	All-India Trade Union Congress	275,000	165
East Africa	Labor Trade Union of E.A.	3,000	
Mexico	Confederacion de Trabajadores	1,200,000	48
New Zealand	Federation of Labor	200,000	238
Palestina Palestina	General Federation	125,000	38
South Africa	Trades and Labor Council	25,000	50
	Cape Federation of Labor Unions	18,000	26
United States	Federation of Labor	5,000,000	120

* Destroyed or Inactive
X Reorganised in England under IFTU Auspices

There were also affiliated with the International Federation of Trade Unions certain international federations of crafts and industries organized in International Trade Secretariats. A list of these follows:

Name	Seat	Last Available Membership Figures (pre-war)	Number of Countries
Internat'l Landwrorkers' Federation	Copenhagen	263,000	15
Mineral Internat'l Federation	London	15,00,000	14
Internat'l Metal Workers' Federation	Berne	1,918,000	16
Internat'l Federation of Stone Workers	Zurich	49,000	8
Internat'l Federation of Pottery Workers		65,000	4
Internat'l Federation of Building and Wood Workers*X	Amsterdam	1,500,000	25
Internat'l Painters' Federation*	Amsterdam	38,000	7
Internat'l Typographers	Berne	165,000	23
Internat'l Federation of Lithographers and kinared trades*	Amsterdam	35,000	15
Internat'l Federation of Bookbinders	Copenhagen	55,000	12
Internat'l Federation of Textile Workers	London	670,000	14
Internat'l Clothing Workers' Federation*X	Amsterdam	640,000	17
Internat'l Federation of Hatters*	Paris	15,000	7
Internat'l Boot and Shoe Operatives and Leather Workers' Federation	London	226,000	14

Internat'1 Union of Food and Drink Workers	Zurich	250,000	15
Internat'1 Federation of Tobacco Workers	Copenhagen	43,000	9
Internat'1 Transport Workers' Federation X	Amsterdam	2,000,000	29
Postal, Telegraph, and Telephone International	Berne	200,000	16
Internat'l Federation of Employees in Public and Civil Services*	Paris	830,000	13
Internat'1 Union of Hotel, Restaurant and Bar Workers	Stockholm	32,000	5
Internat'l Union of Hairdressers	Copenhagen	30,000	8
Teachers' International*	Paris, also Brussels	1,600,000	19
Universal Alliance of Diamond Workers*X	Antwerp	18,000	4
Internat'l Federation of Factory Workers*X	Amsterdam	545,000	14
Internat'l Federation of Enginemen and Firemen*	Amsterdam	24,000	5
Internat'1 Federation of Employees*	Amsterdam	900,000	18

* Destroyed or Inactive
X Transferred Abroad and Reorganized

Also there are other democratio trade unions which are not affiliated with the International Federation of Trade Unions and which have been helpful to us in the past.

The foregoing illustrate the vast scope of the work which is being done by the Labor Section of the Office of Strategic Services in cooperation with the European and American labor movements in obtaining intelligence about the enemy and in carrying on internal warfare against the enemy.

OFFICE OF STRATEGIC SERVICES

INTEROFFICE MEMO

TO: Captain Duncan Lee   DATE: June 1, 1943

FROM: Arthur J. Goldberg   A·J·h.

SUBJECT: Revised Memorandum

Attached you will find the memorandum on the Labor Section of the Office of Strategic Services which I have revised in accordance with our discussions over the telephone.

                        A.J.G.

Attachment

Labor Section
Office of Strategic Services

Acting upon the assumption that this is a people's war, the office of Strategic Services has established a Labor Section to initiate and maintain a people's intelligence service to operate in close contact with the underground labor movements of the Axis and occupied countries. These underground labor movements are important allies in the common struggle against the Axis powers. Although their organizations have been formally dissolved they, nevertheless, wage an unremitting struggle underground and constitute the bulwark of the movements of resistance in the Axis and occupied countries.

The Labor Section of the Office of Strategic Services operates in close cooperation with a joint A.F.L.-C.I.O. Relief committee, headed by Messrs. Mathew Moll and Sidney Hillman, and with the relief committee established by the Railway Labor Executives' Association, representing the twenty-one standard railway organizations of the United States and headed by Mr. J.A. Phillips.

Through these labor channels we have obtained and continuously are receiving a flow of vital and important information about the activities of the enemy.

Declassified by <u>009785</u>
date *8 December 1977*

APPROVED FOR RELEASE
Date *8 December 1977*

The work of the Labor Section encompasses many projects by which intelligence from labor channels is obtained, collected, analyzed and reported to the Joint Chiefs of Staff and to the other military and navel services. Illustrative of these projects is one which emphasizes a widespread plan for the utilization of the underground network of the International Transport Worker's Federation, the International Federation of Trade Union and other democratic trade union organizations which have underground organizations operating in occupied and enemy countries.

The International Transport Workers' Federation, which for brevity is often called the ITF, is the largest international union in the world and has among its affiliated members transport workers in practically every country on the globe. The eighty unions affiliated with the ITF are democratic trade unions of railwaymen, seamen, long-shoremen, tramway and truck drivers and other transport workers throughout the world. Every worker having anything to do with the movement of passengers or goods is eligible for membership in the ITF.

When Hitler came to power, the transport workers' unions in Germany and the various countries occupied by Germany were among the first to be officially dissolved. In spite of this official destruction, however, the organizations, though driven underground, kept in regular communication with ITF headquarters, and the ITF underground communication system between its affiliates and its members has been rather effectively maintained. Until 1939 the headquarters of the ITF were in Amsterdam. In that year they were moved to London where they are at present.

The attitude of the ITF toward the present war is one of militant support to the United Nations. This attitude remained unchanged during the period of the German-Soviet pact. The ITF has at all times resisted communist penetration, and does not follow the communist line.

In France, Holland, Belgium, Luxemburg, Germany, Italy, Norway, Denmark, Sweden, Switzerland, Portugal and Spain, functionaries and agents of the ITF are carrying on underground activities. Unlike the usual agents employed for sabotage or subversion, the members of the ITF do not have to be paid for their work. They are devoted to the task of interfering in every way with the successful exploitation of their countries by the Nazis. Furthermore, because of the strength of the ITF in the railway and maritime fields among the skilled employees of these industries, the members of the ITF have natural cover for their activities.

We are cooperating with the ITF and are utilizing their facilities for penetrating the occupied and enemy countries of Europe. For example, Swedish seamen as part of their job regularly travel to the occupied countries of Europe and even to Germany itself. Swedish railwaymen have direct contract the Norwegian underground and Swiss railwaymen with the German underground. Many of these workers are ITF people and are devoted to the principles of the ITF. We, in collaboration with the ITF, are obtaining intelligence from these sources which should be more helpful in shortening this war.

Among the transport workers perhaps the most important are railway workers. With natural cover, going as a part of their job from place to place, they can, if cooperative and organized, become the key to an information system. Most of them are skilled and cannot be replaced. Many of them are resourceful. They are, on the whole, unusually intelligent. Such evidence as we have has indicated their desire to injure the enemy and to help the United Nations. Occupying key positions in the enemy's transportation system, these railway workers can do more than gather and carry information. They can be of tremendous help as saboteurs.

For many years the Railway Labor Executives' Association, representing the twenty-one standard railway organizations of the United States, has been in close contact with various European railway organizations which are affiliated with the International Transport Workers' Federation. These contacts have been maintained to the present time and the leaders of the American railway labor organizations have exhibited great interest in augmenting and supplementing these contacts during the war in such a way as to be assistance to the prosecution of the war by our Government. At our suggestion the Railway Labor Executives' Association is cooperating closely with the ITF in collecting intelligence through underground channels and in encouraging sabotage and resistance by underground labor groups in the occupied and enemy countries.

The prestige and popularity of America is tremendous among the labor groups in the enemy and occupied countries. Therefore, the participation of American workers will greatly enhance the value of the work now being done and that planned by the ITF. This will make the ITF venture one of transport labor of the United Nations rather than that of transport labor which is European and Insular. Effective resistance and cooperation with our military effort can be multiplied and greatly expanded if it is known that our American workers' organizations are sharing with the ITF in the program.

Beyond the International Transport Workers' Federation and the American Railway Labor Executives' Association, there are those democratic labor unions associated with the International Federation of Trade Unions (IFTU) which maintains headquarters in London and with which the British Trade Union Congress and the American Federation of Labor are associated.

Before the war national labor federations of thirty-three countries were affiliated with the International Federation of Trade Unions.

Also there are other democratic trade unions which are not affiliated with the International Federation of Trade Unions and which have been helpful to as in the past.

The foregoing illustrates the vast scope of the work which is being done by the Labor Section of the Office of Strategic Services in cooperation with the European and American labor movements in obtaining intelligence about the enemy and in carrying on internal warfare against him.

APPENDIX B

Letter from Paul Lindner to UK
Undersecretary of State, August 5, 1941

Re: Request for release from
internment

Paul Inzner,
No. . 966,
house 4,
"P" Camp,
Isle of Man,
August 5th, 1941.

CONFIDENTIAL

The Under Secretary of State,
Aliens Department,
P.O.Box 2,
Bournemouth.

Sir,

I wish to apply for release from internment under Category 19 of the White Paper Cmd. 6233.

I have grown up in a family with an old social-democratic tradition. Both my grandfathers had been leading members of the party already in the years of Bismarck's anti-socialist laws. My parents were brought up in this spirit of the labour movement, and so was I. At the age of nine, in 1920, I joined the social-democratic children's movement, and when I was fourteen I became a member of the S.A.J. (League of Labour Youth). In this organisation I held various positions up to that of a district leader.

When I began to work I joined the German Metal Workers Union and was elected to various posts in the Union as well as in the factory I was working in. After having reached the 16th year I joined the Social-democratic Party where I acted as the representative of the S.A.J. Through these various activities I became well known in the Labour movement, particularly among the young. I often spoke in public meetings where I dealt especially with the Nazi attitude towards the youth. I organised a campaign against the Nazi plans for the conscription of youth for labour service, which was in fact a substitute for military conscription. In the course of this campaign some camps had actually to be closed (e.g. Fürstenwalde). I was hated to such an extent by the Nazis that as early as 1932 a gang of stormtroopers laid an ambush for me near the house of my parents and maltreated me so that I had to be brought to a hospital.

After the establishment of the Nazi Government I worked chiefly in the trade union preparing the groups for the continuation of the underground work. I did not live in my own flat but, on 5th May 1933, I was recognised on the street by a stormtrooper who had me arrested by some of his men and brought to their barracks. Twelve days later I was brought to hospital with a brain-shock, teeth loosened and broken, four missing, kidneys bruised and torn, a bayonet stab in the back, wounded shin bones, and injuries of the skin resulting from flogging and burning on the whole body. After three months I had so far recovered that I could be dismissed. Since then I suffer from kidney haemorrhage reoccurring in shorter or longer intervals.

After a few months' rest I resumed my activities in the trade union as well as in the Labour Youth. In particular, I organised the youth groups under the name of a hiking club (Wanderverein). During the weekend trips I gave lectures in underground methods and we discussed their appliance in each instance. In this period I maintained continued contact with Max Seydewitz (Labour M.P.), at that time living already in Prague, who supplied me with illegal newspapers and books. By the autumn 1933 about 400 young people were organised in groups of this kind.

At that time the Nazis were about to complete the "Gleichschaltung" of all clubs and associations not yet entirely under Nazi control. Their measures were accompanied by very careful examinations of all members of these groups, in the course of which unfortunately some papers were found which caused the Ge- ... "...Wanderverein" as a camouflaged anti-Nazi

organisation. A concentrated search for the "leaders" began, in
pursuance of which my living place was searched and some incriminating material found. The police occupied my flat in order to
arrest me on coming home, but some friends warned me in time, and
I disappeared. A few days later I learned that a warrant with
heavy charges was issued against me.

In these circumstances it was better for me to leave Germany; which, moreover, gave the remaining friends the chance to
discharge themselves at my expense. I went to Czechoslovakia on
27th October 1935 and lived in Prague, where I became the secretary of Max Seydewitz. In this capacity I often travelled to the
frontier to keep contact with the underground social-democratic
groups in Germany and provide them with the necessary material.
To intensify this contact I moved from Prague to Reichenberg, in
January 1937, and later to Teplitz. These activities caused the
Gestapo to arrest my father living in Berlin three times as a
hostage.

During the crisis of September 1938 and in the days after
the Munich Accord I worked with the Czechoslovak Army as a car-
driver motoring inspecting officers and evacuating children from
the territory ceded to the Nazis.

In March 1939, a few days before the occupation of Prague,
I went to England under the auspices of the Youth Refugee and
Relief Council, a section of the British Youth Peace Assembly.
After my arrival in London I was registered with the British
Committee for Refugees from Czechoslovakia, later the Czech Re-
fugee Trust Fund. I was sent to Chatham, Kent, where I was main-
tained by the local branch of the Youth Refugee and Relief Coun-
cil and the Trades Council of the Medway Towns.

At the outbreak of the war I volunteered for A.R.P. work
and was registered as a driver. My services, however, were not
required. On 12th May 1940 I was interned.

In Canada I was foreman in the sewing department of the
camp factory producing articles for the Canadian Army.

I have come back to England in order to help fighting the
Nazi regime, and I should be only too glad to get the opportunity
of doing so by an early release.

Yours faithfully,

CONFIDENTIAL   Paul Lindner.

References, British:

Czech Refugee Trust Fund, New Lodge, Windsor Forest, Windsor, Berksh
Youth Refugee and Relief Council, 90, Sutherland Av., London, W.9
Mrs. Nora Johnson, 35, Charter Street, Chatham, Kent
Mr. F. Elliot, 63, Palmerstone Road, Chatham, Kent
Miss Marjorie Andrews, 33, Gordon Road, Strood, Kent

APPENDIX C

Silver Star certificates awarded to Paul Lindner and Anton Ruh, May 2006

Re: HAMMER Mission

THE UNITED STATES OF AMERICA

TO ALL WHO SHALL SEE THESE PRESENTS, GREETING:

THIS IS TO CERTIFY THAT

THE PRESIDENT OF THE UNITED STATES OF AMERICA
AUTHORIZED BY ACT OF CONGRESS JULY 9, 1918
HAS AWARDED

THE SILVER STAR

TO
PAUL LINDNER
(GERMAN NATIONAL, OSS, ARMY OF THE UNITED STATES)
FOR
GALLANTRY IN ACTION
FROM 2 MARCH 1945 TO 25 APRIL 1945 IN GERMANY

GIVEN UNDER MY HAND IN THE CITY OF WASHINGTON
ON THIS 24TH DAY OF SEPEMBER 2004

THE ADJUTANT GENERAL

SECRETARY OF THE ARMY
(ACTING)

The President of the United States of America, authorized by Act of Congress, July 9, 1918, has awarded the SILVER STAR to

PAUL LINDNER

(THEN GERMAN NATIONAL, OSS, ARMY OF THE UNITED STATES)

For gallantry in action against the enemy from 2 March 1945 to 25 April 1945, in Berlin, Germany, while assigned to the HAMMER Mission (TOOL Missions), Secret Intelligence Branch, Office of Strategic Services. Prior to the team's departure for the HAMMER Mission, Mr. Lindner was placed within various American Prisoner-of-War camps outside of London to gather intelligence from captured German officers and soldiers as well as refine his cover story. Mr. Lindner and his team member were then inserted into Berlin by parachute to gather intelligence on the enemy's situation and movements. The team confirmed the location and operational status of the Klingenberg power plant that was furnishing electrical power to munitions plants, the location and continuing operation of both the Berlin railroad transportation system and Berlin freight yards. Mr. Lindner and his team member were also able to gather intelligence on hidden factories and storage dumps, the effectiveness of Allied bombings, the treatment of Allied prisoners-of-war, and the strength of Nazi control over the civil population. Additionally, the team organized a small group of underground resistance contacts who collected and transmitted intelligence, including valuable information about defense points in the northern section of Berlin. At one point into the mission, Mr. Lindner met for the first time his brother-in-law, a German soldier on leave and the situation became very tenuous as the German soldier quickly learned that Mr. Lindner and his team member were enemy agents. However, after an all-night dialogue, Mr. Lindner and his team member convinced the German soldier to abandon his unit and help aid with the HAMMER Mission. Upon completion of the HAMMER Mission, the team followed OSS instruction and surrendered to the Soviet Army, who then held Mr. Lindner and his team member for two months before finally releasing him into the custody of the U.S. Army. The gallantry displayed by Mr. Lindner was in keeping with the highest traditions of the military service and reflects great credit on himself, the Office of Strategic Services, and the Army of the United States.

THE UNITED STATES OF AMERICA

TO ALL WHO SHALL SEE THESE PRESENTS, GREETING:

THIS IS TO CERTIFY THAT

THE PRESIDENT OF THE UNITED STATES OF AMERICA
AUTHORIZED BY ACT OF CONGRESS JULY 9, 1918

HAS AWARDED

THE SILVER STAR

TO

ANTON RUH
(GERMAN NATIONAL, OSS, ARMY OF THE UNITED STATES)

FOR

GALLANTRY IN ACTION

FROM 2 MARCH 1945 TO 25 APRIL 1945 IN GERMANY

GIVEN UNDER MY HAND IN THE CITY OF WASHINGTON
ON THIS 24TH DAY OF SEPTEMBER 2004

THE ADJUTANT GENERAL

SECRETARY OF THE ARMY
(ACTING)

The President of the United States of America, authorized by Act of Congress, July 9, 1918, has awarded the SILVER STAR to

ANTON RUH
(THEN GERMAN NATIONAL, OSS, ARMY OF THE UNITED STATES)

For gallantry in action against the enemy from 2 March 1945 to 25 April 1945, in Berlin, Germany, while assigned to the HAMMER Mission (TOOL Missions), Secret Intelligence Branch, Office of Strategic Services. Prior to the team's departure for the HAMMER Mission, Mr. Ruh was placed within various American Prisoner-of-War camps outside of London to gather intelligence from captured German officers and soldiers as well as refine his cover story. Mr. Ruh and his team member were then inserted into Berlin by parachute to gather intelligence on the enemy's situation and movements. The team confirmed the location and operational status of the Klingenberg power plant that was furnishing electrical power to munitions plants, the location and continuing operation of both the Berlin railroad transportation system and Berlin freight yards. Mr. Ruh and his team member were also able to gather intelligence on hidden factories and storage dumps, the effectiveness of Allied bombings, the treatment of Allied prisoners-of-war, and the strength of Nazi control over the civil population. Additionally, the team organized a small group of underground resistance contacts who collected and transmitted intelligence, including valuable information about defense points in the northern section of Berlin. At one point into the mission, the other team member met for the first time his brother-in-law, a German soldier on leave and the situation became very tenuous as the German soldier quickly learned that Mr. Ruh and his team member were enemy agents. However, after an all-night dialogue, Mr. Ruh and his team member convinced the German soldier to abandon his unit and help aid with the HAMMER Mission. Upon completion of the HAMMER Mission, the team followed OSS instruction and surrendered to the Soviet Army, who then held Mr. Ruh and his team member for two months before finally releasing him into the custody of the U.S. Army. The gallantry displayed by Mr. Ruh was in keeping with the highest traditions of the military service and reflects great credit on himself, the Office of Strategic Services, and the Army of the United States.

APPENDIX D

Recommendation for Award of *Bronze Star* to Joseph Gould, June 1945

Authority NND47589
By [illegible] NARA Date 9/12/08

SECRET

HQ & HQ DETACHMENT
OFFICE OF STRATEGIC SERVICES
EUROPEAN THEATER OF OPERATIONS
UNITED STATES ARMY
(MAIN)

APO 413
20 June 1945

SUBJECT: Recommendation for Award of the BRONZE STAR MEDAL

TO   : Commanding General, European Theater of
        Operations, APO 887, United States Army.

1. a. It is recommended that JOSEPH GOULD,
0541184, 1st Lt, Infantry, now assigned to the
Manpower Division, United States Group Control Council,
APO 742, United States Army, be awarded the BRONZE STAR
MEDAL.

b. Lieutenant GOULD served as Commanding
Officer of the Secret Intelligence Branch "MILWAUKEE"
Training School for secret agents, and as the Officer
in Charge of the special series of projects, known as
the "Tool Series", of the Labor Division of the same
branch at the time of the service for which this award
is recommended.

c. Name and address of nearest relative:

Mrs. Betty Gould,
95-17 89th Avenue,
Forest Hills, Long Island.

d. Entered United States military service from:
New York.

e. Decorations previously awarded: None

f. The entire service of Lieutenant GOULD has
been honorable since the rendition by him of the service
upon which this recommendation is based.

g. A similar recommendation for this individual
has not been submitted.

2. a. The officer recommending this award has personal knowledge of the service upon which the recommen-
ation is based.

3. a. 1st Lieutenant JOSEPH GOULD while serving with
the Army of the United States, distinguished himself by
meritorious achievement in connection with military operations not involving participation in aerial flight against
an enemy of the United States. The accomplishment of the
service for which the award is recommended, extended from
April, 1944, to April 1945, and has been completed. The
service was performed in London, England, and in France.

b. Detailed narrative of the services for which
this award is recommended:

- 1 -

SECRET

Lt. JOSEPH GOULD joined the Secret Intelligence Branch, Office of Strategic Services, in April, 1944, and was immediately assigned to the Labor Division. He undertook his work with unusual energy and did exceptionally conscientious, thorough, and intelligent work in assuming in large measure the responsibility for the orientation, training and briefing of agents recruited under the FAUST program, which envisaged the introduction of Secret Agents into Germany to develop by contact with underground Labor groups an espionage network that would obtain and report valuable military information to headquarters. Lt. GOULD's task demanded extraordinary skill and care in planning the FAUST operations and in preparing the agents for the success of the plans and safety of the men hinged not only upon skilled evaluation of potential operatives but upon the detailed planning of each phase and painstaking training of the men selected since the agents were to be parachuted inside Germany itself where there would be assistance from persons anxious to aid in the liberation of their home land. The highly satisfactory results obtained from these missions and the safe return of the men can in large part be attributed to Lt. GOULD's full appreciation of the problem and his unusual devotion, originality, and enthusiastic interest in carrying out his tasks. He had a knowledge of German and, although it was not a requisite for the position which he held at that time, he felt that he could render maximum service in the training of his agent personnel if he perfected himself in the language. On a purely voluntary basis and entirely on his own time, he developed such proficiency that at a crucial period in this program it was possible to place him in charge of "MILWAUKEE", the school established for the training of the FAUST agents.

As Commanding Officer of the "MILWAUKEE" School, Lt. GOULD assumed full responsibility for its operation. He personally supervised and directed the organization and development of its training facilities and, exercising great care, directed the recruiting of a special staff competent to thoroughly prepare and brief his agent students for their work in Germany.

In addition to building up the school, with great interest and keen foresight, he took part in devising the special curriculum and adjusting schedules and, at the same time, continued with great success to recruit, train, and brief new agents, and to attend to the over-all administration of the training area. He devoted himself to this task with such energy and interest that the agents trained by MILWAUKEE in the period from its inception in June to August, 1944, were deemed ready to enter Germany a month ahead of the target date previously set for the completion of their training. Thirty students were trained at the MILWAUKEE School, receiving complete briefing in such matters as police regulations, rationing, transportation facilities and controls, housing, and the many details required by a man living in a German community, and, largely through the unfailing efforts of Lt. GOULD and his staff, the men were finally dispatched on secret intelligence missions inside Germany after receiving a training which had been directed at insuring their safety and success.

- 2 -

SECRET

In the fall of 1944, Lt. GOULD, entirely on his own initiative, attempted to contact a very valuable group of politically reliable German nationals with a view to recruiting potential agents for particularly dangerous jobs at strategic points deep inside Germany. Previous efforts to establish liaison with this group had met with no success, and it was entirely due to Lt. GOULD's exceptional tact and diplomacy in skillfully handling these contacts that OSS obtained valuable agent personnel and established a close working relationship with this group. Lt. GOULD was given full responsibility for the training of these recruits and for the development of five missions, and he personally supervised each detail of their schedule from the day they were recruited until they were dropped inside Germany. He worked tirelessly to insure the final success of this program and displayed rare ingenuity and imagination in his briefing and preparation of the men

Realizing that ordinary wireless equipment would be too easily detected by direction-finding apparatus in areas so rigidly controlled, Lt. GOULD decided to dispatch the men with no means of communication other than the newly devised JOAN ELINORE sets, a secret airground communications device which had been developed specially by OSS for the use of their agents in the field. Prior to this time it had been considered necessary to equip all agents with both radio and JOAN ELINORE, and Lt. GOULD conceived the idea to rely solely on this new device, a departure which proved invaluable in the planning of later missions to Germany.

In January 1945, Lt. GOULD found that the targets selected for these teams would not be accessible, as they lay too deep within Germany for the Air Force to dispatch special unescorted missions to parachute the agents at the designated pinpoints. With exceptional perseverance, Lt. GOULD, realizing the importance of the contemplated operations, was determined to see the missions dispatched, and was indefatigable in his efforts to find a type of aircraft suited to the task. Despite great opposition, he carried on, and, finally, in February, 1945, the Air Force agreed to the conversion of an A-26 aircraft for the purpose of dropping Lt. GOULD's teams. The first men were parachuted successfully in the Berlin area, hundreds of miles beyond the region in which it had previously been believed possible to effect a successful drop. Contact was established with this agent team by means of the J/E equipment and maintained successfully at a critical time in the assault on Germany. Vital information was obtained as to conditions in Berlin, the disposition of troops in the Berlin area, and remaining targets for bombing by the Air Force. Other teams were dropped, subsequently, at strategic points deep within Germany and Lt. GOULD maintained full responsibility for servicing these teams while they were in the field. All of these agents were dropped successfully and provided highly significant military intelligence which was not duplicated elsewhere, and which was of great value to the Allies.

- 3 -

SECRET

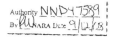

S E C R E T

    Lt/ GOULD'S services were at all times of the highest caliber; and, largely due to his devotion to duty, his interest, and his resourcefulness, important operations were prepared and dispatched, and extremely valuable intelligence was obtained and transmitted to the G-2's of SHAEF and the Army Groups and Armies.

    Lt. GOULD was not wounded while performing the above duties.

    4. Proposed Citation: For the BRONZE STAR MEDAL:

    1st Lt. JOSEPH GOULD, 6341194, Infantry, in recognition of highly meritorious achievements in support of military operations. He assumed complex duties, and displayed a great devotion to duty, unusual initiative, and an unstinting industry in carrying out his assignment successfully. He played an essential part in preparing and activating important missions from which valuable results were obtained.

    5. In order to support this recommendation it has been necessary to divulge in the preceding paragraphs information classified as SECRET. However, the Proposed Citation has been made sufficiently general to permit publication of it separately with the classification of Restricted.

                        JAMES R. FORGAN,
                        Colonel, GSC,
                        Commanding.

- 4 -

S E C R E T

APPENDIX E

P.O.W. Cage report from Paul Lindner,
November 1944

Report about one week's life and experience in a P.W. Camp.

1). The task
2). The preparations
3). What I heard and say
4). My opinion about:

    a) buildings, language, items of conversation
    b) morale
    c) news
    d) the journey to the U.S.A./ fear of the Soviet Union
    e) some types and some typical conceptions
    f) parachutists,
    g) American informers.

5). Conclusions

I. Description of 4 P.W.s who may be used.

II. Suggestions concerning education of P.W.s and how it may be improved

III. Army slang

THE TASK

My task has been to spend one week as a P.W. in a P.W. camp. It was left to ourselves to collect information of any kind, to study whatever we liked and regarded as important.

The first part of my task has been successfully carried out. I have succeeded in staying one week in a camp with about 900 P.W.s without arousing any suspicion against me. For the purposes of "penetration" this is excellent training. When sufficiently trained you can live your own cover story. By adapting it to your surroundings, you can improve it quickly and, after about three days, you can live the normal life of a P.W. without acting too cautiously. In order to find out whether my cover story was tight I had, on the 4th evening, an "expert's" conversation with a parachutist, lasting about two hours. (I went myself as a parachutist.) Though we were talking about training camps, pubs nearby, the training personnel, special qualities of parachutists, details of the jumping down (Rocksprung) from the RK 111 ("Bodenwanne": ground tub), my story was in no danger of being given the lie. On the 5th day, I was introduced to a parachutist from "my" regiment. We discussed "our" officers, street fighting in Mons, Belgium, which we had gone through the same day, and my story proved foolproof. He even remembered having seen me standing sentinel at regiment's H.Q. The P.W.s used to tell so many lies, everyone exaggerating more than the other one, that after only two days you feel able to tell the most atrocious stories yourself. As a newcomer you must swallow all those stories which no one else will listen to.

The second part of my task, i.e. to collect information, is being dealt with in the remainder of this report.

PREPARATIONS

Our main chance of preparing ourselves for our special task was two weeks of interrogating friendly prisoners willing to cooperate with us. My own story was built on what 3 of them had told me.

    a). A 19 year old parachutist provided me with material about training, front service, front experience, and capture.
    b). A 35 year old infantrist told me about conditions in my "home town".

e). A 26 year old infantrist told me about his experience in
factories, about those indispensable for industry, and
other professional details, e.g. scarcity of material,
for instance for a social kinds of steel for tool makers.

On this material of facts, my own life story, age, school
education etc. was based. According to instructions, I built in
my explanation of my knowledge of the English language. While
preparing ourselves we get no advice which, I believe, was good
for our training; we were forced to develop our own ideas and
to take the risk of our own possible mistakes. Inventing the
story, living up to it, and controling it in all details, was
the main result of this story.

WHAT I HEARD AND SAW

The three of us simultaneously went to the camp, living in
the same hut etc. We had met in the hospital. I had a fracture
of the skull and pneumonia. We arrived in the camp in an ambu-
lance, dressed in the usual hospital clothes, taken over by the
guards and, since it was late in the evening, put into a cell
till next morning. From there we were brought to the reception
tents. The American staff had not been informed about our identity
so we were treated like any other P.W. In the reception tent it
was discovered that our identity cards from the "hospital" had not
been filled in correctly, so all details had to be repeated. This
was the first real test for our stories. It seemed to be most
incomprehensible that we had no identity disks and couldn't even
remember our numbers. People seemed to believe that we kept silent
deliberately about this. Nobody now is being released when his
statements are incorrect. We had to leave our fingerprings on
the new cards. This task is left to P.W.s who are allowed to help
with clerical work. Since they have the opportunity of reading
the cards they are informed and question the newcomer, partly of
curiosity, sympathy, or pompousness. From the reception tent,
we were conducted to the cage, i.e. it's office. There an American sergeant-major and his German N.C.O. received us. Since now,
we had been already 24 hours without food, we protested at once
which made a good introduction for us. We got our food in the
kitchen and, then, were assigned to a hut. There, we first had to
report where we were coming from and started, as quickly as possible,
counter-questioning our new comrades. We got quickly in touch with
each other and since we had all kinds of canteen stuff in our
pockets we were able to clear our ways even with cigarettes. It
is easy to get in touch with other P.W.s but "friends" you usually
find among your room mates. During one week, we were living the
life of P.W.s, got accustomed to their way of life, grumbled about
the same things as they did, etc. We were informed by our "comrades" about the special rules of the cage, but it is advisable
to know how beds are made in the hospital because the same method
is being used in the cage. In order to avoid difficulties the
best thing is to do as the American camp personnel do or to avoid
them. Most P.W.s prefer this. You have to salute American officers in the military way. The Hitler salute is not given. When
entering the office you stand to attention and salute. When talking
to, and living with, P.W.s it is necessary to keep in mind that
our task is to learn from them and not to teach them. During my
last two days, after I had become quite familiar and was able to
feel safe, I started several vehement anti-Hitler discussions
because I wanted to know how the P.W.s were going to react to
this. The result was astonishing. People became more intimate
with me. Amongst them was a shore-battery gunner from the navy,
father of two sons who had volunteered for the S.S. The main
impression I got from their replies and other contributions to th

conversations, was that this sphere of thinking was new to them. Apparently they were not accustomed to take part in anti-Hitler discussions, or to express in simple and unmistakable words what they wanted to say against Hitler. Their usual way of expressing themselves is vague and ambiguous so it is difficult to catch them. When, for instance, after an air attack they abuse the "criminals" it remains doubtful whether they mean the allied pilots or the Nazi criminals.

It is easy to become friendly with people belonging to the same service. I got quickly in touch with some parachutists and if there had arisen any difficulties with other people, I certainly would have been able to count on their help. It would have become a fight of "parachutists against navy". On the 8th day we suddenly were removed from the cage and this cut short our relations. We took leave from each other and shook hands.

POSTSCRIPT

Our hospital clothes were good, but it is advisable to have a second set of underwear in your kit bag. One ought to have a number of small implements in one's pockets, for instance, a knife string, pencil, paper, old laces, a piece of bandage, an old magazine, some cloth for shoe cleaning, an empty cigarette case etc. These articles may be of whatever make, English, American, French. Every article for sale in the P.X. is good for the purpose, e.g. towels. German razors are rarely to be found, usually taken away. One ought to have cigarettes or tobacco because it helps making contact, at least: pipe and tobacco, cigarette tobacco and paper, 2 or 3 packets of cigarettes. It is not a matter of how many you have but that you have something to barter your way. The barter value is: 1 good leather - ½ packet of cigarette tobacco. P.X. sweet rations should also be carried. It is usual to hide such "treasures" from your room mates. It appears that only little is being stolen. All rations of this kind are called "canteen" stuff. One must have an explanation ready where one got it. Chocolate is advisable as additional food.

MY OPINION

a) The level of language is very low. Those who have improved their knowledge of German by reading of German literature, or are accustomed to discuss the problems of the Allies in a democratic country ought to try and simplify their language considerably. The best means for this purpose is the use of a dialect and of dialect words. Those who have been living the life of a bandit or, like the occupation army in France, the life of a parasite, speaks also like a bandit or a parasite. The language of the front soldier, up to the highest group of N.C.O.s is just an expression of the Nazi ideology and their methods of warfare; brutality, lack of consideration, vileness, behaviour like a cyclist: treading below and bending your back above. They cowardly obey orders but never forget their own advantage. When remembering France, the fight for freedom, the country, the language, etc., they only mean eating, drinking, and women. At last, they only saw "terrorists" and, now, they feel terribly offended by the French people because all German "descent" has been repaid with stone throws and boxes on the ear.

This is what they usually are talking about. The air superiority of the Allies commands their greatest respect. Innumerable "own experiences" about this are being told. Tales from the front and the garrisons are their usual pastime. Next comes how they have been captured and treated. They generally complain of harsh and bad treatment. In France, they had to camp for weeks in open air, only protected by barbed wire. Not a single

time, any one of them will think of how P.W.s are being treated
in Germany. There is ample discussion of the general rules in
the cage, of the treatment by the American personnel, of the
quantity and quality of the food, and how they suffer from the
cold following the scarcity of coal. The treatment is correct,
matter of fact, and in case of irregularities the Americans
show their hands. There is no doubt that life in the cage is
no pleasure. But in spite of grumbling, the P.W.s accept it and
they vent their fury mainly on their own comrades and not on the
Americans. A group of "permanent inmates", about 80 strong, remains constantly in the cage and carries out kitchen work, administration, and hut supervision, while for the majority it is only
a transition camp. The "permanents" are generally accused of
profiteering in kitchen and store. That is how they explain the
small food rations and there is a general desire that an American
should take over because, then, there would be a fair deal. The
"permanents" are behaving rudely and make every use of their power.
For them, life in captivity means some slices of bread. Every
other P.W., grumbler though he may be, is only too ready to join
the "permanent staff" and, then, to do as they do. With bread
you can buy everything.

Life in the cage is organised according to the Prussian
example. Inspections by American officers are carried out carefully and feared as much as formerly in the German service.
Then the cage is well cleaned and the P.W.s stand rank and file
The "camp leader" appointed by the camp officer, is an old
Prussian N.C.O. He speaks and acts correctly, just like in the
Wehrmacht, but he is backed by the American authority. The P.W.
acts and reacts just as before. He wouldn't think of making use
of the American protection and expressing his thoughts more
freely. It is a great impression I can look back to, this
disappearing for one week in a cage somewhere in England and,
literally, living in another world. The P.W.s still speak the
conqueror's language and live according to their own mentality
of a German soldier and a German subject. They have brought with
them a piece of Germany, Hitler's Germany.

b) It is difficult to talk of morality when you mean people
whose brains are dried up and whose bodies react automatically
when being ordered about. Some P.W.s have some knowledge and
some skill, even expert's knowledge. Some of them have some
practical skill as mechanics, as brewers, as horsemen, as shop-
keepers. Discussions with some of them, e.g. metal workers, can
be quite interesting. But when carrying on with the same man
about politics or other spheres of human knowledge, always result
in complete nonsense. Almost everybody understands that Germany
has lost the war. Nevertheless, they hope for two chances: a
new miracle weapon and a future war between U.S.A., Britain, and
Russia. Their conceptions of "miracle weapons" are widely
different, sometimes absolutely fantastic. Only few P.W.s understand that Germany cannot perform any more miracles. The second
chance is more difficult: when talking of politics, economic
life, production, etc., they only mean victors and vanquished,
and how the booty is going to be shared. They simply cannot understand that the allied powers should be able to decide peace-
fully how the "booty Germany" is going to be carved up. None
of them knows that other nations, too, have paid and sacrificed
enormously in order to stop Hitler's war. One P.W., though being
anti-Hitler, said XXXXXXXXXXXXXXXXXXXXXXXX literally that Germany's
rescue and future is dependent on the future war between the
Allies. When I told him that Germany and the whole world needed
peace and nothing but peace and that, now at last, there should
be an end of this war catastrophe, he replied: "There may be
something about it; I never have looked at it that way."

Most P.W.s cannot be regarded as Nazis. Many of them are
against the Nazis and it is no longer good to be called a Nazi.

But the way they think is still influenced by Nazi propaganda.
Even men who deliberately take their attitude against the Nazis,
are influenced by 12 years of Nazi dictatorship. Life in Nazi
Germany, service in the Wehrmacht, and front life, have caused
everybody to think in a uniform way. Even among those P.W.s willing
to cooperate whom I met during my training time, there was
only one who expressed a clear opinion about the war guilt. He
understood that the German nation as a whole was responsible
towards all other nations. All others strongly protested against
such an imputation.

Another question is how far these P.W.s who, on the basis
of their own experiences, or on political or religious reasons,
are against Hitler, will be able to digest new ideas and, ultimately, will be ready to support their anti-Hitler feelings
with their anti-Hitler knowledge. Here, the Allies ought to have
good chances of success. But the foremost task, at present,
is to win and to terminate the war, and not to reeducate P.W.s.
There will, after all, be nothing that will make a stronger
impression upon the P.Wls than the ultimate victory of the
Allies. Out of the hopelessness of their situation, then,
they will find a way to peaceful occupation especially if the
American personnel in the camps will find means and ways of
encouraging free discussions among the P.W.s and of allowing
them to form their own opinions.

What the P.W.s think about the U.S.A. is almost grotesque.
The Nazis have pressed into their propaganda everything possible
about "degeneration" in the U.S.A., both in words and in pictures: jazz, so alien to the well disciplined Prussian mind,
dancing, the negro question, gangsterism, beggars, slums and
Jews. From "genuine" pictures and reports, the P.W.s have formed
ideas which would be ridiculous if they hadn't had so terrible
consequences. There would be a chance of good success and progress if the P.Wls were chances of studying American conditions
as they really are, by reading books and magazines, and to
learn something about democracy,

  e) There is but little Nazi activity going on in the cage.
The only one you can trace is the way they spread news. Some-
body reads a newspaper and tells the news but misrepresenting
it. "Near Katovice 300 panzers have been destroyed". Everybody talked about this achievement but nobody came to ponder
how this could happen at Katovice. Certainly, Nazis still keep
together, but the difference between them and the majority is
but little and there are many reasons for joining the other
P.W.s. Whether they are Nazis or not, all of them have their
own ideas about German race, German homeland, and German superiority. They are convinced that the Germans are the best soldiers and craftsmen and the war is only being lost because of
the other nations' superiority in men and material. This arrogance which has been prevalent in German quite a long time,
has been increased enormously by the Nazis. Everybody feels important and believes to be the center of the world. Especially
with the youngsters, this Nazi influence can be felt considerably.

I believe a group of ten resolute men would be able to terrorise
a whole camp. Those resisting are only individuals and a group
can crush the resistance. This applies to Nazi terror in the
camps. If a single P.W. makes a stand against Hitler he normally
will be defeated when meeting Nazi opposition or a front of
passivity and neutrality. They are pleased at having saved their
lives, so why should they make things difficult now, One day,
all this will belong to the past. Only when, at last, Hitler's
enemies will join each other in groups of P.W.s, they will be
strong enough to make headway. This would be the first step
towards reeducation, but this step must be taken by the prisoners
themselves.

d) It is of great importance that this cage is only a
transition camp. All P.W.s hope to be brought to a permanent
camp. In the transition camp they can get no mail. In the
permanent camp they expect better food and more activity. Their
live stretches from one list of P.W.s to be removed, to the next
one. It is a grave disappointment when they are not included
in the list. Then they speculate why they have been left out
by the Americans. Some of them claim that the S.S., the Navy,
the parachutists, and obvious Nazis have preference in being
transported overseas. Though they enjoy their not being regarded
as Nazis, the P.W.s claim that, even in captivity, the Nazis
get preferential treatment. The P.W.s have all possible kinds
of reasons why they want to be shipped to the U.S.A. All of
them expect an improvement of their material conditions. The
XXXXXXXXXXXXXXXXXXXXXXXXXXXXXXXX U.S.A. has raw materials
abundantly, and if they are on the spot, independent of transport of the raw materials, then, they believe they will get all
they need. This way of thinking causes some P.W.s in the present
camp even to ask for as little clothing as possible because they
argue that, on arrival in U.S.A., they want to be in need of
clothes and, then, they will get better ones. Some P.W.s hope,
after the war, to be allowed to remain in the U.S.A. Their
thoughts, leading to this desire, are dependent on their ideas
about the future of German prisoners after the war. They are
terribly afraid of being sent to Siberia. They hope for dif-
ferences between the U.S.A. and the Soviet Union and believe
that the U.S.A. will not be interested in helping in the reconstruction of Russia. Consequently: The P.W. either remains
in the U.S.A. or is sent home. But since it is improbable that
P.W. camps will be kept in peace time, some of them will be
given their liberty and then sent home, one group after the
other. Whatever they are thinking, the P.W.s expect, at any
rate, that being shipped to the U.S.A. will be to their advantage, now and in the future.

The other alternative for those unfortunate who are not
being transported to America, is the Labour camp. Many P.W.s
have already been in such camps in England, and they are telling
plenty of stories about the good food they get there. Most
important is that, there, they can steal, or "organise" as they
call it. Apparently food, P.X. articles, and P.W. clothes, are
being dispatched from there by the prisoners. Innumerable stories
are being told of how they succeeded in "organise" chocolate,
tobacco, etc., without being found out. As I said before: the
soldier's ideals in captivity are a slice of bread and a cigarette.

The journey across the Atlantic is being regarded as a dis-
advantage which can't be avoided. The P.W.s believe the U-boat
danger to be serious. Since "England doesn't announce her con-
voys to the German government" and the "ships have no lights",
it may happen that a U-boat torpedoes a convoy. On January 23,
1946, one P.W. tried to get his name cancelled in the shipment
list because he was afraid of the U-boats. In most cases, however, the desire to come to the U.S.A. is strongest. The decisive
point, however, is the terrible fear of the Soviet Union. Two
reasons for this are mentioned:

1) The influence of the Nazi propaganda which, apparently,
has concentrated on the anti-Bolshevik line and, doubtless, has been very successful. If the P.W.s have
grotesque ideas about the U.S.A., what they think about
the U.S.S.R. is simply fantastic. A normal Human brain
ought to eliminate automatically this kind of fantasies,
but Nazi propaganda has succeeded in transforming
normal ways of thinking into morbid phantoms.

2) The fear of revenge. To my great surprise, I found out
that all P.W.s knew about the crimes committed at the
Eastern front, or in the occupied countries of the East

by the Germans. Moreover, all of them know about
Germans murdered in Germany, about slave hells in
Germany from which workers, both Germans and foreigners,
were carried away after having died "a sudden death".
One day we were discussing Buchenwald and the allied
claim that it was the Nazis who had bombed this concentration camp. Then one P.W. said: "I don't believe
the Nazis would waste their bombs for such a thing.
It would have been easier for them to bring the prisoners to our town (Merseburg) and to the underground
factory. From there, every day about 30 people are
killed and carried away. Until such a death, the
concentration camp prisoners can do plenty of useful
work."

I have constantly tried to learn more details from the P.W.s,
but every time they smiled back with a knowing glance and a
twinkle of the eye, saying: "You know yourself, I needn't tell
you."

These are things one doesn't talk about. It is not good
manners to ask for details of a murder. And moreover, they are
afraid of talking. Even now, the P.W.s are afraid because, if
they talk, tomorrow, it may be their turn. As long as the Nazi
terror machine is existing anywhere on earth, few German tongues
will become talkative.

Those living in the West of South of Germany are regarded
as lucky. For those living in the East or South-East Germany,
there is a dark future ahead, in the opinion of the P.W.s.
They regard it as most unjust that German territory should be
ceded. "You can't take away a man's house or the ground it
stands on." Now they begin to understand that the cession of
German territory, the occupation of the whole country, and other
measures of retaliation, are only caused by Hitler's own war and
occupation policy. Differently from those P.W.s, ready for
cooperation, whom I met during my period of preparation, all of
them (except one, named Schulz) are against the cession of German
territory, unconditional surrender, etc. They judge the allied
politics according to their propaganda effect and misjudge that
it is just the "unconditional surrender," which means
definitely the material and mental conquest of Nazism, and this
event will be much more decisive for Germany's future than the
best propaganda slogan. When the unconditional surrender of
the Nazis becomes effective, the stage will be prepared for the
reeducation of the Germans to accept democracy. There is no
chance of coming to a national understanding with Germany as long
as the present German arrogance is the ruling factor. Those
who have murdered millions of human beings and, ultimately, only
with a cynical twinkling of the eyes must get his punishment, lest
he goes on murdering.

The treatment in the camp is a first stage of education:
the P.W.s get as much (or as little) food as the Germans in
their beloved homeland. It would be desirable for them to be
taught that it is not difficulties of transport causing these
restrictions, but the German nation's war guilt.

e) Those in the "cage" were men between 17 and 58, from
all ranks and classes, from privates to sergeant-major. But their
moods and opinions were fairly uniform, just products of uniform
Nazi propaganda. Their feelings were neutralized by what they
had seen, and lived through, at home and at the front. Even the
fate of their families left them almost indifferent. They had
seen so many people die, so many towns crumble into ruins, that
you have a feeling of their being unable to think in any other
terms.

What they think about the Jewish problem must be regarded
as typical. One evening, when sitting round the fireplace, I
had an opportunity of starting this discussion with five men.

Plenty of jokes were made about the best way of committing suicide.
One of them said a "shot in the neck" was advisable. I replied
that he gave this advice to the wrong address and got the answer:
"Yes, that's a matter for the S.S." Another P.W. added that the
S.S. had changed it's name into "J.S." meaning Jews shot. In the
ensuing discussion, the following opinions were expressed:

1) It has been a mistake to start Nazi rule by solving the
Jewish problem. The liquidation of the Jews should have been post-
poned till after victory. As it was, we only brought the Jews of
the U.S.A. and England into the frontline against us.

2) Only the Poles are to have the advantage of the German
Jew policy because they have got rid of their exploiters. The
Poles, later on, will be very grateful for this achievement.

3) It has been a mistake to describe the Jews as an inferior
race. On the contrary, the Germans should have described them as
being of equal value, as well as the Japs. In the history of man-
kind, they have played a valuable part. The Jews are cunning and
tough. Proof of this is the difficulty of exterminating them.
Many Jews would have become Nazis. By exploiting their help, their
tricks, and their international connections, we would have won the
war.

4) The Jews, too, are human beings. They have, of course,
bad qualities of character and smell differently, like the negroes,
for instance, but you could have let them alone and they would
have licked the Nazi boots.

5) The Wehrmacht and Luftwaffe always have protected the Jews.
In the Luftwaffe, we had 6,000 Jews in a repair work-camp. They
worked excellently. When the S.S. came in order to "liquidate"
them, the camp commander put up machine guns because he wanted to
keep them. Near Brest, we had a Jewish Labour company working
marvellously. They did the most difficult work without ever
complaining. Only the S.S. treated them rather badly. Later
they were captured by the Americans.

6) An elderly P.W., from the district of Breslau, a former
business man, took a decent and clear stand defending the Jews.
He was against the war, and probably, against Hitler. He said
Hitler was a megalomaniac and made no secret of his anti-Hitler
feelings. The others didn't take him seriously and laughed at
him. He couldn't pull himself together, didn't wash, etc., and
seemed apathetic.

- - - - - - - - -   - - - - -

Some youngsters showed a surprising readiness to discuss new
ideas. They did not accept their fate as unalterable but tried to
discover the reasons why. They were not so demoralized as the
other P.W.s and had no worries.

f) Parachutists are believed to be real daredevils, partly
because of their age class, partly their training. In the cage,
they are believed to be very unpopular with the Allies. They are
famous for heavy street fighting and, as a parachutist, you are
asked about this many times. Their methods of jumping, of landing,
and their training are different from the American and English
ways of training. I dare say that the American technique is
better. During my training period, I found out that the parachutists have a special way of stringing the laces of their jumping shoes. Twice I was recognised as a parachutist by this way
of lacing my shoes. It was an excellent detail which saved me
much talking and made my story very convincing.

Parachutists, traditionally, are good comrades which, of
course, is to be observed especially when there is a fight on.
All feel proud of their war work: "Whatever you may think about

Hitler and the war, you must have the right heart for a jump from
your air plane" is what one parachutist said to me. Not a single
one of them had the slightest doubt about what I told them and,
usually, it was I who did the questioning. I said I was looking
for a comrade whom I had lost while being captured. Since, during
my training period, I had seen him many times, I could give a
detailed description of him. So I was in a position to put very
precise questions but the replies were very vague. As a rule,
the P.W.s don't know what was going on in France and only remembered their own small place.

g) The P.W.s have a suspicion that "informers" are being
kept among them in order to pass on information to the American
camp authorities. Generally, they try to take care of informers
but this can be explained, to a certain extent, by the general
suspicion everybody has against everybody, the result of the Nazi
spy system. On January 22/23, a new transport was assembled for
shipping to the U.S.A., from our cage about 250 men. Everybody
was surprised that 7 of the "permanent" inmates were included in
the list. Normally, the "permanents" remain in the cage. Later on
a P.W. told me the reason why: these 7 men had started a course
of English. An "informer" had reported this to the Americans as
a "Nazi meeting". So they were shipped to the U.S.A. as being
"suspicious".

I am, of course, not in a position to find out whether this
is true or not, but it is a fact that "meetings" of the "permanents" are being held.

One man being suspected as a spy was shown to me but I could-
n't find out his name. He is tall, moves quickly (possibly a
sportsman), has dark, nearly black hair, strong growth of hair,
narrow face, medium nose (long), white teeth visible when smiling,
characteristic face with energetic features, his body of normal
proportions. He speaks German with Rhineland dialect and I was
told that he speaks good French with "Southern" accent. He belongs
to the "permanents".

Two other P.Ws are also suspected of being informers but
I was unable to find out any details about them. Two of them
allegedly belong to the "permanents", the third one to the cage.

The first mentioned is said to have become a member of the
"permanents", by order of the American staff, not suggested by
P.W.s.

CONCLUSIONS

One week's life in the "cage" is a good school. When living
among Germans and adapting yourself to German surroundings, you
learn more than can be laid down in one report. You get acquainted
with their language and their interests and can describe them.
But it is difficult to give a survey of those innumerable small
remarks you hear, of the impression these men make after having
lived 12 years under such a dictatorship, and how these beings have
developed under the influence of the war. Another difficulty is
that, many times, you feel tempted to state things which your
wishful thinking wants you to discover, or that you collect "impressions" answering to your own ideas about Hitler's Germany. It
therefore, is most important to keep to facts and not to impress
sions. The P.W.s in the cage are a good cross-section of the
average man in Germany. Those P.W.s cooperating with us, and
employed for propaganda, and interrogated during our time of
preparation, are by far not such a good cross-section. There is
a great difference between the average P.W. in the cage and other
special groups. For our purposes, the average P.W. is much more
important and instructive.

What I found about the morale of the P.W. and signs of
demoralization, their selfishness, their autocratic behaviour,
and their corruption, allows for conclusions to be drawn which

XXXXXXXXXXXXX may be useful for our future activity. The same
applies to the chance of exploiting anti-Hitler tendencies and the
slogan "pro-German and therefore anti-Hitler".

Just to put down a personal impression: Allied soldiers,
when defeated, become harder and better soldiers, German soldiers
are worn out, become hopeless and lose their fighting spirit.

I. Description of 4 P.W.s who may be used.

SCHIERZ, Winfried, in cage A on Jan. 23, 1945.

19-20 years old, middle class man, Grammar school education,
wanted to study science of technique, airman on Eastern and Western front, strong anti-Hitler tendencies, apparently influenced by
parents and friends, describes Brüning as the last genuine representative of Democracy, knows that Brüning is in U.S.A. and hopes
he (who?) will come and speak in P.W. camp.(?). Vague but decent
way of thinking as to the Jewish question, strictest opposition to
S.S. and its methods, tries to think independently, discusses with
his friend (next below) history, literature, mathematics, etc.,
hoping to withstand obscurantism of military service, feels distinctly German and can't understand American and English opinions about
Germany. He might be useful for propaganda work. Was taken prisoner near Strassburg. Has good knowledge of Luftwaffe. A good
voice, speaking without dialect. Hometown Merseburg.

Further intensive interrogation necessary because I could not
show my hands. It is possible that, in the beginning, he will be
uncommunicative if interrogated by American personnel. Clever
and cunning interrogator needed.

SCHMELZER, Alfred, on Jan 23, 1945, transferred from cage A
to cage B. 19-20 years old, naval cadet (to become officer), training finished as teacher at elementary school, intelligent, from
Lauma, friend of Schierz" (see above). Strong anti-Hitler tendency,
reserved, independently thinking and tries to form his own world
philosophy. Speaks English, probably influenced by parents.
Reserved and critical towards the Allies, but hopes that the U.S.A
democracy will take the lead. Was forced into Officer's career,
in spite of his antipathy against the bad repute of the officers.
Has a good voice, free of dialect, has good knowledge of navy and
education problems. Must be more interrogated and is likely to
cooperate if treated in the right way.

Both chaps try to get rid of the Nazis and their ideologies.
In an anti-Nazi camp they, probably, will develop quickly. Still
under the influence of Nazi propaganda and education. Both have
the advantage of not being careerists, contrary to most people
in the anti-Nazi camp. It might be good to keep them together and
use them together.

MUNCK, Wilhelm, on Jan 23, 1945, in cage A, infantrist, 35
years old, electro-welder at I.G. Farben, Halle. Anti-Nazi. Probably an old enemy of Hitler's. Strictly anti-militaristic. Not
bound to a political party, perhaps originally a trade unionist.
His family and parents are anti-Nazis. He told me how, for several
years he successfully avoided getting into a Nazi organization.
Clear understanding of war situation, knows that Allied victory
is imminent, and hopes for it. Embittered and reserved. Quiet
type. Thinks independently. Has no clear knowledge of allied
politics. Worked 6 months as guard in concentration camp Torgau.
There was one K.Z. for Wehrmacht members, another one for political
prisoners. Attaches great importance to his having been only a
member of the guards outside the camp. Knows much about treatment
in the camp and must have seen horrible scenes. He says, "It was
high time for me to leave; otherwise I should have gone mad."

Probably willing to cooperate. Good speaker but with slight
Saxon dialect. May be of good value at working out programmes, etc

A good source of information. Can be used for other purposes, e.g.
in camp administration. At any rate, further interrogation is
advisable where he should be taught that the allies expect the
anti-Nazis to cooperate more. No careerist!

KATISCH. Kurt, 33 years old, peasant, from the district of Leipzig.
Strictly against the war, anti-Nazi, good-natured, ready to help.
Hopes for an allied victory, if only in order to end the war.
Knows about France, the homeland, German officers. Willing to work
Probably prepared to cooperate. Further interrogation may make
sure whether he can be used for propaganda, but can, at any rate,
be employed for more collaboration in the cage or in Labour camps,
even for confidential work. Quiet, reserved type, should be
subjected to clever and friendly interrogation.

Postscript. These four suggestions have been discussed by the
three of us (Bill, Dolf, Phil). The result of our discussions
is laid down in the valuation given above. (Since we left the
camp, the four men have been taken over by the camp commander).

II. Suggestions concerning education of P.W.s and how it may be
                         improved

    When making a suggestion, it must be taken into account that
the camp commander is very short of staff.

    1) There should be given an opportunity of publishing the
daily war reports in the cage. It is not very useful to send a
newspaper into the cage because only few people can read it and
the Nazis have the opportunity of distorting the news. It would
be better to put up a board and to phasard the news visible for
everybody.

    2) A kind of newspaper publishing the P.W. broadcasts. In
the anti-Nazi camp, this material could be easily collected. This
paper (also publishing news) ought to ask the P.W.s to
work out their own material for broadcasts. In this way, the anti-
Nazis would have an opportunity of offering their own services
and proving the sincerity of their intentions. Furthermore, German
anti-Nazis would be in a position to influence the P.W.s and, thus
to speed up the liveration from Nazi influence. Last, but not least,
the broadcasts would be improved because, doubtless, there will be
many P.W.s giving us good chances for good propaganda.

APPENDIX F

German and English translation of *Der Spiegel* article titled FALSE FRIENDS
November 1, 2004

US-Präsident Bush (in der Normandie 2002)
Orden für Kommunisten

ZEITGESCHICHTE

Falsche Freunde

Tausende deutscher Exilanten kämpften im Zweiten Weltkrieg für die Amerikaner gegen Hitler. Auf Betreiben Hillary Clintons zeichnet der US-Präsident nun erstmals zwei von ihnen aus. SED-Dokumente belegen: Beide waren sowjetische Agenten.

Spione Ruh, Lindner (1945): *Ehrung durch den Klassenfeind*

Die Stimmung der drei Männer auf dem kleinen Flugplatz Watton bei Cambridge war angespannt. Die beiden Deutschen nahmen noch einen großen Schluck Brandy aus dem Flachmann ihres amerikanischen Führungsoffiziers, ehe sie bewaffnet und mit Helm in den schwarz gestrichenen A-26-Bomber stiegen. Es war, wie der US-Geheimdienstler später berichtete, ein aufwühlender Augenblick.

Der nun beginnende Einsatz von Anton Ruh, 33, und Paul Lindner, 34, zählte zu den gefährlichsten Missionen, die deutsche Emigranten für die Alliierten im Zweiten Weltkrieg übernommen haben. Mit Fallschirmen sprangen sie im Morgengrauen des 2. März 1945 einige Kilometer nordwestlich Berlins ab, um in der Reichshauptstadt Hitler-Gegner zu kontaktieren

und Informationen für alliierte Bomber zu sammeln.

Acht Wochen versteckten sich Ruh, ein gelernter Steindrucker, und Lindner, von Haus aus Dreher, in einer Laubensiedlung in Berlin-Britz. Sie teilten der Londoner Außenstelle des amerikanischen Geheimdienstes OSS die Lage von Munitionsfabriken mit, informierten darüber, dass das Kraftwerk Klingenberg noch in Betrieb war, und legten nahe, die Berliner S-Bahn zu bombardieren.

Von großer Bedeutung war keine dieser Informationen, doch nur wenigen der 38 Teams, die das OSS in der Endphase des Zweiten Weltkriegs über Deutschland absetzte, gelang es, überhaupt Kontakt mit London herzustellen. Nach dem Sieg der Alliierten sollten Ruh und Lindner für ihren Mut ausgezeichnet werden. Die Eh-

rung kam aus unbekannten Gründen nie zu Stande.

Das will jetzt, knapp 60 Jahre später, die Regierung von US-Präsident George W. Bush nachholen. Den beiden längst verstorbenen Hitler-Gegnern ist postum der „Silver Star" verliehen worden, eine hohe militärische Auszeichnung. Es ist das erste Mal, dass Deutschen, die auf Seiten der Amerikaner kämpften, eine solche Anerkennung zuteil wird.

Bedanken können sich die Familien der Geehrten dafür bei dem New Yorker Rechtsanwalt Jonathan Gould und der US-Senatorin Hillary Clinton. Advokat Gould, dessen Vater einst die beiden Widerstandskämpfer das Agentenwesen lehrte, hatte bei Recherchen zur Familiengeschichte herausgefunden, dass Ruh und Lindner nach 1945 leer ausgegangen waren. Er wandte sich deshalb an die prominente Politikerin, die den Bundesstaat New York im Senat vertritt. Hillary Clinton bat ihrerseits die konservative Bush-Regierung um Prüfung – mit Erfolg.

Vergangene Woche traf der Bescheid bei ihr ein. Obwohl Ruh während des Kalten Krieges in der DDR zum Botschafter aufstieg und auch Lindner in der SED Karriere machte, hatte das zuständige US-Verteidigungsministerium offenbar keine Bedenken.

Was freilich weder Clinton noch Gould oder die Militärs wussten: Die beiden für die Ehrung vorgeschlagenen Deutschen kämpften nicht nur im Namen der Freiheit gegen Hitler, sie kundschafteten zugleich im Auftrag Moskaus den amerikanischen Bündnispartner aus.

Dass Ruh und Lindner auf zwei Schultern trugen, reklamierten die ostdeutschen Kommunisten schon in den siebziger Jahren als Erfolg im Kampf gegen die Nazis für sich. Doch Zweifel schienen angebracht, denn Übertreibung und Irreführung gehörten zum Handwerkszeug der Machthaber jenseits der Mauer. Dem SPIEGEL vorliegende SED-Dokumente liefern nun aber die Gewissheit: Ruh und Lindner spionierten tatsächlich für die sowjetischen Genossen.

Beide Kommunisten mussten 1953 vor der Zentralen Parteikontrollkommission der SED aussagen. DDR-Diktator Walter Ulbricht misstraute der ideologischen Standfestigkeit jener Genossen, die vor Hitler in westliche Länder geflohen waren, und ließ sie überprüfen. Lindner und Ruh wurden nach ihrem Einsatz für das OSS befragt. Da berichteten sie von ihrem Doppelspiel.

Schon Anfang der dreißiger Jahre hatten die beiden Berliner für den Geheimdienst der KPD gearbeitet. Kurz vor ihrer Dienstverpflichtung auf amerikanischer Seite schwor sie der amtierende KPD-Verbin-

Rotarmisten in Berlin, Waffenbrüder Stalin, Roosevelt in Jalta 1945: *Hitler-Gegner ohne Berührungsängste*

dungsmann zu den Sowjets ein: „Ab jetzt musst du dich so betrachten, dass du für unsere sowjetischen Freunde arbeitest, und behandele die Fragen so, dass du unter Befehlsgewalt der Roten Armee stehst."

Der militärische Nachrichtendienst Moskaus wollte vor allem die Methoden ausspähen, mit denen die amerikanische Konkurrenz Agenten trainierte. Lindner informierte bereitwillig über das Ausbildungsprogramm: montags Taktikschulung, mittwochs Umgang mit SS-Patrouillen, freitags Studium von Landkarten.

Die beiden Kommunisten hatten sich im Spätsommer 1944 vom OSS anwerben lassen, als die Amerikaner verzweifelt deutschsprachige Agenten suchten, um sie hinter der Front abzusetzen. US-Truppen näherten sich der Grenze des Dritten Reiches, doch Washington führte in Hitlers Imperium nur eine Hand voll Spione, weil US-Oberbefehlshaber Dwight D. Eisenhower davon ausgegangen war, dass der Krieg schon auf französischem Boden siegreich enden würde.

US-Leutnant Joseph Gould – vor dem Krieg Gewerkschaftsfunktionär in der Filmbranche – erhielt den Auftrag, sich auf der Suche nach Kandidaten unter deutschen Emigranten in London umzutun. Dass deren Herz oft links schlug, war bekannt, aber das OSS hatte keine Alternative.

Als gewiefter Großstädter beschloss der 29-jährige New Yorker Gould, zuerst Londoner Buchläden anzulaufen. Ein Händler in der New Bond Street vermittelte ihm schließlich einen Kontakt. Gould geriet an den deutschen Sowjetagenten Erich Henschke alias Karl Castro, der sofort seine Führungsleute informierte. Die waren, so Henschke laut SED-Unterlagen, „begeistert".

Bald konnte der Mann Moskaus dem Amerikaner eine Kandidatenliste vorlegen. Die Lebensläufe waren sorgfältig frisiert – angeblich alles Sozialdemokraten oder Ge-

werkschafter, sozusagen Kollegen Goulds; von KPD-Mitgliedschaft kein Wort.

Gould suchte sieben Männer aus, darunter auch Lindner und Ruh. Für das damals üppige Gehalt von 331 Dollar im Monat und eine satte Lebensversicherung heuerten sie beim Klassenfeind an.

Im November 1944 begann die Ausbildung. Die Doppelagenten trainierten Fallschirmspringen und lernten im OSS-Lager in Ruislip bei London, wie man Papiere fälscht und Menschen lautlos tötet. Sie bekamen Schießunterricht und übten das Dechiffrieren codierter Botschaften, die später die BBC senden sollte. Vor allem an den dafür notwendigen Schlüsseln waren die Sowjets interessiert; Lindner gab das Wissen weiter.

Ob Ausbilder Gould ahnte, wen er vor sich hatte, lässt sich nicht mit Sicherheit beurteilen. Lindner gewann den Eindruck, dass der OSS-Mann insgeheim mit dem Kommunismus sympathisierte: „Man hatte annehmen können, dass er ein amerikanischer Genosse ist." Unter ihrem Kriegspräsidenten Franklin D. Roosevelt hatten die Amerikaner kaum Berührungsängste. Um Hitler zu bezwingen, erklärte OSS-Chef William Donovan einmal, würde er auch den sowjetischen Diktator Josef Stalin „auf die Lohnliste setzen".

Im Januar 1945 schickte der Geheimdienst die Emigranten, die nie gedient hatten, in Landser-uniformen für einige Tage in ein Kriegsgefangenenlager – ein Test. Als die Männer unter den Wehrmachtsoldaten nicht auffielen, konnte die Operation mit dem Codenamen Hammer beginnen.

Von den Amerikanern bekamen Ruh und Lindner 14 000 Reichsmark, zwei Diamanten und rund hundert Kilogramm Kaffee für den Schwarzmarkt mit auf den Weg; von den Sowjets erhielten sie nur die Order, in Berlin Kontakt zu einem Verbindungsmann aufzunehmen und dessen Anweisungen zu folgen.

Anwalt Gould *Einsatz für Vaters Schützlinge*

Doch der sowjetische Kontaktmann erschien nicht; und an die Amerikaner konnten Ruh und Lindner ihre Beobachtungen in Berlin auch nicht wie gewünscht durchgeben. Zwar hatte sie das OSS mit der neuesten technischen Errungenschaft versorgt, dem Joan/Eleanor-Funkgerät, benannt nach den Freundinnen der beiden Erfinder. Der Handy-Vorläufer ermöglichte es, mit der Besatzung eines Flugzeugs in zehn Kilometer Höhe zu sprechen.

Aber nur einmal kam eine brauchbare Verbindung zu Stande, und der Großteil des Gesprächs drehte sich um Nachschubwünsche der beiden Agenten, denen der Proviant auszugehen drohte. Es habe eben eine Weile gedauert, ehe sie sich eingerichtet hatten, sagte Lindner 1953 im SED-Verhör und räumte ein: „Als wir zur Entfaltung kommen konnten, war der Krieg vorbei."

Am 24. April marschierte die Rote Armee in Neukölln ein. Ruh und Lindner gaben sich sofort als Freunde der Sowjetmacht zu erkennen, was ihnen die Russen vor Ort allerdings nicht glaubten. Sie durften die Einheit nicht verlassen und wurden als US-Agenten Mitte Juni 1945 den Amerikanern bei Leipzig übergeben. Diese schafften ihre Schützlinge in die OSS-Dependance nach Paris und ließen sich dort berichten, wie der Einsatz gelaufen war. Dann wurden Ruh und Lindner entlassen, sie kehrten für einige Monate nach England zurück und zogen schließlich in den Ostteil Berlins. DDR-Botschafter Ruh erlag 1964 einem Herzanfall in Bukarest, Lindner starb 1969 in seiner Heimatstadt.

Lange wohl war einigen Amerikanern freilich nicht gewesen, als sie die beiden ziehen ließen. Sie ahnten bereits, dass der neue Feind im Osten stand, und fürchteten, dem Waffenbruder von einst könne das hochmoderne Joane/Eleanor-Funkgerät in die Hände fallen.

Ganz überflüssige Sorge. Ruh und Lindner hatten den Apparat zwar kurz vor Kriegsende vergraben, weil sie eine Verhaftung fürchteten. Als aber Sowjetagent Henschke 1947 von ihnen verlangte, das Gerät wieder auszugraben, mühten sich die Spione vergebens. Sie fanden die Stelle nicht mehr.   KLAUS WIEGREFE

False Friends

Thousands of German exiles fought with the Americans against Hitler during the Second World War. The American president has now honored two of them on Hillary Clinton's instigation. Socialist Unity Party documents show that both were Soviet agents.

The mood was tense among the three men gathered at the small airfield in Watton near Cambridge. Both Germans took a deep swill of brandy from the hip flask of their American commanding officer before boarding, armed and helmeted, the black A-26 bomber. It was, as the U.S. intelligence officer later reported, a stirring moment.

The now-commencing mission of Anton Ruh (33) and Paul Lindner (34) counted among the most dangerous Allied operations undertaken by German emigrants during the Second World War. They parachuted from the plane a few kilometers northwest of Berlin at dawn on March 2, 1945 to contact opponents of Hitler and collect information for Allied bombers in the capital.

For eight weeks Ruh, a trained lithographer, and Lindner, a lathe operator, hid in Berlin-Britz. They notified the London Branch of the American intelligence agency OSS about the state of munitions factories, informed them that the Klingenberg power plant was still active, and suggested bombarding of Berlin's commuter rail system (*S-Bahn*).

None of this information was of particular importance, but only a few of the 38 OSS teams deposited into the Germany during the war's concluding months succeeded in making any contact whatsoever with the London office. After the Allied victory Ruh and Lindner were to be honored for their bravery. For reasons unknown the distinction never took place.

Now, 60 years later, the administration of American President George W. Bush wants to make up for it. Both of the long-dead anti-Hitler combatants have been posthumously awarded the "Silver Star," a notable military decoration. It is the first time that a German fighting on the side of the Americans has received such recognition.

The families of the honored can thank the efforts of New York lawyer Jonathan Gould and American Senator Hillary Clinton for it. While researching his family history, attorney Gould, whose father once taught the two resistance fighters the life of an [secret] agent, learned that Ruh and Lindner had been left empty-handed after 1945. For this reason he turned to the prominent politician representing the State of New York. Hillary Clinton then asked the conservative Bush administration for a review of the case — with success.

Last week she received their decision. Although Ruh rose to the position of ambassador in East Germany and Lindner made his career in the Socialist Union Party, the deciding officials in the American Ministry of Defense had no apparent objections.

What of course neither Clinton nor Gould nor the military knew was that the Germans nominated for the distinction fought not only in the name of freedom against Hitler, but reconnoitered simultaneously on Moscow's behalf against their American ally.

In the seventies the East German Communists credited themselves for Ruh's and Lindner's double agency, which they saw as proof of success in the fight against the Nazis. But then doubts arose, since exaggeration and deception belonged to the tools of those in power on the other side of the wall. The materials acquired by *Der Spiegel*, however, show with certainty that Ruh and Lindner were actually spies for the Soviet Comrades.

In 1953 both Communists had to testify before the Central Party Control Commission of the Socialist Union Party (SED). Walter Ulbricht, dictator of the German Democratic Republic, mistrusted the ideological steadiness of those Comrades who'd fled to Western countries before Hitler, and had them closely scrutinized. Lindner and Ruh were asked about their mission for the OSS; they then gave account of their duplicity.

Both Berliners were already employed by German Communist Party intelligence during the early thirties. Shortly before pledging their services to the American side they were committed to the sitting Communist Party liaison for the Soviets: "from now on you must recognize that you work for our Soviet friends, and treat the questions with the knowledge that you stand under the direct authority of the Red Army itself."

The military intelligence corps in Moscow wanted above all to spy on the methods with which their American rivals trained their agents. Lindner informed eagerly about the training program: tactics school Mondays, how to deal with SS patrols Wednesdays, cartographical studies Fridays.

Both Communists let themselves be recruited by the OSS, as the Americans desperately sought German-speaking agents to place behind the front. U.S. troops were nearing the borders of the Third Reich, yet Washington commanded no more than a handful of spies in Hitler's Reich because Dwight D. Eisenhower, Supreme Allied Commander of the Armed Forces, had expected the war to end victoriously on French soil.

U.S. Lieutenant Joseph Gould—a union official in the film industry before the war—was instructed to look for candidates among the German emigrants in London. It was known that their hearts leaned a little to the left, but the OSS had no alternative.

A streetwise city man, the 29 year old New Yorker decided to begin at the bookstore. A merchant on New Bond Street finally got him in touch with someone. Gould met the Soviet agent Erich Henschke, alias Karl Kastro, who immediately informed his superiors. They were, according to Henschke in the SED files, "enthusiastic."

Soon Moscow's man had a list of candidates ready for the American. Their backgrounds were carefully doctored—allegedly all of them had been Social Democrats or unionists, colleagues of Gould, so to speak. Of their membership in the German Communist Party (KPD), not a word.

Gould selected seven men, among them Lindner and Ruh. They were hired by the "foe of the classes" at the then-luxurious salary of $331 a month plus a full life insurance policy.

Training began in November 1944. The double agents learned how to parachute, and at the OSS camp in Ruislip near London how to falsify papers and to kill people silently. They received shooting lessons and practiced deciphering encoded messages that the BBC was to later send. The Soviets were interested above all in the necessary codes; Lindner passed this knowledge on.

As to whether their teacher Gould had an idea of whom he was dealing with—there's no way of telling for sure. Lindner had the impression that the OSS man secretly sympathized with the Communists: "One could guess that he is an American Comrade." Under their war president, Franklin D. Roosevelt, the Americans scarcely feared such contact. In order to defeat Hitler, the head of OSS William Donovan once declared that he would even add the Soviet dictator Joseph Stalin "to the salary list."

In January 1945 the intelligence service dressed the emigrants, who had never served, in German uniforms and sent them into a POW camp for a few days—a test. When it was confirmed that the men did not stand out to the *Wehrmacht* soldiers, the operation codenamed "Hammer" could begin.

Ruh and Lindner received 14,000 Reichmarks, two diamonds, and around one hundred kilograms of coffee for the black market from the Americans to carry in with them; from the Soviets, they received only the order to contact a liaison in Berlin and to follow his instructions.

But the Soviet liaison never appeared, and Ruh and Lindner could not pass on their observations to the Americans as wished. It is true that the OSS supplied them with the latest technological feat, the Joan/Eleanor transmitter-receiver, named after the girlfriends of both inventors. This precursor to the cell-phone made it possible to speak with the crew of an airplane ten kilometers up.

Yet only once was a serviceable connection established, and most of the conversation revolved around the supplies requested by both agents, whose provisions were threatening to run out. It had taken a while before they had set themselves up, Lindner said during his 1953 SED hearing, and conceded, "By the team we were ready to unfold [begin], the war was over."

On April 24 the Red Army marched into Neukölln. Ruh and Lindner immediately presented themselves as friends of the Soviet powers, which the Russians did not believe on the spot. They weren't permitted to leave the unit and were handed over in Leipzig mid-June 1945 as U.S. agents to the Americans. The OSS charges were both sent to Paris, where they were debriefed on their mission. After they were released they returned to England for a few months, then moved in the end to East Berlin. GDR ambassador Ruh suffered a heart attack 1964 in Bucharest, Lindner died in his hometown.

Of course some Americans were not entirely at ease when the move of both men was permitted. They already suspected that the new enemy was in the east, and feared that the highly modem Joan/Eleanor radio might fall into the hands of their former brothers in arms.

A superfluous concern. Ruh and Lindner had indeed buried the apparatus shortly before the end of the war because they feared imprisonment. When in 1947 the Soviet agent Henschke demanded, however, that they dig it up, the spies' efforts were in vain. They no longer found the place.

APPENDIX G

Recommendation for award of the *SILVER STAR* to PICKAXE mission Agents Waiter Struwe and Emil Konhauser, June 19, 1945

S E C R E T

HQ & HQ DETACHMENT
OFFICE OF STRATEGIC SERVICES
EUROPEAN THEATER OF OPERATIONS
UNITED STATES ARMY
(MAIN)

APO 413
19 June 1945

SUBJECT: Recommendation for Award of SILVER STAR

TO : Commanding General, European Theater of Operations, APO 887,
U. S. Army

1. a. It is recommended that Walter STRUWE, German civilian,
attached to the Office of Strategic Services, European Theater of
Operations, APO 413, United States Army, be awarded the SILVER STAR.

   b. STRUWE was serving as a secret agent at the time of the
service for which this award is recommended.

   c. Name and address of nearest relative:

        Leonie Struwe (wife)
        32 Granville Road
        Fallowfield, Manchester 14

   d. Entered military service from Manchester, England, as a
civilian with the Office of Strategic Services.

   e. Decorations previously awarded: None

   f. The entire service of Walter STRUWE has been honorable since
the rendition by him of the service upon which this recommendation is
based.

   g. A similar recommendation for this individual has not been
submitted.

2. a. The officer recommending this award has personal knowledge
of the service upon which this award is based.

   b. This recommendation is supported by official records of the
Office of Strategic Services.

3. a. Walter STRUWE, while serving in close collaboration with the
Army of the United States, distinguished himself by gallantry in action.

S E C R E T

    Following the invasion of France, the Labor Division of the Secret Intelligence Branch of the Office of Strategic Services, pursuant to a SHAEF approved plan, was engaged in introducing undercover agents into Germany for the purpose of securing military and other intelligence desired by the attacking Allied army groups.

    WALTER STRUWE, a German citizen who had been active in the anti-Nazi underground movement of that country, volunteered for one such project. He was assigned a team-mate with whom he was to be parachuted to the vicinity of Frankfurt-am-Main. The rapid advance of the Allied armies made this plan impracticable, and on 2 April 1945, the target city for the team was changed to Landshut, in what was expected to be the German southern redoubt, an area under rigid Gestapo surveillance.

    They were able to obtain only a rudimentary briefing on the area because their departure was imminent. In spite of the eleventh hour change in plans necessitating the discarding of safe addresses and contacts previously obtained, STRUWE and his team-mate volunteered to operate in this important transportation hub. On 4 April 1945 dressed in civilian clothes and equipped with false identity documents, they were introduced behind the German lines by a parachute drop into the area where they could anticipate no aid from persons on the ground.

    The drop was accomplished on a moonless night, which added greatly to the hazard. Immediately after landing, STRUWE attempted to make contact with his team-mate, but failed. Only because they had previously arranged to follow a certain route from the landing point to Landshut, did they meet on the second day.

    Their supply container, which was parachuted with the men, unexpectedly added to the danger. It was impossible to locate the container in the darkness, but it had to be found and buried. It was finally located at dawn. In spite of the danger incurred by remaining in the neighborhood of the drop, STRUWE and his partner spent most of the next day in the vicinity before they had an opportunity to dispose of the container and the parachute.

    Upon entering Landshut, the two men investigated the possibilities of legalizing their positions by registering with the authorities. They found that most of the foreign workers were assigned to farmers or to work in other cities after a few days. In order to be most effective in their work, STRUWE and his partner lived in a hiding place in a forest and carried on without registering.

    STRUWE had in his possession secret communications equipment, the discovery of which would have been instantly compromising. In order to establish contact with the Office of Strategic Services communications system, it was necessary to repair to a comparatively secluded spot in open country, set up, and operate the equipment - all on a precise time schedule. This STRUWE and his coworker accomplished on seven different occasions, notwithstanding the always imminent danger of detection. During the last contact on the night of 28-29 April, the men were situated directly between the opposing fire of American tanks and the German artillery battery in the vicinity of Tiefenbach. Although their position was extremely dangerous, the men stayed with their equipment as long as it was possible to convey any intelligence.

S E C R E T

Among the observations and intelligence conveyed to the Office of Strategic Services in London (and in turn relayed to the appropriate authorities) by the men were the following:

All railway traffic through Landshut was paralyzed by the severe airraid on 16 April 1945; between 5,000 and 6,000 soldiers were stationed in Landshut; during the 12 days prior to 26 April, an entire Waffen-SS division passed through Landshut bound for Munich; in addition 400 to 500 soldiers and officers of other branches passed through Landshut daily for the same destination; soldiers in a boat were occupied at the left pillar of the upper Isar bridge, probably mining it.

Before Landshut was taken by the American Army, STRUWE and his team-mate were able to give important information to the American G-2 regarding the defences of the city. Among the observations passed on were:

Fresh troops appeared in the city on 27 April pursuant to a last minute decision to defend the city; tank blocks were erected on all strategic roads and the Isar bridges mined or blown up; the position of a German artillery battery and of a key observation post in a woods along the Isar.

At a meeting of the Operations Committee of the Office of Strategic Services in charge of intelligence procurement, it was decided to send a message of congratulations to STRUWE and his team-mate, then still in the field, on the excellence of their work. All agreed that the two men were outstanding in their high motivation and ability.

In the performance of the services described above, STRUWE spent 26 days behind enemy lines and he was not wounded.

4. Proposed Citation: For the SILVER STAR

WALTER STRUWE, for exceptionally meritorious and courageous action in volunteering for and successfully carrying out a secret and dangerous mission behind enemy lines, which benefitted the Armies of the Allied Nations in the prosecution of the war.

5. In order to support this recommendation, it has been necessary to divulge in the preceding paragraph information classified as Secret. However, the proposed citation has been made sufficiently general to permit publication of it separately with the classification Restricted.

JAMES R. FORGAN
Colonel, OSC
Commanding

S E C R E T

HQ & HQ DETACHMENT
OFFICE OF STRATEGIC SERVICES
EUROPEAN THEATER OF OPERATIONS
UNITED STATES ARMY
(MAIN)

APO 413
20 June 1945

SUBJECT: Recommendation for Award of SILVER STAR

TO : Commanding General, European Theater of Operations, APO 887,
U. S. Army

    1. a. It is recommended that EMIL KONHAUSER, German civilian,
attached to the Office of Strategic Services, European Theater of
Operations, APO 413, United States Army, be awarded the SILVER STAR.

    b. KONHAUSER was serving as a secret agent at the time of the
service for which this award is recommended.

    c. Name and address of nearest relative:

        Johanna Hopf Konhauser (wife)
        Friends Adult School
        Seattle, Yorkshire, England

    d. Entered military service from: Not applicable

    e. Decorations previously awarded: None

    f. The entire service of EMIL KONHAUSER has been honorable
since the rendition by him of the service upon which this recommendation
is based.

    g. A similar recommendation for this individual has not been
submitted.

    2. a. The officer recommending this award has personal knowledge
of the service upon which this award is based.

    b. This recommendation is supported by official records of the
Office of Strategic Services.

    3. a. EMIL KONHAUSER, while serving with the Army of the United
States, distinguished himself by gallantry in action.

    b. Detailed narrative of the services for which this award is
recommended.

    Following the invasion of France, the Labor Division of the
Secret Intelligence Branch of the Office of Strategic Services, pursuant
to a SHAEF approved plan, was engaged in introducing undercover agents into
Germany for the purpose of securing military and other intelligence
desired by the attacking Allied army groups.

    EMIL KONHAUSER, a German citizen living in England,
volunteered for one such project. KONHAUSER had been a leader of the anti-
Nazi underground in Germany until 1939. It was originally planned that
he and a team-mate would be dropped by parachute into the neighborhood of
Frankfurt-am-Main and operate there until the Allied armies approached.
Then they were expected to move to Nuernberg to obtain additional intelligence there.

    Before the men could be dropped, Frankfurt was already a
battle area, and the American Army was well on its way toward Nuernberg.
On 2 April 1945, the target city for the team was changed to Landshut, an
important transportation center far in advance of the Allied lines.

S E C R E T

Although KOHMAUSER and his team-mate knew nothing about
Landshut and the surrounding area, and although the entire area was under
the close scrutiny of the Gestapo, they volunteered to operate in that
city. On 4 April they were dropped by parachute into the vicinity of
Landshut in civilian clothes and with highly secret communications equipment, the finding of which by the enemy would have subjected the men to
torture and death.

The parachute drop was accomplished on a moonless night without
signal lights or any other possible aid from persons on the ground. The
darkness presented three great dangers: It was impossible to tell when
the ground would be hit; the two men on the team would undoubtedly lose
contact with each other upon landing; and the supply container which was
dropped with the team would be lost.

Because of careful plans previously made, KOHMAUSER was able
to find his partner on the next day. Their supply container which was
likewise dropped by parachute was located with the coming of daylight,
but it could not be reached because it landed on an open field where
movements might be observed. In spite of the danger of remaining in the
vicinity of the landing place, KOHMAUSER and his team-mate spent most of
the day in the area before they had an opportunity to dispose of their
supplies.

Although the two men were adequately supplied with forged
documents explaining their presence in Landshut, German regulations provided that all transients register with the authorities. KOHMAUSER and
his partner learned, however, that foreign workers were allowed to remain
in Landshut for only three days after registering, and then were assigned
to work for farmers or in other cities. Since legalizing their position
for the sake of their own safety meant that their usefulness would be
greatly diminished, KOHMAUSER and his team-mate found a hiding place in a
forest in which to live, and operated in the city without legal cover.

The communications sets carried by the men were of a highly
secret type, the discovery of which would have been instantly compromising.
In order to transmit intelligence, it was necessary to repair to a com-
paratively secluded spot in open country, set up, and operate the
equipment on a precise time schedule. Despite the great danger of
detection involved, the men appeared for each of the seven communications
contacts scheduled, one of the most noteworthy records made. During the
last contact on the night of 28-29 April, the men were situated between
the opposing fire of American tanks and the German artillery battery in
the vicinity of Tiefenbach. In spite of their extremely hazardous position,
they operated their equipment for the full contact period.

Among the observations and intelligence conveyed to the Office
of Strategic Services and in turn relayed to the appropriate authorities
were the following:

All railway traffic through Landshut was paralyzed by the
severe airraid on 16 April 1945; between 5,000 and 8,000 soldiers were
stationed in Landshut; during the 12 days prior to 25 April, an entire
Waffen-SS division passed through Landshut bound for Munich; in addition
400 to 500 soldiers and officers of other branches passed through Landshut
daily for the same destination; soldiers in a boat were occupied at the
left pillar of the upper Isar bridge, probably mining it.

S E C R E T

Before Landshut was taken by the American Army, KOMHAUSER and his team-mate were able to give important information to the American G-2 regarding the defenses of the city. Among the observations passed on were:

Fresh troops appeared in the city on 27 April pursuant to a last minute decision to defend the city; tank blocks were erected on all strategic roads and the Isar bridges mined or blown up; the position of a German artillery battery and of a key observation post in a woods along the Isar.

At a meeting of the Operations Committee of the Office of Strategic Services in charge of intelligence procurement, it was decided to send a message of congratulations to KOMHAUSER and his team-mate, then still in the field, on the excellence of their work. All agreed that the two men were outstanding in their high motivation and ability.

In the performance of the services described above, KOMHAUSER spent 26 days behind enemy lines and he was not wounded.

4. Proposed Citation: For the SILVER STAR.

EMIL KOMHAUSER, for exceptionally meritorious and courageous action in volunteering and successfully carrying out a secret and dangerous mission behind enemy lines, which benefitted the Armies of the Allied Nations in the prosecution of the war.

5. In order to support this recommendation, it has been necessary to divulge in the preceding paragraphs information classified as Secret. However, the proposed citation has been made sufficiently general to permit publication of it separately with the classification Restricted.

JAMES R. FORGAN
Colonel, GSC
Commanding

APPENDIX H

Memorandum from Lt. Commander Stephen Simpson

Re: Dispatch of the CHISEL Mission aircraft, March 20, 1945

CHISEL Mission Dispatch Report from OSS mission conducting officer Lt. Joseph Gould, March 20, 1945

Memorandum by Lt Comdr Stephen Simpson co-inventor of the "Joan-Eleanor" system concerning the loss of the A-26C on the first Red Stocking mission.

On March 19th orders were given and cancelled several times to fly the CHISEL mission (the first A-26 operation). It was brought to everyone's attention that the A-26 needed a 100 hour check and the radio altimeter needed recalibrating. The Loran and Gee navigation systems needed checking and that Lt Emmel had insufficient in the A-26 – he had only flown it twice at night.

Major Tresemer had only been in an A-26 once before and had been completely bewildered by "ground pilotage" at such a speed. None of the crew – pilot, navigator or bombardier had ever flown together before, and were unfamiliar with the ship as a whole.

It was finally decided to put the ship into the hanger for repair and inspection. At 4 o'clock Comdr Simpson heard a rumour that Col Upham had again changed his mind and proceeded to headquarters to find that this was true. Upon advising Col Upham that both engines were down, that the altimeter was not operating properly he was told to call the hanger and get the ship back into commission and have it ready by 7.30.

The whole crew advised the Colonel that it would be impossible to get the flight plan and mission organised by that time, but the colonel stated that this was an order from Headquarters and it had to be done. The weather section added to the unease of the crew, stating that a bad front would be crossing the area and conditions on the continent were not good.

The mission finally got off the ground at approximately 10.00 after instructions from Comdr Simpson and Lt Fogarty on operating the special apparatus in the ship they were not familiar with. Final statements were made by the pilot, navigator and bombardier to Col Upham that the trip was not feasible.

The aircraft did not return from the mission, it was found after the war on a moor in Germany with the remains of the crew. Although this train of events may sound inconceivable it shows the almost impossible decisions expected of a commanding officer during those hectic times. Allied and German commanders had to issue orders that were virtual death sentences to their airmen. Commander Simpson's report was filed and marked "Top Secret".

This article was previously published in the November 1999 edition of Flypast

~~SECRET~~

20 March 1945.

MEMO from Lt. (jg) Carl Devoe
      Lt. Joseph Gould
      Labor Division, SI.

SUBJECT: Dispatch of the CHISEL Mission.

Submitted herewith in essentially chronological form is an account of the dispatch of the CHISEL Mission, on 19 March 1945.

At 3.25 p.m. on 19 March the Labor Division was informed that the CHISEL Mission was to be dispatched on the evening of the same day.

This mission had been alerted for imminent dispatch during the dark of the moon. On or about 6 March Lt. Gould and the agent reported to Watton for dispatch on that night. The report of a scheduled weather ship arriving at Watton a half hour before dispatch brought about a decision to postpone the dispatch. This report was first brought to the attention of Commander Simpson by Major Walsh, one of the two navigators who were members of the crew. Commander Simpson asked Lt. Gould to meet with him and Major Walsh. The situation was discussed, the greatest weight being given to Major Walsh's opinion. Commander Simpson with complete agreement on the part of Lt. Gould, decided to call off the dispatch of the mission for that night.

For a week subsequent to this cancellation, the CHISEL mission was alerted for imminent dispatch. On about 13 March the Labor Division was informed that dispatch for this mission was indefinitely delayed. The next word concerning dispatch of this mission came at 3.25 p.m. on 19 March 1945. At no time during the period 13 to 19 March was any notification of alert or imminent dispatch forwarded to this Division.

Five minutes after the notification referred to, the agent was physically in hand at the Labor Division's holding apartment for this purpose. At approximately 4.20 p.m. through Capt. Thompson, Lt. Gould was informed of a message from Major Stearns. This message was to the effect that Major Stearns wanted the agent and Lt. Gould to report "to Area "O" or some area" and that the dispatch would be an early one. Lt. Gould requested that the information be made more specific, particularly as to details of movement from London to the point of dispatch. Approximately 15 minutes later Lt. Turano called to say that one piece of parachute gear had not been forwarded to the point of dispatch, and requested that this be taken in Lt. Gould's care. Lt. Gould agreed to this and asked that the

~~SECRET~~ APPROVED FOR RELEASE Date/____/___

- 2 -

gear be brought to his office? During this period of time, and
at the suggestion of the Operations Office, Lt. Gould was responsible
for arranging transportation. Having no accurate time guide he originally
laid on transportation for 7 p.m. At his request for information from
the Motor Pool he was informed that the only male civilian driver, Dick,
was under the control of the Communications Office. Lt. Gould asked
Capt. Thompson to clear with Capt. McWaters for use of this vehicle;
during this conversation between Thompson and Gould it developed that the
departure from London would have to be earlier than at 7 p.m. since
dispatch was scheduled for 10 p.m., and the car was ordered to report to
Lt. Gould at 5 p.m. Lt. Turano's piece of parachute gear was delivered
at 4.50. At approximately that time Lt. Burke came to Lt. Gould's office
and informed him that the agent and Conducting Officer were to proceed
to Area "O", and that Major Stearns would be present there.

The agent and Lt. Gould left the holding apartment at 5.45 p.m.
Arrival at Area "O" was at 7.50 p.m. Major Stearns was not present and a
Non-commissioned officer in charge informed Lt. Gould that Major Stearns
had phoned to say that he expected Lt. Gould and his party at Harrington
(one half hour's drive away) before 8 p.m.

The plan for dispatch included dinner at Area "O". This consisted
of heated "C" Ration, Canned Corn, Coffee and Oranges. In view of the time
schedule this meal was hastily consumed. Departure from Area "O" was at
approximately 8.5 p.m.

The party arrived at Group Operations Office, Harrington, at
8.40 p.m. The agent was left in the car, while Lt. Gould reported to
Major Stearns. Lt. Gould asked where the dressing was to take place.
Major Stearns' conversation indicated that no plans had been made on this
score, and pointed to the office of Lt. Col. Fish, suggesting that it be
done there. This office faces the map room of the Group Operations Office,
where a considerable number of Operations Personnel were present. Lt. Ancrum
followed Lt. Gould to the car to assist with baggage and on return from the
car led the party to the Intelligence Office; during the course of this
Lt. Ancrum indicated that Major Stearns had changed his mind as to where the
dressing was to take place.

The Intelligence Office consisted of two small rooms with an
open window passage in the wall between. The office to be used for dressing
was empty but the adjacent office referred to included a number of
operating personnel. Nevertheless, dressing was immediately begun and the
agent was in the clothing of his mission by approximately 9.25.

Shortly after entrance into this room Major Stearns appeared and
asked to talk with Lt. Gould. Gould stepped outside and was asked by
Major Stearns whether he (Gould) had brought the necessary gear with him.
On enquiry it developed that Major Stearns was referring to the entire kit of
parachute clothing, including the strip-tease, cushions, etc. Lt. Gould
repeated the exact message as Lt. Turano had given it to him and referred

- 3 -

deginitely to the fact that the only piece of equipment he was charged with bringing to Harrington was one parachute, enclosed in a burlap sack. Major Stearns indicated that he had no idea as to where the rest of the gear was, that he had been informed by London that Lt. Gould was bringing all the gear with him. Approximately 10 minutes later Major Stearns appeared again, asked for Lt. Gould and wanted to know if Lt. Gould was certain that he had brought no other parachute gear with him. Lt. Gould repeated his reply of 10 minutes before and returned to the business of completing the agent's dressing.

At approximately 9.30 p.m. Major Stearns reappeared with an assistant and the necessary gear. He informed Lt. Gould that this material had been located in the bomb-bay of the plane.

During the course of the dressing a considerable number of individuals entered the room and remained present. At least five officers, no one of whom appeared at any time during the process to have any direct concern with the business at hand, were included among those present. Also, the operating personnel in the adjacent office continued to view the scene. Immediately prior to the location of the parachute gear, the two navigators and the pilot came into the room and proceeded to present the final pinpoint information. The agent confirmed his understanding, Lt. Gould presented additional information concerning the area and the appropriate sections of the maps involved were cut out for the agent's use. One of the navigators was Major Walsh, the only member of the crew known to Lt. Gould. No introductions were made as far as the agent was concerned. Towards the end of the dressing process Col. Upham, the Group Commander, came into the room.

At 9.50 p.m. the agent was completely prepared and the party proceeded by car to the plane with Major Stearns in the front seat. A number of other cars followed and the immediate vicinity was thoroughly lighted. With Stearns approval Lt. Gould and the agent left the car to proceed to the plane. On arrival at the bomb-bay, they were instructed to return to the care and wait; the walk to and from the plane was entirely visible to both the ground crew and the attending group of personnel.

During the subsequent period Lt. Gould returned to the bomb-bay where he encountered the dispatcher and suggested that the dispatcher consult with the agent, Major Stearns agreeing to the validity of this idea. The dispatcher was brought back to the car and the consultation was held. At about 10.50 p.m. Major Stearns came to the car and signalled that the agent was to be placed into the plane. This was done.

Some 15 minutes later the engines were started, the surrounding automobiles having been withdrawn to the other side of the run-way. Cmdr. Simpson had been present in the vicinity of the plane from the time of the party's arrival and during this time was mainly to be found in the interior of the plane.

Lt. Gould discussed the prevailing situation with Cmdr. Simpson at the first opportunity which was after the agent had been placed in the bomb-bay. Cmdr. Simpson discussed the situation in the frankest terms. He

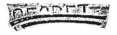

- 4 -

declared that he did not wish to share any responsibility for the dispatch of this mission. In the course of his conversation a series of events and items of information was brought out. According to Cmdr. Simpson the plane had been undergoing an operational check during the afternoon of 19 March; he indicated that there had been considerable disassembly. He spoke frankly of certain telephone calls and other forms of pressure, eventually devolving to the Group Commander, Col. Upham, and indicated that some time during the course of the afternoon Col. Upham had received what amounted to a direct order from a general officer to fly the mission, whereupon Col. Upham issued orders of similar tenor and effect. As a result Major Walsh was ordered for duty on this mission, from his unit at Watton. Other members of the crew, it was indicated, had not had sufficient rest. At one point during the course of the preparations for the mission, and presumably during the difficulties of shaping up the crew, Col. Upham had indicated that he would pilot the ship himself; in view of the Col's brief flying time in the A-26, certain navigator members of the crew refused to go. How eventually the crew was finally selected was not indicated. Also it appeared that it was only through Cmdr. Simpson's suggestion that a developed and pertinent weather report was secured for this mission, from Watton. Cmdr. Simpson said that he was not of the opinion that the Harrington apparatus included the necessary S-2 approach and experience for a pinpoint dispatch; the Commander felt that both the facilities and the personnel at Harrington, as of this time, were designed for operations of mass dispatch and for pinpoints involving considerable area, (two miles by one in dimension). In the opinion of Lt. Gould, Cmdr. Simpson was obviously uncertain as to the condition of the plane.

Certain general impressions as to the attitude of the crew are also offered in this report. Lt. Gould had met Major Walsh on a number of occasions including, those of dispatch and return of the A-26 on the HAMMER Mission. In all instances, Major Walsh gave the impression of a highly intelligent and personable officer; invariably, the agents concerned were impressed by his presence and attitude. Throughout the period of dispatch of the CHISEL Mission, Major Walsh appeared to be most concerned and worried. In general, this can also be said of the other members of the crew.

The plane left the run-way at 11.17 p.m. Expected time of arrival was 2.45 a.m. on 20 March. Total possible time in the air according to fuel capacity was given as 6 3/4 hours. By 0615 a.m., the control tower had had no indication of the return of the plane.

JG:dj.

APPENDIX I

Letter from Kurt Goldstein to Jonathan Gould, September 21, 2006

Re: Kurt Gruber (German and English translation)

Internationales Auschwitz Komitee

KURT-JULIUS GOLDSTEIN
Ehrenpräsident   27 September 2006

JONATHAN S. GOULD
Attorney at Law
603 West 1156th Street. #198
NEW YORK, NEW YORK 100125
(212)531-4852

Sehr geehrter Herr Gould,

In Beantwortung Ihrer telefonischen Bitte sende ich Ihnen mit Freude den folgenden kurzen Bericht über meinen, leider so früh und tragisch verstorbenen Freund KURT GRUBER..

Kurt Gruber war der Leiter des antinazistischen Jugendverbandes in den ich im August 1928 eingetreten bin. Von diesem ,Zeitpunkt an, habe ich an allen Aktivitäten des Jugendverbandes, die sich gegen das Aufkommen des Nazismus in unserem Heimatgebiet, westliches Westfalen, richteten, unter der Leitung von Kurt Gruber teilgenommen. Ich erinnere mich an eine Serie von Heimabendvorträgen von Kurt Gruber unter dem Thema „Was. wir von Hitlers' „Mein Kampf" zu erwarten haben".

Als ich von 1942-45 im Lager Auschwitz war, habe ich oft an Kurt Gruber denken müssen, weil er uns in diesen Vorträgen auf die antisemitischen Pläne, die Hitler in diesem Buch entwickelt hat, aufmerksam machte, denn wir waren viele jüdische Jugendliche in diesem antinazistischen Jugendverband.

Die Heimatstadt von Kurt Gruber war Ahlen in Westfalen. Die Arbeitersiedlungen dieser Industriestadt waren fest in den Händen linker Organisationen. Im Jahre 1929 wollte die Hitlersche-SA einen Aufmarsch durch diese Arbeitersiedlungen machen. Dies wurde durch eine Aktion linker Organisationen, des Reichsbanners, des antifaschistischen Kampfbundes der Sozialistischen Arbeiterjugend und unserer antinazistischen Jugendvereinigung, verhindert. Kurt Gruber war einer der Organisatoren dieser erfolgreichen Aktion. Er war auch der Verfasser von Flugblättern gegen die Nazis, die unser Jugendverband zu allen Reichstags-, Landtags- und Kommunalwahlen herausgab. Unter der Leitung von Kurt Gruber gingen wir auch in Versammlungen der Naziorganisationen, wo Kurt Gruber als Diskussionsredner gegen die Nazis auftrat. So arbeiteten wir bis Ende 1930 zusammen. Zu diesem Zeitpunkt wurde Kurt Gruber in die Bezirksleitung Ruhrgebiet unserer Organisation gewählt. Mir wurde seine Nachfolge übertragen. Wir sind dann bis Januar 1933, als die Nazis ihr Terrorregime in Deutschland errichteten, in engem Kontakt miteinander geblieben.

Ich würde mich sehr über eine postume Ehrung meines Freundes freuen und verbleibe

Hochachtungsvoll

KURT JULIUS GOLDSTEIN

International Auschwitz Committee [etc.]

Kurt-Julius Goldstein
Honorary President
September 27, 2006

Jonathan S. Gould [etc.]

Dear Mr. Gould:

In response to your request over the phone, it is my pleasure to send you the following short report about my friend Kurt Gruber, who died so young and so tragically.

Kurt Gruber was the director of the anti-Nazi youth federation that I joined in August, 1928. From this time on, I participated under the leadership of Kurt Gruber in all activities of the youth federation that were directed against the rise of Nazism in our home region, western Westphalia. I remember a series of club-evening lectures by Kurt Gruber on the subject of "what we have to expect from Hitler's *Mein Kampf.*"

When I was at the Auschwitz camp between 1942 and 1945, I often came to think of Kurt Gruber, because in these lectures he turned our attention to the anti-Semitic plans that Hitler had developed in this book, for there were many of us young Jews people in this anti-Nazi youth federation.

Kurt Gruber's hometown was Ahlen in Westphalia. The working-class neighborhoods of this industrial town were firmly in the hands of leftist organizations. In 1929, Hitler's SA wanted to hold a march through these neighborhoods. This plan was frustrated by an intervention of leftist organizations, the Reichsbanner [an organization mostly of WW I soldiers for the defense of the Republic that was nominally nonpartisan but dominated by Social Democrats], the Anti-fascist Kampfbund of the Socialist Workers' Youth [the youth organization of the Social Democratic Party] and our anti-Nazi youth federation. Kurt Gruber was one of the organizers of this successful intervention. He was also the author of pamphlets against the Nazis which our youth federation issued before all elections for the Landtag or parliament of the Land as well as municipal elections. Under Kurt Gruber's leadership we also went to the conventions of Nazi organizations, where Kurt Gruber appeared as discussant against the Nazis. We worked together in this fashion until late in 1930. At this point, Kurt Gruber was elected to the district leadership for the Ruhr area of our organization. I was appointed to succeed him. We continued to be in close contact until January, 1933, when the Nazis created their terror regime in Germany.

I would be very pleased by a posthumous honor for my friend, and remain with the very best regards,

[signed]
Kurt Julius Goldstein

APPENDIX J

Recommendation for the award of the *Bronze Star* to Kurt Gruber, June 1945

SECRET

HQ & HQ DETACHMENT
OFFICE OF STRATEGIC SERVICES
EUROPEAN THEATER OF OPERATIONS
U.S. Army
(MAIN)

APO 413
18 June 1945

SUBJECT: Recommendation for award of the BRONZE STAR MEDAL
(POSTHUMOUSLY)

TO   : Commanding General, European Theater of Operations,
United States Army, APO 887.

1. a. It is recommended that KURT GRUBER, German
civilian, formerly serving with the Labor Division of
the Secret Intelligence Branch, Office of Strategic
Services, ETOUSA, be awarded the BRONZE STAR MEDAL
(Posthumously).

b. KURT GRUBER was serving as a Secret Intelligence Agent for the Labor Division, SI Branch, ETOUSA at
the time of the act for which this award is recommended.

c. Name and address of nearest relative:

Jessie Campbell Leith Gruber (wife)
188 Byres Road,
Glasgow, Scotland.

d. Entered military service from: not applicable

e. Decorations previously awarded: None

f. The entire service of KURT GRUBER has been
honorable since the rendition by him of the service upon
which this recommendation is based.

g. A similar recommendation for this individual
has not been submitted.

2. a. The officer recommending this award has personal
knowledge of the service upon which this award is based.

b. This recommendation is supported by official
records of the Office of Strategic Services.

3. a. KURT GRUBER, German civilian, while serving in
close collaboration with the Army of the United States
distinguished himself by heroic achievement in connection
with military operations not involving participation in
aerial flight against an enemy of the United States.

3. b. Detailed narrative of the service for which
this award is recommended:

In December 1944, the Labor Division, Secret Intelligence Branch, OSS, ETOUSA, formulated a project for
establishing contact with an anti-Nazi underground organization of German coal miners known to be functioning in
the Ruhr. The potential value of the organization for
intelligence purposes was estimated to be great, and this
value was thought to justify an effort to overcome the
complex problems involved in dispatching an agent into the
region to establish relations and transmit intelligence.

Handwritten margin note:
w/o from Jan Council office
30 Sept 44
(a sealed address
10 of august 45
7 mar 50 high St
Jordan, NW?
Scotland

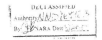

SECRET

The hazards and difficulties involved in making an initial contact with the clandestine miner's group arose from the facts that, due to the nature of the operation, no reception committee was possible; the drop had to be a blind one, and names and addresses of possible collaborators could not be supplied. Disruption of life in the target areas through the constant and heavy Allied bombings also increased the agent's difficulties in locating the few contacts known personally to him.

The great danger and difficulties of such an undertaking were fully discussed with GRUBER. It was emphasized that it would reflect no discredit upon him to refuse the assignment for he was a coal miner, deemed essential, and deferred from military service. In addition, as a German national he could have felt his employment in an important war industry as an adequate contribution to the Allied war effort. However, displaying outstanding courage and a great desire to make an invaluable contribution to the allied prosecution of the war, GRUBER volunteered for the mission.

To the task at hand GRUBER brought a store of experience and qualifications rarely equalled. He had lived in the Ruhr from his birth in 1912 until the summer of 1934. He was himself a coal miner, and had personally organized among the German miners more than 100 local groups dedicated to fighting Hitlerism during the turbulent years 1931 and 1933. He had himself worked underground with the remnants of these groups during 1933 and 1934; and if any survivors of them were active in the 1944 organization, he would know them and be known to them. In addition, GRUBER was acquainted by experience with the problems of living and travelling illegally in Nazi Germany; for between 1934 and 1938, he made ten trips from Czechoslovakia to Berlin to establish and maintain contacts with German underground groups in that city.

GRUBER agreed to be parachuted into Germany wearing civilian clothes as an integral part of his "cover" story. The knowledge that discovery by the Gestapo would mean torture and perhaps death as an enemy agent did not deter him; and, after the necessary training, including practice parachute jumps, GRUBER was dispatched on the night of 19 March, 1945. The plane did not return, nor has any trace of it been found since; and GRUBER and the crew are presumed dead. Attempts to contact GRUBER by means of the communications equipment which he carried were unsuccessful, and recent investigation in the Ruhr area has yielded no trace of him. It is now assumed that he lost his life either in a crash of the plane or at the hands of the Germans while carrying out his work. The heroism he displayed in leaving his wife and the safety of his civilian work in England to undertake such an extremely dangerous mission was of the highest order.

4. Proposed Citation: For the BRONZE STAR MEDAL: (Posthumous)

Mr. KURT GRUBER, civilian, in recognition of his outstanding gallantry and devotion to the Allied cause. He volunteered for a special and extremely dangerous assignment, and sacrificed his life in attempting to carry it out. His bravery and desire to serve the Allied Armies was of the highest order.

5. In order to support this recommendation, it has been necessary to divulge in the preceding paragraphs information classified as Secret. However, the proposed citation has been made sufficiently general to permit publication of it separately with the classification restricted.

JAMES R. FORGAN
Colonel, GSC,
Commanding.

APPENDIX K

Undated memorandum from OSS
Assistant Director G. Edward Buxton To
Joint U.S. Chiefs of Staff

Re: OSS Penetration of Germany

MEMORANDUM OF INFORMATION FOR THE JOINT U.S. CHIEFS OF STAFF
SUBJECT: OSS Penetration of Germany

    1. During the eight months preceding the unconditional
surrender more than 100 OSS intelligence missions penetrated
into Germany to obtain information on the enemy's situation and
movements, on hidden factories and storage dumps, on the
effectiveness of Allied bombings, on the treatment of Allied
prisoners-of-war, and on the strength of Nazi control over the
civil population. Information from these missions reached
Allied military headquarters promptly and in a steady stream
throughout the rapid advances in March and April and into the
last weeks of crumbling Nazi resistance.

    2. The activities of these missions were directed and
coordinated from the principal OSS headquarters in England,
France, and Italy, in cooperation with OSS offices in Switzerland
and Sweden and the OSS units in Brussels, Belgium and Eindhoven,
Holland. In addition there were OSS detachments on the staffs
of the Sixth and Twelfth Army Groups, the First, Third, Seventh
and Ninth Armies and the 18th Airborne Corps of the First
Allied Airborne Army. All were in radio contact with each
other to assure quick and immediate dissemination of intelligence.

    3. Long-range penetration was begun in September 1944 when
an intelligence agent was parachuted into the Ruhr area where he
successfully made contact with Socialist anti-Nazi elements.
The first operative to reach Berlin proper crossed through the
lines of the Western Front in November and by February had

Germany in November. Entry of operatives across the Swiss
border was initiated in December. Three missions dispatched
from Sweden were by February operating successfully in
Hamburg, Berlin and Leipzig. Also in February another mission
from Italy was parachuted into Austria near Innsbruck to report
on traffic through the Brenner Pass. Aside from reporting
intelligence these missions served as pathfinders for further
penetrations.

4. Additional intelligence was obtained through contacts
with potential anti-Nazi groups. Austrian resistance centers
supplied information on German installations in Austria as well
as on defenses of the Nazi "redoubt" area. Operatives dispatched from Sweden joined with secret German anti-Nazi nuclei
among labor union men.

5. Shorter-range intelligence penetrations were carried on
by the OSS detachments with the Armies. "Tourist" agents were
infiltrated through the German lines on two- or three-day missions
to gather information on the enemy's tactical situation and
report to OSS officers on their return. In January the intensified
German counter-activity and the heavy use of land mines made it
preferable to parachute the "tourists" ahead of the lines. The
Seventh Army officially commended OSS for the timely and
accurate intelligence received from such sources.

6. After the crossing of the Rhine high-frequency ground-
to-air radio-telephone was used to supplement coded wireless-
telegraphy for communication with agents. Radio-telephone not

quently in daily radio-telephone communications with OSS officers
in specially equipped American bombers on clandestine missions.
The effectiveness of this system was proven in March when an
agent urged immediate bombardment of a railroad station through
which heavy enemy traffic was passing. The bombardment took
place the next day and by night-fall the agent's eye-witness
account of the damage was received at Air Force Headquarters.
This action drew a commendation from the Eighth Air Force.

7. By mid-April, when organized resistance along the
central and southern German front began to disintegrate, the OSS
penetration program was adapted to permit last-minute changes
whereby agents could be prepared on very short notice to be
parachuted many miles deeper inside Germany than originally
planned. In this manner OSS kept pace with the speed of the
Allied advance and continued until the surrender to intensify
reliable first-hand intelligence coverage of areas still in enemy
hands by newly dispatched "tourist" agents.

8. In addition to agents reporting by radio, "sleeper"
teams were dispatched into enemy territory to "lie low," observe
local military and political conditions, and upon being overrun
to report directly to Allied intelligence and civil affairs
officers. Other such teams were assigned to observe atrocities,
prisoner-of-war camps, and Nazi attempts to go underground.

9. Over 30 intelligence operatives were by 1 May
successfully installed in the German "Redoubt" area, in
preparation for extensive reporting on that region had the
Germans sought to make a last stand in the Austrian Alps. Further
They provided useful information on enemy troops preparing for
surrender, on war criminals seeking to escape or hide, and on
caches of weapons, food, materiel and Nazi loot.

> G. Edward Buxton
> Acting Director

APPENDIX L

HAMMER Mission dispatch report from OSS mission conducting officer Army Lt. Joseph Gould, March 12,1945

12 March 1945.

FROM   Lt. Joseph Gould
              Labor Division, SI.

SUBJECT   HAMMER Mission.

          The HAMMER Mission was dispatched to Berlin on the
morning of 2 March 1945.

          This account will make only passing reference to the events
which preceded the midnight of dispatch.   The agents, who shall be
known as Phil and Toni, are Germans.   They are political refugees,
relatively young, men with wives and each the father of a child.
Phil agreed to undertake the mission in October, 1944.   Toni, who is
his friend, was recruited during the following month.   Their courses of
training were eventually joint.

          The Plans and Operations staff, OSS, London, granted approval
to the HAMMER Mission on 17 November 1944.   On 14 February 1945 Phil and
Toni had completed their intensive courses of training.   Initial cover
conferences were held on 7 February, and on the morning of the 15th
February the agents entered upon final briefing and communications training.
The latter consisted mainly of familiarisation with the Joan-Eleanor
device.

          On that same morning of February 15, a crew of men were
working secretly at Watton aerodrome, on an A-26 attack bomber.   The
aeroplane had been painted a jet and shiny black, and outwardly this was
perhaps the only indication that it was shortly to fly a special mission.
Inside her, the A-26 was being reconstructed.   Forward of the long
bomb-bay and partially over it a plywood platform had been set into the
bottom of the plane.   Around and to the rear of this platform were
installed the riggings for a series of static lines.   The signal lights
were installed.   Under the command of Lt. Cdr. Stephan H. Simpson a few
men at Watton were planning, checking, planning again...

          In the course of this the HAMMER Mission was test-flown.
The black A-26 took off from Watton many times during these days.   Four
of these times it went to Berlin.   On these flights the men of the A-26
were planning their course and their tactics.   There were four in her
crew, Major Walsh, the squadron navigator, Lt. Walker, the pilot,
Lt. Wishke, navigating, and the tail gunner, Derr, who was also to serve as
dispatcher. Only the most courageous and highly skilled hands could have
brought the HAMMER Mission safely and accurately to its pinpoint,

- 2 -

forty-seven kilometers away from Berlin, seven hundred feet over
ground.

On 24 February, (T   Elder, Marine Corps, made the first
live jump out of an A-26.   at day the plane received its first actual
tests in dropping packages and bodies.   The plans, the tests and the
revisions were successful.   The general plan had been refined to
absolute detail.   As the plane came over the target, the bomb-bay doors
would swing down, and the ready light would flash.   The bomb release
button would instantaneously release the package, turn on the green light
and move the dispatcher into action.   Tapped on their helmets by
dispatcher, the men would push themselves off the platform and down into
space.   Time for dispatch: three seconds.

We arrived with Phil and Toni at Watton shortly after 9.30 on
the evening of March 1st.   At the supper table Phil and Toni were
introduced to Derr.   Together they determined the details of the final
3 seconds of dispatch, and somewhere during the meal came to an agreement.
Commander Simpson nodded his approval, while Captain Thompson and
Sgt. Elder checked silently.   Immediately after supper the men were
brought to a small house where they dressed for their mission.   Out of
two small canvas bags had come the essentials of this process: their
clothes, their documents, a few diamonds, money, their pistols.   At
  30 p.m. they left the small house and were driven to the operations hut.

As we left the car we looked out over the field to the right.
It was raining lightly, and through the dark ground-haze the only distinctly
visible object was the high, huge, squarish tail of the A-26 fifty yards
away from the hut.   We pointed out the plane to Phil and Toni.

Lt. Turano and Sgt. Elder were waiting for us inside the
operations hut, each of them at a mound of parachute gear.   Immediately we
entered they went to work.   Five minutes later the engines of the plane
began to warm up, and through all of the long serious minutes of
preparation which followed the sharp, incessant sound of her motors filled
the room.

At 11.50 p.m. Phil and Toni were dressed for their journey.   Over
his overcoat each had the heavy, camouflaged canvas of the strip-tease.   Into
their pockets had been placed the essentials of their arrival into Germany.
Over it all were the white straps and the tan bundle of their parachute.
They smoked, and men were talking to them quietly.

Three minutes before midnight Commander Simpson opened
the door and gave the signal.   In a moment we were in a rapidly-moving
station wagon, and in the next instant standing in the propeller blast
of the A-26, now poised and roaring on the runway.   We saw the reddish
light shining out of her bomb-bay as we walked, leaning against the blast,
   the plane.   We moved under the doors and hoisted Phil and Toni to their

- 3 -

seats, to the plywood floor. There was too much sound for talking, and it was not the time. We reached up from the runway to shake hands with Toni and Phil. Then we ducked under the bomb-bay doors

We returned to the station wagon at the side of the runway. For long minutes, the plane stood on the runway, her engines raging. Now the night was absolutely clear. Ten minutes before, the weather ship had returned from Berlin to say that the weather over the target area was perfect for the operation. Suddenly we saw the A-26 begin to move. Then she began to taxi rapidly, and then she was racing down the runway. She was almost out of sight before we saw her rise, climb quickly and bank off to the north-east.

The HAMMER Mission had taken off at 0001, 2 March 1945.

The expected time of return was 0430. We took some sleep at about 1 a.m., and at 4.15 were awakened to meet the plane. It was almost exactly 4.30 when we stepped out of the doors of our quarters. That same instant we heard her, then saw her circling high. We had not taken more than a few steps when she was back, very low. We knew it was Walker. He had his ship on one wing and on that one wing he buzzed the field as his Colonel had never heard it buzzed before.

It was our first sign of how well things had gone. The next indication came as the ship wheeled to a halt, when Derr's enormous figure came up out of the blister on top. We saw him silhouetted and then we saw his two gloved fists shoot straight in the air. Inside the gloves were his thumbs, straight up. The mission was in.

While Cmdr. Simpson typed the operations report, the story tumbled out from Walker and Walsh, and from Mishko, who was given to saying little. Walker had flown her in at a steady rate of 300 miles an hour or better. He had flown her low, so low that most of the time their "G" had not been functioning. He had flown her on her side, twisted her, banked her through to confuse the enemy radar. They reported "no enemy action". They had arrived at the target at 0205. The report of the weather ship had been exact - three-tenths clouds, a bright moon, clear visibility. The pinpoint had been doubly confirmed - visibly and by the navigational "G". They had made a pass over the target, circled it to look again, gone back for the final pass, and on the final run the bomb-bay doors had swung down. Then, at lower than 700 feet, Phil and Toni left their plywood platform to enter Germany.

JG:dj.

Joseph Gould,
1st Lt. AUS.

Index

Note: Page numbers in *italics* indicate figures on the corresponding pages.

Abbey, M. xvii
African American POW camp
  guards 53
Albin, F. 85
Alpenfestung concept 57–58
Andrews, M. 8
Arandora Star xix
Ardennes Forest attack 5–6

B-17 Montblanc/Missing Aircraft 74
Beau, L. 74
Berliner Zig 30
Bessinger, M. 86–87
Beurton, L. 15
British Broadcasting Corporation
  (BBC) radio 5, 12
British Committee for the Rescue of the
  Czech Refugees (BCRC) xviii, 64
British Youth Peace Assembly xviii
Bronze Star: awarded to Joseph Gould
  27–29, 137–141; recommendation
  for award to Kurt Gruber 177–179
Bross, J. A. 25
Buchholz, A. xviii, xix, *97, 98*; dispatch
  of the MALLET mission and 93–97;
  post-war life of 98; recruitment of
  92–93
Buchner, M. 93, 97
Bursztin, L. 51
Bush, G. W. 26
Buxton, G. E. 101; memorandum on
  the OSS Penetration Campaign by
  180–183

BUZZSAW mission 81; dispatch of
  84–85; Leipzig destination of 84;
  training for 83–84; *see also*
  Fischer, W.

Campbell, J. 70
Casey, W. J. xiv, xiv–xv; Ardennes
  Forest attack and 6; PICKAXE
  mission and 54, 56; political conflict
  within OSS London and 6; post-war
  life of 31
Center for Defense Information 31
Central Intelligence Agency 28–29,
  31, 69
Chaplin, C. xvi, 31
CHISEL mission 62; aftermath of
  69–84; aircraft used in 68, 72–73,
  77–78; breakthrough in investigation
  of 71–73; dispatch memorandum
  on 168–173; Hudson Upham and
  67–69, 73–74, *77*; recruitment
  and training of Kurt Gruber for 66;
  tragedy marring the dispatch of
  66–68; *see also* Gruber, Kurt
Churchill, W. xix, 15, 55
Clinton, H. 18–20, 25–26, 48n102
Cold War, the: end of 14; outbreak of 21
Columbia Pictures xvi
Communist Party, Germany 21, 81–82,
  92, 95, 101
cover stories 1–2
Czech Refugee Trust Fund xviii, 8, 17,
  51, 82

Der Spiegel 19–20, 23, 154–160
Disney Co. xvi
Donovan, W. J. xiii–xiv, 4, 6–7, 28, *32–33*; memorandum from Arthur Goldberg to, 1943 113–128; post-war life of 31; search for Werner Fischer and 86
Dulles, A. xiii

East Germany 21
Eva, E. 98
exiles, German: communist 21; internment of xix; recruitment of xv–xix; resettled in the West 21

False Friends 22, 154–160
FAUST Plan xv
Film War Service Council xvii
Fischer, H. 88, *89*
Fischer, W. xviii, xix; attempts to determine what happened to 87–88; dispatch of the BUZZSAW mission and 84–85; Leipzig destination and 84; mission training 83–84; profile of 81–83; search for 85–87
Forgan, J. R. 59, 69
Forgan, W. J. 28–29
Frauenheim, M. 72–73
Free German Movement 6, 82, 93
Fuchs, K. 30

German Penetration Campaign: Buxton's memorandum on the 180–181; contributions to the Allied war effort 100–102; limited nature of intelligence gained through 101; origins of xiv–xv; OSS recruitment of German exiles for xv–xix
Godart, G. 52
Goddard, D. R. 4
Goebbels, J. 57
Goldberg, A. xiii–xiv, 6–7, *39*, *41*; memorandum to General William J. Donovan, 1943 113–128
Goldberger, S. *38*
Goldstein, K. J. 62–63; letter to Jonathan Gould, 2006 174–176
Gottwald, H. 11

Gould, Jonathan 18–20, 26–27, 48n102; letter from Kurt Goldstein to 174–176
Gould, Joseph xvi–xviii, xix, 5, 9, 18, 22, *37–41*, 99n17; on Adolph Buchholz 95; awarded the Bronze Star 27–29, 137–141; as conducting officer for HAMMER mission 1; end of HAMMER mission and 14–15; Kurt Gruber and 65, 66–67; post-war life of 30–31; recruitment of Adolph Buchholz by 92; recruitment of Werner Fischer by 81; search for Werner Fischer and 86; Simpson's memorandum on dispatch of the CHISEL mission to 168–173
Gross, A. 4, *37*
GRU 1, 15, 18, 22, 85, 96, 99n17
Grubendorf, E. 73
Gruber, E. 62, 64
Gruber, Karl 63, *76–77*
Gruber, Kurt xviii, xix, *74*; birth and youth 62–63, *75*; escape to England 64–65; Jennifer Campbell Leith and 65, 66, 69, 70–71, *75*; letter from Kurt Goldstein to Jonathan Gruber on 174–176; life in the underground 63–64; Medal of Freedom awarded to 69–70; mission aftermath and 69–71; murder of brother of 63, *76–77*; new life and family in Glasgow 65; recommendation for award of Bronze Star to 177–179; recruitment and training for the CHISEL mission 66–67; tragedy marring the dispatch of the CHISEL mission of 66–68

Hagen, P. xiii–xiv
Hager, K. 18, 93
HAMMER mission 67, *77*, 92; beginning of 9–11; in Berlin 7–9; Bronze Star awarded to Joseph Gould for 27–29; communication technology for 4–5, *36*, *37*; finale of 12–14, 23; German attack in the Ardennes Forest as intelligence failure of 5–6; political conflict within OSS London and 6–7;

postscript on 29–31; at risk 11–12;
Silver Star medals presented to
families of HAMMER agents 1,
18–20, 25–27, *43*; "Sonya" and the
GRU after 14–25, 47n93; training
for 1–4
Henschke, E. 16–18, 19, 21–25, *43*;
Adolph Buchholz and 93, 95–96;
post-war life of 30; Werner Fischer
and 85–86
Himmler, H. 55
Hitchcock, A. 31
Hitler, A. xviii, 3, 21, 26; Alpenfestung
concept and 57–58; death of 94;
declaration of war on the United
States by 55; persecution of Jews
by 54
Holocaust, the 54
Honecker, E. 29
Huth, G. 94

I Am a German Coal Miner 65
internment of German exiles xix

Jackson, R. 31
Jacobus, H. 87–88
J/E transmitter-receiver communication
technology: BUZZSAW mission use
of 85; HAMMER mission use of
4–5, *36–37*; MALLET mission use
of 94, 96; PICKAXE mission use of
56, 57
Joyce, C. 70

Kahle, H. 22, 93
Kanin, G. xvii, *39*
Kastro, K. *see* Henschke, E.
Kaylor, J. 87
Kersey, M. 26–27
Kindertransport 93
Konhäuser, E. xviii, 51, *59*; dispatch of
the PICKAXE mission and 55–59;
flown to Paris for mission debriefings
58–59; POW camp report of 52–53;
Silver Star award recommendation
for 161–167
Kopkow, H. 5
Kruse, H. 72–73, *78*
Kuczynski, J. xvii–xviii, 14–16,
21–23, *42*, 95; post-war life of 29

Kuczynski, R. xvii
Kuczynski, U. 14–15, 21–23, *42, 42*,
47n93; post-war life of 30; *see also*
Werner, R.

Landshut 54–55
Lauterbach, E. G. 83
League of Labor Youth 7
Leipzig 84
Leith, J. C. 65, 66, 69, 70–71, *75*
Lindner, F. 10, 31, *34*; aw 48n102
Lindner, I. *34*
Lindner, M. 17, 27, *34, 43*
Lindner, Paul xviii, xix, 17, *33–34,
35*; Adolph Buchholz and 93, 96;
awarded the Silver Star 1, 18–20,
25–27, 132–136; beginning of
the HAMMER mission and 9–11;
on Erich Henschke 23, 25; *False
Friends* article on 22, 154–160;
HAMMER mission at risk and
11–12; HAMMER mission finale
and 12–14, 23; Hammer mission
in Berlin and 7–8; letter to UK
Undersecretary of State, August 5,
1941 129–131; mission training of
1–4; post-war life of 29–31; P.O.W.
Cage report, 1944 142–153
Lindner, Paul, Sr. 31, *34*

MALLET mission 92–93; dispatch of
93–97
Manhattan Project 15
Matern, H. 21, *98*
Medal of Freedom 69–70
MGM xvi

National Committee for a Free
Germany 6
National Labor Relations Board xvi
National Redoubt 57–58
Neubert, P. 88
Neus Deutschland 87

Office of Strategic Services (OSS)
40–41, 180–183; Ardennes Forest
attack and 6; formation of xii–xiv;
logo of *32*; memorandum from
Arthur Goldberg to General William
J. Donovan, 1943 113–128; mission

communication technology and 4; origins of the German penetration campaign and xiv–xv; political conflict within London 6–7; recruitment of German exiles by xv–xix
Office of War Information (OWI) xii–xiii
order of battle 1

Paramount Pictures xvi, 31
Pearl Harbor attack xvi
PICKAXE mission: debriefings on 58–59; dispatch of 55–59; Landshut destination of 54–55; POW camp reports 52–54; profiles of agents involved in 50–51; training for 51–52
Pickford, M. xvi, 31
POWs, German: on African American camp guards 53; on fear of the fate of their families in Germany 54; on German prospects of losing the war 2, 52–53; on the Holocaust 54; Konhäuser and Strüwe as 52–54; on life in the prisoner of war camps 4; on the morale of the German Army 2–3; on Nazi war crimes 54; Paul Lindner's Cage report, 1944 142–153; on the persecution of the Jews 3; PICKAXE mission reports on 52–54; on the resistance of European countries occupied by Nazi Germany 4; on the Soviet Union 3–4; on the United States military 3; Werner Fischer's report on 83–84
Premke, G. 72

Rangel, C. 29
RCA Laboratories 4
Reagan, R. 31
Ribbentrop, J. von 82
RKO xvi
Roosevelt, F. D. xii–xiii
Ruh, A. xix, *33*, *43*, 101; awarded the Silver Star 1, 18–20, 25–27, 48n102, 132–136; beginning of the HAMMER mission and 10; on Erich Henschke 17–18, 23, 25; *False Friends* article on 22, 154–160;

HAMMER mission at risk and 11–12; HAMMER mission finale and 12–14, 23; Hammer mission in Berlin and 8–9; mission training of 1–4; post-war life of 29
Ruh, D. 27, *43*

Schmidt, H. 87, *89*
Screen Publicists Guild xvi–xvii, *38–39*
Silver Star medal: awarded to Ruh and Lindner 1, 18–20, 25–27, *43*, 48n102, 132–136; Strüwe and Konhäuser and 161–167
Simpson, S. 4, 67–68; CHISEL mission dispatch memorandum by 168–173
Skala, F. 51–52
Sonya's Report 15–17, 22, 47n93
Sorge, R. 15
Soviet Union, the: German POWs on 3–4; Ruth Werner and 15; "Sonya" and the GRU after HAMMER mission and 14–25
Sparacino, R. 19–20, 26, 48n102
Strüwe, W. xviii, xix, 50–51, *60*; dispatch of the PICKAXE mission and 55–59; flown to Paris for mission debriefings 58–59; POW camp report of 53–54; Silver Star award recommendation for 161–167
Supreme Headquarters of the Allied Expeditionary Force (SHAEF) xv

Time magazine 58
Timken, W. R. 26, *43*
TOOL missions *see* German Penetration Campaign
training, mission *40–41*; BUZZSAW 83–84; CHISEL 66–67; HAMMER 1–4; PICKAXE 51–52
Truman, H. 31
20th Century Fox xvi

United Artists Corporation 31
United States military, German POWs on the 3
Universal Pictures xvi
Upham, H. 67–69, 73–74, *77*

Walch, J. *77*

Wall Street Journal 14

War Activities Committee of the Motion Pictures Industry xvii

Werner, J. 15, 16

Werner, R. 15–17; *see also* Kuczynski, U.

Wiegrefe, K. 19, 22

Will Germany Crack xiii

Winant, J., Jr. 55, 59, *60*

Winant, J., Sr. 55, *60*

Zedler, D. 26–27, *43*

For Product Safety Concerns and Information please contact our EU
representative GPSR@taylorandfrancis.com Taylor & Francis Verlag GmbH,
Kaufingerstraße 24, 80331 München, Germany

Printed and bound by CPI Group (UK) Ltd, Croydon, CR0 4YY

11/04/2025

01844009-0002